T0327688

The Art of Business Valuation

The Art of Business Valuation

Accurately Valuing a Small Business

GREGORY R. CARUSO

WILEY

Published by John Wiley & Sons, Inc., Hoboken, New Jersey.
Published simultaneously in Canada.

For general information on our other products and services or for technical support, please contact our Customer Care Department within the United States at (800) 762-2974, outside the United States at (317) 572-3993 or fax (317) 572-4002.

Wiley publishes in a variety of print and electronic formats and by print-on-demand. Some material included with standard print versions of this book may not be included in e-books or in print-on-demand. If this book refers to media such as a CD or DVD that is not included in the version you purchased, you may download this material at http://booksupport.wiley.com. For more information about Wiley products, visit www.wiley.com.

Library of Congress Cataloging-in-Publication Data is Available:

ISBN 978-1-119-60599-7 (hardback)
ISBN 978-1-119-60600-0 (ePDF)
ISBN 978-1-119-60601-7 (epub)

Cover Design: Wiley
Cover Image: © suksunt sansawast/Getty Images

Printed in the United States of America

SKY10025957_032921

Contents

This book, *The Art of Business Valuation: Accurately Valuing a Small Business* is an important guide and desk reference for valuing small businesses under $10 million in revenues. The vast majority of businesses are this size, yet most business valuation books, even the ones claiming to be for small businesses, do not address the unique factors impacting these small and very small businesses (also sometimes called micro-businesses). The author's business broker and valuation background provides a practical view of technical valuation issues from someone who has had to then "find the number" in the market. Yet this is not a book about price. It is about business valuation, namely, finding a business value for a specified interest as of a specified date to a specified standard of value.

My contribution to this work has been to provide insight and modification as an experienced practitioner, instructor, and mentor, from a more technical accounting business valuation view. The book's focus on small businesses does not mean that methods or techniques have been simplified or ignored. What has been provided is a thorough examination of how valuation methods really work, with the data that is really available for these businesses. Things like, how to work with less than perfect financial information, how to find a highly supportable multiplier using available data, when to use the market or the income method, how to meet valuation standards, and more. Included in the book are detailed figures, tables, explanations, and on the related website working Excel files and even sample reports that provide a framework that can be adapted to most business valuation needs.

Lastly, while an exact "opinion" may only be supportable and *not* be accurate, our methods, work product, and reports can and should be accurate. That is the standard we all must strive for every day in every engagement. That is why accurate is in the sub-title.

Clearly, the best a valuator can do is issue an "opinion." Therefore, there will be varying viewpoints on the topics and methods presented here. In fact, there will be situations where the facts and assumptions would dictate that we use different techniques than the ones recommended here. That illustrates the importance of professional judgment. That is the Art of Business Valuation.

We find this variety of viewpoints and challenges to our thoughts to be exciting and invigorating. It makes business valuation better. With this view in mind, please contact us at ron@theartofbv.com with your thoughts on the book and the valuation of small businesses. We also would be pleased to receive additional reports, studies, techniques and other viewpoints that can be posted on our related website www .theartofbusinessvaluation.com. This way, we can all continue to learn, grow, and improve together.

**Ronald D. Rudich, CPA/ABV/CFF, MS, MCBA,
CVA/ABAR/MAFF, CM&AA, CMEA, BCA**

My father was the CEO of a $750,000,000 revenue general contracting firm when he retired 25 years ago. With 20 job-sites under construction, he was king of just knowing where the problem was—and getting someone to solve it—before it became a threat to the company. After all, large general contractors work on 5% or less gross profit. One "bad" job can wipe out a year's profits. Excelling in this environment, one of his favorite maxims was: "I would rather be approximately right than perfectly wrong."[1]

His maxim came out of jobsites full of technical engineers who each solved their system problems perfectly but with no regard for how the building as a whole would work. All too typical were pipes that were shown running through the structural steel that held the building up. What made this more difficult was the fact that often there was nowhere else for the pipes to go. This was offset by the more practical guys in the field who had to make it all work.

This tension between technical perfection and seeing the big picture still exists today in construction and it also exists in business valuation. It is all too easy to get lost in technical details. After all, business valuators tend to be technical people with extensive technical training. Being able to work between these two worlds—the technical and the practical—is the art of contracting for my father and the *Art of Business Valuation* for us.

In most approaches to business valuation, an equation or model is created where a company being valued is compared to other similarly known data. In the asset approach, it is other asset sales. In the market approach, it is sales of other businesses. In the income approach, it is investment options of investors.

The problem with small and very small businesses is that there is an information gap on both sides of the equation. Small businesses tend to have poor data collection. Compilations of the collected data are based on the suspected data. Yet, that is all there will ever be. Small businesses will not be expected to provide GAAP-based audited statements. Therefore, much of this book is about how to work with suspicious company data and other relevant information to close the gap.

Yet most businesses are small and very small businesses. Using 2012 data with $10 million of revenues as an upper limit, 96% of the businesses with payroll are very small. In fact, revenues of $5 million and below cover 93% of the total businesses and revenues under $1 million cover 75% of the firms in the United States.[2]

Even with imperfect data, these owners are still engaged in planning for the future. They are taking out loans. They are adding and eliminating partners who often are lifelong friends or family members, adding volatility to the mix. They are getting divorced. Some are even eventually selling. All of these common activities require an accurate business valuation.

That is the genesis of this book.

HOW DOES ONE ACCURATELY VALUE SMALL BUSINESSES?

How do we as business valuators, business brokers, accountants, lawyers, owners, and other interested parties prepare, review, evaluate, or use an accurate business valuation for small and very small businesses in a clearly difficult environment?

The answer in just a few words may be: "I'd rather be approximately right rather than perfectly wrong."

After all, we are never going to accurately predict the future. But we can accurately value a business. Accurately valuing a business is using credible cash flows and methods properly based on professional judgment as to material matters.

Accurate does not mean with the advantages of hindsight that we predicted the future precisely. It means we performed our work to high ethical and professional standards based on what is known and knowable, as of the valuation date.

The book is not about how to value mid-sized or large businesses. Much has already been written on that. Even though the methods are the same, valuing larger businesses involves focusing on different specific analyses, different parts of the data, and different risks than valuing small and very small businesses.

A few key elements that both continue through the entire book and should always remain part of the focus when preparing or using a business valuation are:

- Does this make sense?
- What are we valuing?
- What method provides the best comparisons?
- How can we improve one or both sides of the valuation equation?
- How can we tie our value found into a price as a sanity check?
- Does this make sense?

Note the circular effect of these key areas of focus. "Does this make sense?" is listed twice. That question should be listed after every other area of focus and after every question asked, document reviewed, assumption made, and so forth "Does this make sense?" is the essence of the art of business valuation. "Does this make sense?" is the most interesting and most infuriating thing about business valuation.

At its heart, a business valuation is a mix of facts and assumptions to estimate a value based on future results, as of a given day. Integral to the process is the addition of assumptions—after all, we *are* looking to the *FUTURE*. It is said the stock market is valued on the future 18 months. So are private businesses. This brings in assumptions. Layers of assumptions.

The future will rarely be the same as an accurate business valuation. But, by following a systematic process filled with plenty of "Does that make sense?" questions, we can build and document and report accurate business valuations even when any one piece of the puzzle does not quite fit. We can master our art.

Improving the Art of Business Valuation should be the goal of every valuator. Hopefully this book will assist valuators and other users in that endeavor.

HOW TO USE THIS BOOK

Depending on who you are and what you want to accomplish, there are different ways to use this book. This book is more than a book. It also includes a related website with links to a business broker-level estimate of value, a sample annotated calculation report, a sample annotated summary conclusion/opinion report, various checklists and Excel files for many of the calculations and methods shown in the book.

Some suggestions on how different readers could use this book are:

- **New valuation analyst.** The book, along with the sample reports, and using Statements for Standards for Valuation Services (SSVS) No. 1 as a checklist, is a great way to prepare your first few business valuations, assuming they are for typical companies under $10 million in revenues. Keep in mind every valuation is different, so assume you are 85% complete if following these suggestions. Hitchner, Pratt, Mercer, Trugman, and others have written or contributed to more encyclopedic and technical area books. Use them for reference liberally. Do find someone to review your work if you are on your own.
- **Experienced business valuator.** You will find most of this book VERY basic. But many valuators are not familiar with more up-to-date small business market methods. For most

businesses and situations under $1.5 million to $3 million in value, this is the most reliable methodology. In addition, an attempt has been made to present current positions on current income method matters, such as multiple sources of capitalization rate buildup method data, tax affecting, and a review of projections.

- **Certified public accountant (CPA), analyst, or other advisor to a business owner or business buyer.** There are chapters on working with business brokers, transactions, due diligence, increasing business value, the sales process, listening, negotiation, and, of course, business valuation. These are all to the point yet comprehensive enough for many small and very small business situations.

- **Business owner.** Read the chapters on increasing business value, how to sell or buy a business, negotiation, and listening, which are all likely to be helpful and well worth your time. Do hire competent experts. Use this to have a working knowledge and be able to manage your experts.

- **Business broker.** Depending on your level of interest in business valuation, you might want to read how to apply the market method and how to best work with small business financial statements. This was my initial level of interest and work in business valuation. You will also find helpful chapters on asking questions and listening, the business brokerage process, negotiation, Small Business Administration (SBA) loans, and due diligence. Great summaries and checklists are provided. Finally, as you progress and want to have better tools and estimates, you may find the whole book helpful.

- **Attorney.** If you primarily work with small business owners in litigation, growth, or exit planning, this book will provide helpful background. Chapter 14, How to Review a Business Valuation, provides insight into how valuations might be tilted to favor one side or another, either inadvertently or intentionally.

DISCLAIMER

This is a book about business valuation. Business valuation is a curious mix of facts, assumptions, comparisons, methodologies, and theories, used to estimate a value to set standards, as of a specific date. If any part of the mix varies even a small amount, the suggested solution and the calculated result are likely to change substantially.

In addition, in many areas of business valuation, there are multiple methods and theories which may be correct and equally suitable. Finally, the theory and accepted practices are always changing. An effort has been made to reflect current thinking as of the publication date but change is constant.

The need for professional judgment cannot be understated in business valuation. Therefore, use this book as the resource it is. But, liberally use other resources and always follow Standards. Finally, no tax, legal, financial, valuation, or other specific advice is being given. Always use your best judgment and, if you are unsure, check with experts.

NOTES

1. Regarding the source of this quote by Richard Caruso, a variation is often claimed to be by Warren Buffett but my dad was saying it long before that. Officially traced to John Maynard Keynes, "It is better to be roughly right than precisely wrong." Before that, John Banham, a British industrialist, was quoted as saying, "We are in danger of valuing most highly those things we can measure most accurately, which means we are often precisely wrong rather than approximately right." This seems to have particular meaning for valuators. Finally, the original quote is attributed to Carveth Read (1848–1931), a British philosopher and logician, "It is better to be vaguely right than exactly wrong."
2. 2012 Census Data Employer Firms. *See* https://www.sba.gov/advocacy/firm-size-data

Acknowledgments

I would like to acknowledge the following friends and professionals who went out of their way to assist me in the development and writing of this book. They contributed substantial personal time and significantly improved this book. Each has brought their outstanding technical backgrounds, personal brilliance, and experience to the book. I thank each of you.

Michael Gregory, ASA, CVA, former PE, Certified General Appraiser

Cheryl Hyder, CPA, CFF, ABV, CFE, CVA

James M. King, CBI

P. Dermot O'Neill, CPA, ABV, CVA, MAFF, ABAR

Ronald D. Rudich, CPA/ABV/CFF, MS, MCBA, CVA/ABAR/MAFF, CM&AA, CMEA, BCA

Alan Zipp, JD, CPA, CVA, CBA, CFE

I would also like to acknowledge my wife, Robbin Caruso, for unending support.

I acknowledge my parents Barbara Singel and Richard Caruso, who taught me that, "I would rather be approximately right than perfectly wrong."

I would like to thank my long time partner Eddie Davis for his support. Parnell Black and Brien Jones for giving me the opportunity to edit "Around the Valuation World" webinar. That involvement led to writing this book.

Lastly, I would like to acknowledge Shannon Pratt, Jim Hitchner, Chris Mercer, Nancy Fannon, Fred Hall, Jim

Alerding, Roger Grabowski, Jim Harrington, Lance Hall, Aswath Damodaran, and the many, many, unnamed consummate professionals who have both raised the bar for the business valuation profession and provided teaching and thought leadership. I aspire to perform at their level.

The Art of Business Valuation

CHAPTER 1

What Is My Business Worth?

In theory, the value of a business or an interest in a business depends on the future benefits that will accrue to it . . .
—Shannon Pratt, *Valuing a Business*, 4th Edition
(New York: McGraw-Hill, 2000)

What is my business worth? This is the essential starting point for business valuation.

VALUE IS NOT PRICE

Price is what someone is willing to pay for the business. Price includes the quality of the sales process, negotiation, emotion, economic demand, timing, luck, and financing. Price for private businesses often includes terms with post-closing price adjustments based on continued business performance or adjustments due to failures of representations and warranties. These terms are hard to translate into useful data. There are no mechanisms to determine downstream what actually gets paid for earn-outs and seller notes.[1] There is no verifiable data on how often representations and warranties result in post-closing price adjustments. The importance of emotion in the sales process cannot be overstated. It takes tremendous energy to buy or sell a business. This is diametrically opposed to the valuation process.

VALUE IS ...

Valuation consists of applying established analytical methods and preset assumptions to what is known or knowable about a company in order to estimate its value as of a specific date. These assumptions rarely resemble real-world sales situations. Value and valuations are useful for sale and exit planning discussions but they do not represent prices. In the same way, value is useful when there will not be an arm's length sale. Value is the best that can be done for situations such as adding or removing owners, divorce, litigation, and required compliance situations, for example bank loans, estate and gift taxes, Employee Stock Ownership Plans (ESOPS), fairness opinions, and the like.

Value and price are related but not the same. The only way to determine its price is to buy or sell a business.

Most of this book is about how to value a business. Chapter 13 addresses working with business owners to prepare them and the business with an exit strategy. The chapter concludes by explaining ways to sell small businesses in the market for a price profitably.

NOTE

1. Earn-outs are adjustments to the price based on results that occur after a sale closing. Seller notes are sometimes adjusted or not paid after closing. Each of these can be viewed as an adjustment to the price paid. There is no mechanism for these post-closing price adjustments to be reported to the transaction databases.

CHAPTER 2

Valuation Basics

This chapter covers the basic business valuation assumptions and methodologies that are the necessary building blocks of every estimate of value.

VALUATION IS MODELING

Business valuation is the process of taking a subject company and, through the application of different models, estimating a value. Different models work best in different situations. Each model is generally referred to as a method in business valuation. Selecting the correct model is done using professional judgment, reviewing all available information along with the standards of value and purpose of the valuation.

A key concept is that business valuation models tend to be comparisons. In each case, there are two sides to the comparison: the subject company and the comparables. It is important to try to align the two sides as closely as possible. When that is not possible, it may make sense to use another model. Sometimes there is no model that is close and more professional judgment than is typical will be required.

There is no perfect method, only useful methods. However, even a useful method can be applied in a misleading way. At every level, selection of the model and then proceeding to choose and screen the inputs for comparison, are key to a supportable valuation.

All comparisons have shortfalls. There is no perfect data on either side of the modeling equation. Our job as valuators is to impartially align the two sides and then account for variances where possible, using the method to project into the future.

What is important is considering what will improve our model. Ask the right questions, use the right model, select inputs for apples to apples comparables and then adjust as reasonable. Finally, ask, "Does this make sense?" Work with the case until the answer is YES. That is the truest application of "I would rather be approximately right than perfectly wrong" and that is the Art of Business Valuation.

THREE PRIMARY APPROACHES TO BUSINESS VALUATION

There are many models or methods for valuing a business. These fall into three main approaches.[1] It is important to select the best model or method in order to obtain the most accurate business valuation.

There are three primary approaches, each with different methods for valuing a business. The approaches are the market approach, the income approach, and the asset approach:

1. **Market Approach.** The market approach uses the theory of substitution. Market comparable sales are substituted for the company being valued. In practice, this means that market comparable cash flows and financial information are compared and substituted for the subject company to estimate a value. This is the primary means used for valuations of small and very small businesses.
2. **Income Approach.** The income approach examines what an investor would pay for a business, based primarily on its cash flows. Investors have many choices of how to deploy

their money. Using financial data collected since 1926, the risk and reward actions of investors are used to estimate the value of the subject company.

3. **Asset Approach.** The asset approach estimates the current value of the individual assets of the business. These approaches tend to ignore or underestimate the value of intangible assets, such as goodwill. For this reason, the asset method is often referred to as a floor value. If the business is not generating value based on its cash flows in the market approaches and income approaches, then the assets may be sold, establishing a floor value or high liquidation value. The asset method tends to be used when the subject company may be considering whether to stop operating, owns valuable assets such as real estate, definable and protectable intellectual property, valuable equipment, e.g., excavation companies, or the company is a holding company.

Types of Business Valuation Engagements

Business valuation engagements fall into two different categories: the calculation of value and the conclusion of value. These are revisited in more detail in Chapter 12, Details for Business Valuators.

Calculations of Value. *Calculations of value cover a large range of work product agreed to by the valuator and the client.* Calculations may vary from the simple flat spreadsheet estimate of value (see Tom's Residential Air, provided on the associated website), to something just short of a conclusion or opinion of value in breadth and scope. In all cases, the client needs to be notified that calculations require less valuation procedures and the resulting estimate may vary from what a full valuation engagement would have found.

Conclusion of Value. These are commonly thought of as Opinions of Value but the American Institute of Certified Public Accountants (AICPA) reserves the word "opinion" for audits exclusively. *Conclusions are complete valuation engagements* where the valuation analyst had access to all the necessary data in order to determine the estimate of value. The underlying work and analysis are thorough and complete. Report levels may vary depending on agreement and use.

VALUATION THEORY BACKGROUND

Business valuations for all sizes of business are built on a framework of assumptions. The highest level building blocks of these assumptions are identified and defined in the business valuation report. This section defines some very significant assumptions on which business valuations are built.

STANDARDS OF VALUE

Standards of value is a subtle concept that permeates every assumption made throughout the business valuation. *Who is the buyer and who is the seller?* Every buyer and every seller will have biases and limitations, along with advantages, that will be reflected in the final value found.

A simple way to look at this is to think what would happen if you are selling a high speed but somewhat dangerous race car. A race car driver is going to have a very different view of the value than a family looking for a safe way to transport three kids. At some point the family may buy the race car because it is considered a bargain, but only to resell it because it dos not suit their purposes. Clearly who the buyer is matters. Who the seller is can work very much the same way.

Professional judgment is understanding what is important. That begins with understanding who are the parties to the transaction you are valuing.

Different businesses have different risks and rewards which will be acceptable or unacceptable to different buyers and sellers. Different businesses will also require different levels of sophistication to manage. Different buyers will have different expectations of advantages or disadvantages in running the business that should result in different expected levels of profitability. Therefore, the individual characteristics of the buyer and seller drive many elements and assumptions in valuation. Real-world examples are:

- Gas stations and convenience stores are often sold to people for whom English is a second language. These businesses do not require as much conversation as a consulting business.
- Tax practices are usually sold to CPAs or enrolled agents or other types of accountants and tax preparers.
- Industrial distribution companies can be sold to a variety of people depending on the size and level of complexity of the products distributed.

There is one other piece to this puzzle of standard of value. Namely, is the value being estimated the value to the seller, the value to the buyer, or both? The two parties to the theoretical transaction may have very different views of the value of the business. In the real world of buyers and sellers, most businesses are not for sale, which is just another way of saying the business is worth more to the owner than to buyers who are just other potential owners.

Let's look at some common standards of value:

Fair Market Value

What is the definition of fair market value?

Fair market value is the price at which the property would change hands between a willing buyer and a willing seller, when the former is not under any compulsion to buy, and the latter is not under any compulsion to sell, both parties having reasonable knowledge of relevant facts. Court decisions frequently state in addition that the hypothetical buyer and seller are assumed to be able, as well as willing, to trade and to be well informed about the property and concerning the market for such property.[2]

An alternative definition is:

> *Fair market value is the price, expressed in terms of cash equivalents, at which property would change hands between a hypothetical willing and able buyer and a hypothetical willing and able seller, acting at arm's length in an open and unrestricted market, when neither is under compulsion to buy or sell and when both have reasonable knowledge of the relevant facts.*[3]

Critical to the understanding of fair market value is its inherent subjectivity, which even the Appraisal Foundation acknowledges. According to the Uniform Standards of Professional Appraisal Practice (USPAP):

> *Value expresses an economic concept.* As such, it is never a fact, but always an opinion *of the worth of a property at a given time in accordance with a specific definition of value.*

Fair market value is about a fictitious buyer AND a fictitious seller. It is important to remember that we are dealing with the actual business and other surrounding actual facts but even the "seller" is not our actual owner. Our owner for personal reasons might never sell, but the assumption is our fair market value seller will make a deal at some price.

With small businesses it often is helpful to try to visualize the buyer and seller under this standard. Some businesses can be purchased by almost anyone, such as a convenience store or liquor store. These require few special skills and anyone with the drive and money could buy them. Many businesses take some level of expertise or licensure. Law firms tend to be purchased by other lawyers or law firms. As businesses get larger, more expertise and skill are required by buyers. Looking at a possible real-world buyer often makes it easier to apply professional judgment about how the buyer would treat various facts and unknowns or unknowables about the business.

Note that market value in real estate valuation and fair market value in business valuation do not have the same definition. In real estate appraisal, market value includes the assumption of "highest and best use." Real estate appraisals assume a reasonable marketing period as part of the definition of market value instead of a marketability discount that is often used in business valuation under a fair market value standard of value.

Many people assume fair market value includes highest and best use. When working with clients or other users, make sure they understand the value you are calculating is based on the assumptions about the buyer and seller. Talk to them about what fair market value really means in business valuation.

Market Value

IFRS, the International Financial Reporting Standards, contain a reference to market value. Market value has a definition similar to fair market value in real estate:

30.1. Market Value is the estimated amount for which an asset or liability should exchange on the valuation date between a willing buyer and a willing seller in an arm's length transaction, after proper marketing and where the parties had each acted knowledgeably, prudently and without compulsion.

30.2. The definition of Market Value shall be applied in accordance with the following conceptual framework: (a) "the estimated amount" refers to a price expressed in terms of money payable for the asset in an arm's length market transaction. Market Value is the most probable price reasonably obtainable in the market on the valuation date in keeping with the market value definition. It is the best price reasonably obtainable by the seller and the most advantageous price reasonably obtainable by the buyer. This estimate specifically excludes an estimated price inflated or deflated by special terms or circumstances such as atypical financing, sale and leaseback arrangements, special considerations or concessions granted by anyone associated with the sale, or any element of value available only to a specific owner or purchaser.[4]

This appears to be much closer to price and to the real estate appraisal definition of fair market value than standards of value currently used in America.

Investment Value

Investment value is the value of a known company to a known specific buyer. In effect, it is the opposite of fair market value where both parties are fictional. In this case both parties are known. The buyer may be a financial buyer or may have recognizable synergies. An investment value definition is: "The value to a particular investor based on individual investment requirements and expectations."[5]

Actual pricing situations with known parties are investment value.

Synergistic Value

The definition of synergistic value is:

70.1 Synergistic Value is the result of a combination of two or more assets or interests where the combined value is more than the sum of the separate values. If the synergies are only available to one specific buyer, then Synergistic Value will differ from Market Value, as the Synergistic Value will reflect particular attributes of an asset that are only of value to a specific purchaser

70.2 If the synergies are available to multiple market participants, then the Synergistic Value may be consistent with the Market Value, as the price the asset should exchange on the valuation date between a willing buyer and a willing seller would likely reflect the value of any synergies available to multiple market participants.[6]

Can a Synergistic Value Also Be a Fair Market Value? To go back to the race car analogy, who is a fair market buyer? Is it anyone wanting a car? Is it only those people wanting race cars? Exactly how broad or narrow is the definition of people wanting race cars? While this question seems silly, contrast this with Synergistic Buyers. At what point is a race car driver synergistic? This leads to the question that has been raised: "Are all market sales synergistic since they were purchased by the most motivated buyer not the typical motivated buyer?"

In *BTR Dunlop Holdings, Inc. v. Commissioner (Dunlop),*[7] the U.S. Tax Court ruled, among other things, that a valuation analyst must look at the pool of potential buyers when determining the fair market value of a target entity.

With respect to *Dunlop*, there were six potential buyers, all of whom had a synergistic incentive to acquire the target entity. Therefore, based on the synergistic pool of potential buyers, the Tax Court ruled that a hypothetical willing and able buyer would enjoy the benefits of synergistic value upon acquisition. This indicates that, when it comes to valuing a target entity, a valuation analyst must first examine and understand the market of potential buyers.

A pool of potential buyers comprised exclusively of financial entities (e.g., a private equity fund) would likely find no synergistic value in the target entity. If this were the case, the fair market value standard of value would be more appropriate.[8]

Fair Value

There are at least two different definitions of Fair Value. The first, according to FAS157, for General Accounting and Auditing Standards (GAAS) purposes, namely, for financial reporting:

> *5. Fair value is the price that would be received to sell an asset or paid to transfer a liability in an orderly transaction between market participants at the measurement date.*

It is an exit price for a particular asset or liability. It could be a stand-alone asset or liability or a collection of assets and liabilities, such as a reporting unit or whole business. Part of the fair value definition is that the asset or liability price will have a reasonable time on the market. Therefore, there would not be independent discounts for marketability.

The second definition of fair value is specified by many state codes and court decisions for the purposes of corporate and divorce litigation. In most of these cases, fair value of the interest is calculated to be fair market value of the entire business divided on a pro rata ownership interest basis. However, there is no universal definition.

Example

One example is from Maine. According to the Supreme Judicial Court of Maine:

> The valuation focus under the appraisal statute is not the stock as a commodity, but rather the stock only as it represents a proportionate part of the enterprise as a whole. The question for the court becomes simple and direct:
>
> What is the best price a single buyer could reasonably be expected to pay for the firm as an entirety? The court then prorates that value for the whole firm equally among all shares of its common stock.[9]

Fair value in court cases provides indemnification to the minority owner who is unable to stop a majority owner from taking an action, but no longer wants to be an owner after the actions are taken.[10]

Intrinsic Value

Intrinsic value is occasionally used in litigation. It is used in Virginia divorce cases. Here is a quote from the lead case, *Howell v. Howell*:

> *Intrinsic value is a very subjective concept that looks to the worth of the property to the parties. The*

methods of valuation must take into consideration the parties themselves and the different situations in which they exist ... Commonly, one party will continue to enjoy the benefits of the property, while the other will relinquish all future benefits. Still, its intrinsic value must be translated into a monetary amount. The parties must rely on accepted methods of valuation, but the particular method of valuing, and the precise application of that method to the singular facts of the case must vary with the myriad situations that exist between married couples.[11]

It is difficult to apply that standard of value. It has been summarized by Virginia practitioners as "Fair Value along with whatever the judge wants to consider and find." Others have said it is a "crap shoot" or "beauty contest". Be prepared.

It is important to note that there are two types of courts in the United States (except Louisiana), courts of "equity" and courts of "law." Courts of equity are supposed to make things right and produce fair and equitable results. Courts of law are presumed to apply the law even if the result does not seem fair or equitable.

Divorce courts are courts of equity. This means the court (often a judge or jury) is doing its best to be fair. Sometimes fair in the larger context of the case may mean ignoring or reading things into the best business valuation that are not there.

Liquidation Value

What is the definition of liquidation value?

Liquidation value: the net amount that can be realized if the business is terminated and the assets are sold piecemeal. Liquidation can be either "orderly" or "forced.[12]

The adjusted equity value found by the asset approach may be deemed to be a high liquidation value. There are tiers of liquidation value, each assumed to be lower than the last. Orderly liquidation will decrease this value based on "reasonable" costs with a somewhat restricted time to liquidate assets. Forced liquidation will further decrease value based on the additional costs and sellers "must sell now" situation.[13]

Standards of Value in Litigation and Divorce

Many small business valuations are performed for litigation and divorce situations. In those situations, state statutes and the relevant courts have often defined the standard of value. Usually these standards are fair market value or fair value. But, beware, sometimes the court will use one standard of value in name and apply a different standard of value in practice.

Therefore, whenever doing a business valuation for litigation, confirm the name and the definition of the standard of value being used in the state or local jurisdiction. Ask your client's attorney for the standard of value to be applied. If they do not know the standard of value to be applied, check on your own. Just Google the case law under a search such as, "Business Valuation, Standard of Value, Divorce, New Jersey." You may also look it up in a resource such as "Standards of Value: Theory and Applications."[14] Just make sure standards have not changed since the publication's date. Read the definition and even the leading case so you understand what the standard of value really is—not just what the term is.

Conclusion: Standard of Value

Standard of value is a subtle concept that permeates every assumption made throughout the business valuation. Who is the buyer and who is the seller? Every buyer and every seller will have biases and limitations along with advantages that will be reflected in the final value determined. Professional judgment begins with a clear understanding of the relevant parties in the transaction.

Make sure you understand the standard of value to be applied in the business valuation process. If the work is for litigation, make sure you understand the definition used for the standard in the jurisdiction. Fair value is NOT always your definition of fair value. The standard of value is a basic building block level of assumption that affects every other assumption and calculation made.

PURPOSE OF THE VALUATION

The purpose of the valuation and the standard of value are often linked together. Namely, the purpose will often define the user and often the user has specified a standard of value. For example, Gift Tax purpose will be prepared for the Internal Revenue Service (IRS) and maybe the tax court. IRS regulations and related court rulings specify that fair market value is the standard of value. Another example is corporate, or partnership, or limited liability company dissolutions will often specify a fair value standard of value under state law.

But, the purpose of the valuation does not always specify the standard of value. For instance, a business valuation for mergers and acquisitions (M&A) purposes can have a fair market value, investment value or synergistic value.

While not as all-defining as the standard of value, the purpose may influence the methods used and assumptions made. For instance, a valuation for internal M&A purposes is likely to be based on the market method. The same valuation for litigation may be based on the income method.

PREMISE OF VALUE

The premise of value answers the question, does the valuator expect the company to continue as a going concern or does the valuator expect the company to cease operations? Going concerns are expected to continue operating into the future. Companies that are not going concerns are expected to be liquidated usually for asset or liquidation value as discussed above.

The Three-Legged Stool

Ron Rudich, CPA, ABV, CFF, CVA, and an instructor for the NACVA/CTI, always teaches that there is a three-legged stool concept that valuators must know and follow.

1. Standard of value.
2. Premise of value.
3. Purpose of the valuation.

If any of these are incorrect, then the valuation will go "off the rails" and the conclusion will be suspect.

ANALYTICAL FRAMEWORK OF BUSINESS VALUATION

Below is a general framework for how to proceed with a business valuation, with cross-references to the relevant chapters in this book. What is not shown is the iterative nature of the process. Changes in one part of the valuation may cause changes throughout other parts. For instance, changes raising the cash flow might result in a lower multiplier if "soft data" does not support the overall found value. This iterative process is integral to business valuation.

- Define the Work (Chapters 3, 12)
- Examine the Company
  - Historical Financial Data (Chapters 4, 11)
  - Normalization of Financials (Chapters 5, 11)
  - Financial Ratios (Chapter 4)
  - Soft Data (Chapter 4)
    - Internal (e.g., People, Processes)
    - External (e.g., Economy, Industry)
    - Forecasts (Chapter 8)
- Select Approach
  - Market (Chapter 6)
  - Asset (Chapter 7)
  - Income (Chapter 8)

- Estimate Value (Chapter 12)
- Examine Interest/Discounts (Chapter 9)
- Goodwill (Chapter 10)
- Final Review (Chapters 14, 15)

This outline will be expanded in the book.

Chapter 13 covers preparing an owner and the small business for a sale and touches on the business purchase and sale process.

MECHANICS OF PREPARING A VALUATION

This section will cover an efficient method for preparing business valuations. Different practices will have different levels of delegation of these tasks. In larger practices, the signor may be providing oversight, guidance, and editing. In many practices, ministerial portions of the work are done by assistants and true valuation portions requiring professional judgment are done by valuators.

Obtaining the Engagement

Depending on the type of engagement, this usually involves a call with the client or the client's advisor. The level of technical discussion will depend on who is on the other end of the call and the purpose. The following questions need to be determined to prepare an engagement letter and provide a quote.

- What is the subject entity?
- What is the interest being valued?
- Who is the client?
- What is the purpose of the engagement?
- Who are the other parties authorized to use the report? (This is often clear from the purpose.)

The following points are always considered in price estimation:

- The size of the business in terms of people and revenues?
- A detailed review of available statements and quality level (e.g., tax returns prepared by owner or accountant, compilation, reviewed, or audited. Cash basis, GAAP, or some other basis). This is often more difficult than it sounds.
- An investigation of contractors, or as businesses get larger, ask for one year's tax returns and internal statements to see what we are working with. Some firms ask for most of the valuation data prior to quoting.

Other items that need to be determined to provide a quote are shown below.

- Standard of value
- Compilation or opinion
- If a compilation, what work needs be performed to meet user requirements and meet the client's needs and valuation standards? While standards provide flexibility for calculations, standards provide that work may not produce a misleading result. The Statements on Standards for Valuation Services (SSVS) also require objectivity in dealing in all professional services (SSVS No. 1, 14).

Can the engagement be performed for a fixed fee or are there so many unknowns that an hourly rate is required? This often bends into clients' desires and purpose. As businesses get larger, there tend to be multiple entities, investments in other businesses, and other loose ends that make fixed fees quite difficult. With small and very small businesses, outside of supporting discretionary add-backs, usually there is only so much documentation and information to be obtained, reviewed, and worked with.

Engagement Agreements. These are essential when doing a business valuation. Engagement agreements specify the work to be performed along with all the other crucial information. They are important to define the limits of your engagement and your ultimate liability for errors or problems. Many firms have several engagement agreements for different purposes, standards, and reporting levels.

When doing fixed fee work, it is important to specify exactly the work that is being performed for the fee. Clear specifications are important for both the work being developed in a calculation, the calculation report deliverable, and the cost. For an opinion or conclusion, the work must meet standards and is already defined. But the report level must be specified and the payment terms stated. When preparing an opinion or conclusion, the valuator has agreed to do the work necessary to render the opinion. That is a work specification.

However, if the valuation is being done for a fixed fee, the work included in the fee may not be everything that is required or desired. For instance, forensic work in litigation to verify underlying numbers is likely to be outside the scope of the fixed fee valuation and report work. Clear specifications of the work included in the fixed fee can provide the best of both worlds by allowing the analyst to quote a fixed fee for known work and the ability to bill for unknown work. Just be very clear in the specification of what is included in the price and be clear with the client so they understand the specific terms.

Documentation. Often the most difficult part of the process to manage is obtaining documentation. Sometimes clients have little or no motivation to provide the documentation. This can be particularly egregious in divorce and litigation situations. Another variation is "compliance," i.e., providing documents under court order where the other party sends the documentation but cut-offs, cash or accrual basis, and the like are mysteriously different. Even when clients are motivated, they tend to be busy and in small companies the book-keeper and owner are each likely to have three other responsibilities.

It is good practice to tell clients at the time of the engagement that there are generally two major document requests. The original one at the beginning and a supplemental one to further support matters that arise from initial review. Clearly, there may be more document requests but in most cases this creates the expectation on the client's behalf to expect a second round of documentation. Often creating a reasonable expectation is half the battle.

The owner/management interview is often done in two steps for small and very small businesses. Many valuators use a questionnaire for the basic interview. The questionnaire covers business organizational matters, potential add-backs, accounting matters, and so on. Sample questionnaires are on the website for this book. Most valuators develop their own questionnaires to fit what they think is important. An important consideration is to develop one that actually gets completed. With small and very small businesses, long questionnaires tend never to be completed. For larger businesses with true financial staff, more detailed questionnaires will be useful. Later, after initial review, a true interview may be set up or additional questions and document requests sent to answer remaining questions.

Documents, when saved into the computer, should be saved with file names that are meaningful. As firms get larger, standardization of folder layout and file names becomes a must. Anyone who may need to access files to prepare, review, or figure out what was done three years later must be able to understand the folder and file structures.

Around this time, initial research should be performed. Economic reports, industry information, comparable data, build-up data, and any other necessary research should be performed, reviewed, and placed in the file.

Once the initial documents have been received, the financial data should be entered into the worksheets. Initial draft adjustments and rough-cut valuation estimates may be calculated. This provides a better understanding of the case and provides time to think about assumptions and other professional judgment matters.

Initial Review. The folder should be reviewed based on data received to date, and should specify what other documents are going to be needed. Often these will revolve around verifying add-backs. Sometimes additional detail is needed with payables or receivables. Sometimes notes and items in the financial statements or tax returns will also indicate loose ends that need to be followed up. Remember, in an opinion of value, standards require doing all the work necessary to issue the opinion.

Questions to ask yourself at preliminary review:

- Does this make sense?
- What is unclear or inconsistent?
- What seems unusual for the business, industry, and so on?
- Is data clear and organized? If not, how can we supplement and test reasonableness?
- What additional data from the company or third parties will help?
- What is missing? What advantage or risk is not being seen at all? Remember your biggest risk is what you do not see at all.
- How will the report be sanity tested? How will the value found be tied on some level to the world of price?

While work must be done in a linear fashion, there is an iterative nature to business valuation. Major assumptions provided by standards and purpose are mixed with company and financial information to then hone new assumptions and questions. This cycle may go on two or three or more times. It can be much like solving a complex math equation. This is truly the Art of Business Valuation.

Once all the initial documentation, research, and financial data and the questionnaire replies have been entered, the analyst will follow this up with email questions and/or a phone or in person conference. Make sure that the notes include who the parties are, the date and start time, and the matters covered. Contemporaneous notes are very helpful. Some younger valuators record the calls with permission. (Always get permission and make the request for permission the first part of the call.) Zoom or other computer/video conferencing is becoming common and is quite effective.

The draft calculations should be updated with revised figures derived from original financials, support documents, and answers to questions. Critical assumptions and judgment issues should be worked through. A second draft of the computations should be completed.

Report Writing. The report can be started. Most small and very small business valuations are based on some level of standardized template report. Specialized software for business valuations often contain templates.[15] Sometimes the calculations are included in the report and sometimes they are attached as exhibits. The report detail and level will vary with what was agreed in the engagement agreement.

In most cases (again unless clearly otherwise specified in an engagement agreement letter or if it falls in a category reporting exception), it is important to write up all assumptions used in preparing the report. All professional judgment matters should be discussed. Methodologies used to verify add-backs, if any, should be reviewed. The valuator should create a road map that can be followed by others as to how the value was determined. This gives users and reviewers the ability to see what was done, replicate results when desired, and modify if they believe that is in order.

Usually writing the report will generate a few more questions and perhaps the need for more documentation. Get these resolved as soon as possible at this stage.

Complete the report. Put all the exhibits and other information into the report. Review the report to make sure all critical matters are addressed and that the value found is fully supported. The aim is to make a case for your value found that is fully supportable and credible and can be reproduced by other qualified valuators. The AICPA Professional Standards are very rule-based. For that reason, SSVS can serve as a checklist for your work. The NACVA has developed checklists which are useful for this purpose also. Finally, Chapter 14, How to Review a Business Valuation also can be used to check your work.

Proofing and Publishing the Work. Have the report proofed. Point out any matters that may be questionable or where you are still considering alternatives to the reviewer so they may focus on them.

Make final modifications and publish and send to the client. In some instances it may make sense to provide the work to the client or attorney as a draft. This may be even more the case with small and very small businesses. Often, upon reading the report, no matter how many times you asked, new helpful information comes out at the time of the review. Sometimes these legitimately change the value found.

Make further changes and issue the final report and opinion or calculation of value. Most business valuators are paid in full prior to issuance of the final report. For small assignments often the retainer obtained at the start covers the entire fee. This simplifies collection and removes any concern about "contingent payments."

PROFESSIONAL JUDGMENT

> USPAP STANDARDS Rule 9-5 Comment, The value conclusion is the result of the appraiser's judgment and not necessarily the result of a mathematical process.
>
> (2018–2019 USPAP)

As clearly stated in the above USPAP Standard, judgment is key. Yet how does one apply judgment to develop an accurate business valuation? The topic of professional judgment is further developed in Chapter 12, Details for Business Valuators.

You're Never Going to Be Exactly Right

There are many reasons why finding the "exact" answer is not going to happen. The biggest reason is the premise that valuation is about future cash flows from a going concern. One thing most small businesses owners will agree on is that they really cannot predict future cash flows. If an owner with 20 years' experience cannot *correctly* predict his next year's cash flow, how can we?

We cannot. But we can make a *reasonable* prediction of cash flows and we can apply *reasonable* (again they are unlikely to be what happens with hindsight) multipliers and capitalization rates to produce very meaningful and accurate opinions of value or conclusions of value as the AICPA and other bodies specify. After all, the best we are expected to do is give an "opinion."[16] This is never going to be demonstrably correct like a simple tax return or audit. It is rarely going to be consistent with what actually happens over the next few years.

Focus on What Matters

Business valuation requires a high level of professional judgment; this is the "art" in what valuators do. There are many elements and applications of professional judgment. This element is very different from book-keeping, basic taxes, or much of auditing. There is often no clear right or wrong. For a more detailed discussion of professional judgment and what matters, see Chapter 12, Details for Business Valuators.

Much of professional judgment boils down to focusing on what matters. If we ask the right questions and use reasonable assumptions and valid logic, we are going to meet our professional obligations and standards while providing a valuable service to our clients and third parties. This is "accurate" in business valuation. Accurate is not exactly predicting the future. That is never going to be achievable.

Asking the Right Questions

One of the keys to business valuation is asking the right questions. The perfect answer to the wrong question yields an inaccurate result. In fact, in litigation, often the two sides are answering very different questions when preparing business valuations for evidence. Hence, the very different results.

Key questions that should be reviewed—several times—during the valuation process include:

- What interest am I valuing?
- How does this interest relate to the overall company?
- What additional risks or benefits exist for the interest that are different from the company?
- What is my purpose?
- Who is my user?
- What do they need to know and why?
- What is my standard of value?
- How might the standard of value buyer/seller vary from the buyer/seller in my comparable data?
- Is this really the best comparable data set and method?
- What am I missing? (That question cannot be emphasized enough.)
- What more do I need to know?
- What risks/advantages does this company have?
- How do those vary from my comparable data?
- How can I adjust for that variance?
- How can I sanity check this?
- Does this make sense? (Ask yourself this question over and over again.)
- Is the valuation date set or might it move as part of the process?[17]

Most major errors in business valuation are the result of missing facts or patterns and misinterpreting those facts or patterns, not from the improper application of the model. For instance, failing to factor in falling fuel prices into a bus company valuation that results in a very high valuation.

Note that these questions are not specific financial questions but much more modeling and seeing the big picture to improve the results type of questions.

Remember it is better to be "approximately right as opposed to perfectly wrong."

NOTES

1. The three most common valuation approaches are: the income (income-based) approach, the asset (asset-based) approach (used for businesses, business ownership interest, and securities) or the cost approach (used for intangible assets), and the market (market-based) approach. SSVS 100, Valuation Approaches and Methods .31
2. IRS Revenue Ruling 59-60.
3. *International Glossary of Business Valuation Terms.* Retrieved from http://www.bvappraisers.org/ glossary/glossary.pdf.
4. Exposure Draft: IVS 104–Bases of Value.
5. *International Glossary of Business Valuation Terms.* Retrieved from http://www.bvappraisers.org/ glossary/glossary.pdf.
6. Exposure Draft: IVS 104–Bases of Value.
7. 78 T.C.M. 797 (1999) T.C. Memo. 1999-377.
8. *See*   http://www.willamette.com/insights_journal/13/summer_ 2013_7.pdf.
9. *In re Valuation of Common Stock of McLoon Oil Co.,* 565 A.2d 997,1004 (Me. 1989).
10. *Della Ratta v. Larkin,* 856 A.2d 643 (2004) ; 382 Md. 553
11. *Howell v. Howell* 523 S.E.2d 514 (Va. Ct. App. 2000).
12. *International Glossary of Business Valuation Terms.* Retrieved from http://www.bvappraisers.org/ glossary/glossary.pdf.
13. Auction costs may include: advertising, hiring an auctioneer and staff, costs to conduct the auction, tagging assets, preparing a brochure for the auction, supervised viewing of assets, etc.

14. J. Fishman, S. Pratt, and W. Morrison, *Standards of Value: Theory and Applications* (New York: Wiley, 2013), Appendix C. Retrieved from https://onlinelibrary.wiley.com/doi/pdf/10.1002/9781119204244.app3

15. I use ValuSoft. It provides a very good platform and the report writer allows for easy changes. At this point, I have many templates for different methods and situations. See https://www.valusource.com/

16. ASA, SSVS 100.

17. Both divorce and some planning purposes may have "moving" valuation dates as the process continues.

CHAPTER 3

Why Is Valuing Small Businesses Different from Valuing Larger Businesses?

The problem with valuing small and very small businesses is that there is an information gap on both sides of the model or equation.[1] Small and very small businesses are just not very good at data collection, much less providing it to third parties. Most small business owners manage by walking around. In addition, the best owners have a few indicators that tell them where they stand; perhaps incoming orders and cash balance; perhaps today's cost of goods. They have their one or two simple indicators and a feel for the business. This way owner/operators can run great businesses and keep overhead down. While this limits long-term growth, it creates significant overhead efficiencies. Consequently, this lack of data makes economic and business sense.

Therefore, even "reliable" sources cannot have data that is better than what the businesses have. Having reviewed hundreds of small business financial statements and tax returns, one of the few things I am sure of is that little of the data available from small businesses meets standards that larger companies must comply with, both to keep control of the business and for compliance with requirements like employment law, safety standards, loan covenants, taxes, and so on.

Many owners drive costs down in all areas, including bookkeeping and tax compliance. The result of this is many tax returns are prepared by certified public accountants (CPAs), enrolled agents, and others who do not review the underlying financial information unless it is clearly deficient. They just enter the data. If they do review and clean up the data, adjusting entries often do not make it back to the internal books. Reviewed or audited financial statements are rare. Supplementary data beyond accounts payable and accounts receivable aging, and third party provided payroll reports are the exception.

In addition, many well-run small businesses tend not to have any formal business plan, forecasts, operating agreements, shareholder or buy-sell agreements or written direction forward. Many small business owners are convinced that these are a waste of time because they cannot predict the future. Based on the fact that most small businesses have a very limited range of products or services, limited geographic range, and have a comparably small number of customers, small business is subject to the winds of change, be it economic change, industry demand, or technological change (i.e., the Amazon effect).

There tends to be increased susceptibility to concentrations in small business. Customer concentration, supplier concentration, even referrer concentration can cause shocks to small business when the resource is lost.

Another concentration is the smaller and more limited management teams. These managers are often well trained at their day-to-day tasks but do not have broader training to move up as the business grows. This too can slow growth and create problems if someone leaves.

Yes, we could walk away from these challenges but that would not leave a lot of small businesses to value. In many cases of divorce, Small Business Administration (SBA) loans, small business sales, and other planning situations, the above

TABLE 3.1 Employer Firms, by Size of Firm, 2012

Receipt size class	Firms	% Firms	Total %
Total	5,726,160	100.00	
<100,000	1,160,026	20.26	20.26
100,000–499,999	2,288,643	39.97	60.23
500,000–999,999	878,945	15.35	75.58
1,000,000–2,499,999	733,402	12.81	88.38
2,500,000–4,999,999	298,715	5.22	93.60
5,000,000–7,499,999	110,951	1.94	95.54
7,500,000–9,999,999	57,463	1.00	96.54
10,000,000–14,999,999	60,995	1.07	97.61
15,000,000–19,999,999	31,500	0.55	98.16
20,000,000–24,999,999	20,160	0.35	98.51
25,000,000–29,999,999	13,523	0.24	98.75
30,000,000–34,999,999	9,860	0.17	98.92
35,000,000–39,999,999	7,362	0.13	99.05
40,000,000–49,999,999	10,633	0.19	99.23
50,000,000–74,999,999	14,490	0.25	99.48
75,000,000–99,999,999	7,100	0.12	99.61
100,000,000+	22,392	0.39	100.00

Source: Census data, 2012.

limitations are ever present. After all, as of the last date when data is available, as shown in Table 3.1, 96.5% of all firms have less than $10 million of revenues, 93.6% of all businesses have under $5 million of revenues and 75.5% of all businesses have under $1 million in revenues. Clearly most businesses are small businesses. These challenges are present in the vast majority of small and very small business valuations.

This is a very different environment than larger businesses with controllers and finance officers who often produce and review sophisticated operations, accounting, and finance data. This data is then taken and either reviewed or audited by third party accountants. This produces reliable data that can be compared to other similar-sized reliable company data. Again, the comparable data set is larger, more organized companies. Clearly this improves both sides of the valuation equation (the compared and the comparables) and in many ways makes it easier to produce an accurate or at least more supportable business valuation.

Larger companies often have multiple product lines, broad geographic areas, and many, many more customers, reducing concentration risk. Planning and forecasts are part of larger businesses process. Plans are implemented and forecasts are reasonable and tested over time.

Therefore, the emphasis and focus on many small business valuations should be directed at determining the reasonableness and likelihood of future cash flows. A high level of professional judgment must be applied in making adjustments to the cash flows and in applying valuation approaches. For most small business valuations, approximate is as exact as anyone will ever get.

When valuing smaller companies, the application of common sense and judgment in determining both cash flows and proper valuation theory is essential. It is even more important than in larger businesses where financial statements are prepared by knowledgeable people and then reviewed or audited by outside firms.

Therefore, the Art of Business Valuation is to keep asking the question, "Does this make sense?" until the honest answer is "Yes."

IS THIS A BUSINESS OR A JOB?

The independent contractor world has created a fuzzy line between a modern job and a small business. In theory, independent contractors have their own businesses. Yet, do they really? Despite what Uber is selling to their drivers, their drivers have jobs. (This is not a statement on payroll tax matters.) No matter how much money an Uber driver makes, there is nothing to sell. Uber drivers have no independent goodwill.

Anyone with a suitable car and driver's license can become one. This is an easy example.

What about a dog walking business with one owner who does all the walks and makes $75,000 per year? The answer may depend on whether the owner has a contract with a company that does everything except the actual walking or if the owner has direct contracts with the dog owners. Is this a business? If the owner has multiple direct contracts (even if oral), this can be sold.

According to the Financial Accounting Standards Board (FASB), the definition of a business is:

> *805-10-55-3A A business is an integrated set of activities and assets that is capable of being conducted and managed for the purpose of providing a return in the form of dividends, lower costs, or other economic benefits directly to investors or other owners, members, or participants. (FASB No. 2017-01, January 2017 Business combinations (Topic 805))*

The FASB's definition is for use in accounting for Business Combinations. In the FASB's case, since this is for accounting purposes after a sale or purchase, the ability to sell the assets or business is assumed.

A small business exists for our purposes as business valuators when:

- Client relationships are transferable, or
- There is technical knowledge or processes that are transferable, and
- There is the possibility of making money in the foreseeable future.

Namely, "profits, people, and processes," as my partner Eddie Davis likes to say.

At the point when the dog walking business's revenues are $225,000 and the owner handles sales functions and has other people do the walking, assuming the owner takes a reasonable salary, this looks like a nice very small business.

Under this standard there are many small businesses that look like "jobs" to outsiders or many highly paid professionals. Let's take look at a "job" that may be familiar to many valuators: Accounting practices.

There is a very good market for small accounting practices that essentially earn the owner the equivalent to a salary for mid-level professional staff at a mid-sized local firm. Most of the owner-operators work as hard as, or harder than, their equivalent at the local firm so it is not a matter of a difference in hours or dollars per hour. Perhaps the owner just does not fit in corporate America. Small accounting firms sell rapidly and easily. Apparently there are a lot of these people.

Here is an example that makes economic sense to the buyer.

Example

Bob is an immigrant, who was a doctor in his old country but between licensing and language issues, he is not going to get far here. So he works at a convenience store as a clerk for $20,000 per year. He belongs to an investing club and has an opportunity to buy the store where he works. Now he will make $35,000 during the five-year loan payoff period and thereafter close to $100,000 a year once the debt is paid. If a person has limited options, this is a very good economic decision.

The opposite has happened with small primary care medical practices. At one time there was a good market for them. Now most young physicians would rather make $150,000 with benefits by having a job rather than owning a small practice and maybe making $175,000. Because they have a choice other than being business owners to make a good living, the small medical practice has lost almost all value.

This directly ties into another essential point—who is our buyer? What are their motivations and, just as important, what will they *never* buy? Most important is, how does that impact the data we are comparing and the ultimate price?

This is distinct from selling assets such as a vehicle. Yes, a vehicle is necessary for a transportation business but the fact that it was or can be used in a business does not make the car a business. For most small businesses, the tangible assets are comparatively easy to obtain and, while necessary, they do not usually contribute much to business value.

Similar but different is the very high level of technical skills that cannot be transferred. A fine artist could have a wonderful "business" or practice or career but great difficulty in its transfer. Relationships and technical knowledge, if they can be duplicated and transferred when they produce income, have business value. Again, back to Eddie Davis: "profits, people, and processes." Many independent contractors will fail this definition of a business because the client is not transferable or the technical knowledge is not transferable.

Some may meet those standards but not have the possibility of making enough money to transfer. It is difficult to transfer small dollar amounts of relationships and technical knowledge. *For many very small businesses, the training and transition costs are higher than the entire likely business value.* Buyers have a similar issue with the amount of effort to perform due diligence. Often due diligence costs are more than the very small businesses is worth. Particularly if you have to perform due diligence on three or four businesses to buy one. This is an effective barrier to business value in very small businesses. In those cases, the client at best has a business with no value or more likely has a job.

NOTE

1. Also commonly referred to as micro-businesses. Because the owners and consultants and valuators who typically work with these businesses usually refer to them as small or very small businesses we will use those terms throughout the text.

CHAPTER 4

Assessing the Subject Company

This chapter addresses the information collection and basic analysis of the subject company. A firm understanding of the company, supported by documentation, is necessary in order to effectively make comparisons under both the income and market methods. What we are really assessing is, according to Eddie Davis: "people, processes, and profits."

No matter how complex a company or situation may seem while working through a valuation, when complete, the valuation analyst should be able to provide a concise and clear analysis. If the analyst cannot do that, then more work is needed. Being able to simplify is a major indication that you are achieving the Art of Business Valuation. Companies are people, processes, and profits. This chapter is about understanding the company.

DOCUMENTS NECESSARY FOR A BUSINESS VALUATION

An engagement to estimate value results in either an opinion or conclusion, or a calculation. In all these cases, the estimate needs to be based on the combination of facts and the opinions of key people inside and outside the company, the assumptions provided to the valuator as well as the assumptions made, and estimates performed by the valuator. Here we are going to look at the documents, forms, and possible interviews used to build a foundation for the statement of value.

Sample Detailed Document Request

A detailed document request could be worded like this:

> *We have been engaged to prepare a valuation. Please provide all information requested below. If the information does not exist, please note on the form and return with the information. Thank you for your patience and assistance.*

- Brief history of the company
- Last 3/5 years tax returns with all schedules including depreciation schedule
- Last 3/5 years financial information including:
  - income statement
  - balance sheet
  - statement of cash flows if prepared
  - audit/review/compilation report, notes and schedules, etc., if prepared.
- Internal year to date financial statements with prior year comparison data
- Trailing twelve months (last twelve months) income statement if available
- Current accounts payable and accounts receivable aging
- Copy of all notes payable
- W-2s or 1099s for owner and/or key manager
- Equipment list with estimated current market value
- List of top 10 clients and last year's revenues from each
- Summary of key customer or supplier contracts, including term, minimum and maximum amounts, classifications of owner/company if applicable, extensions (particularly

important for government contractors, may be referred to as "vehicles")

- Work in Process or Work in Progress (WIP) schedules if used by industry, company (construction contractors, software writers, some manufacturers)
- Business plan
- Cash flows, budgets, forecasts, projections for future, current and past 3 years
- File copy resumes of owners and top tier employees along with organization chart
- Breakdown and back-up for
  - all compensation to owners
  - all compensation to owner's family
  - all benefits to owners
  - all benefits to owner's family
  - all duties and time spent for owner's family.
- Unusual one-time charges (e.g., large one-time legal expense)
- Copies of LLC operating agreement or all corporate charter information, by-laws, and minutes
- Any buy-sell agreements or shareholders agreements
- Related transactions details
- Any purchases or sales of stock
- Information on Key Man life insurance policies
- Real estate leases
- Appraisals of the real estate used if owned by an owner of the company or the company
- Franchise documents and, if for a sale, prospective franchise documents for buyer
- Any franchise industry analysis or information provided in last 3–5 years
- Any valuation performed within the last 5 years
- Information and back-up on any:
  - advantageous or disadvantageous contracts
  - contingent or off-balance sheet liabilities or assets
  - trademarks or other intellectual property

- litigation
- information on prior offers or sales of stock or LLC interests
- if in construction or manufacturing, bid waterfalls, contract backlog reports
- Web URL
- Anything you feel would materially affect the value of the firm
- Completion of questionnaire form

Subject Company Backbone or Primary Documents

Subject company backbone documents are those documents that provide the framework of the business valuation. They are the starting point of the analysis. They provide documentation to build a historic financial model of the subject company. When collecting the documents and entering and reviewing them, remember the following:

- What is the likely cash flow that is going to be chosen for modeling and comparison?
- What are the likely valuation methods that will be used?
- What information is needed to create a reasonable comparable subject company based on the above two criteria?
- What is not being asked for or looked at that could materially move the needle up or down?
- Has a reasonable level of support documentation been requested, particularly for add-back adjustments?
- Does this make sense?

Now a little more detail on key documents. Many of these documents are addressed in much more detail in Chapter 11, "Accounting Issues with Small and Very Small Businesses."

- **Tax returns.** For many small and very small businesses this is often the only financial document that has been reviewed by a third-party financial person. Sometimes even these are prepared by the owner. Fortunately, that is rare. Because they are examined by an independent or semi-independent person and because they are filed with the government, they have the presumption of being the most accurate and useful source of financial data in most cases. They sometimes are still wildly wrong. Examples of errors include no opening inventory (but they purchased and sold inventory over the year) when a company with inventory was purchased. Inventory starting and ending amounts that never vary. Uncollectable accounts on accrual basis that have never been written off and are far in excess of the contra account. The list goes on and on.

- **Internal financial statements.** Larger businesses will have both financial statements and tax returns. Many small businesses really do not. Usually the accountant will make year-end adjustments so the tax returns and the financial statements tie together but not always. Balance sheets tend to be less complete than income statements. Ask for both. If the tax returns appear in order and were prepared by an outside firm, that is likely to be the best data available.
- **Compiled, reviewed, or audited financial statements.** Few small companies have audited financial statements. Those with loans or bonding may have reviewed financial statements. Where available, notes attached to properly prepared audited or reviewed financials or occasionally compiled financials are one of the most useful sources of data available. In some cases, notes are more useful than the financial statements as they provide clarity about the stated amounts and many details on operations and liabilities. This quality financial statement is a luxury. If these statements (particularly reviewed or audited) are accrual-based and the tax returns are cash basis or quite different, the valuation may be based on these statements and not tax returns. Audited financials are better than tax returns. They are just as rare as hens' teeth with small and very small businesses.

- **Forecasts.** If the company has forecasts, this may become a backbone document. They should be requested in all circumstances. Most small businesses will not have forecasts. In general, that is OK. Review of forecasts is covered in greater detail later in the book.
- **Discretionary and other add-back questions and support.** Many small businesses bury or hide their discretionary owner's expenses/benefits. Seller's discretionary earnings (SDE) is the most important cash flow figure with small and very small businesses. These expenses and adjustments may not be easy to find. Ask for a chart or list of owner benefits and perks. It is common to require additional follow-up support documents for these adjustments.
- **W-2s or 1099s for owner, owner's family, and/or key managers.** If the owner's salary is not shown as a breakout (or if all owners' salaries are not shown), the W-2 will provide salary support. If the owner is not an owner/operator, then often the key manager's compensation can be substituted for the owner in the seller's discretionary earnings formula. While salaries are not supposed to be paid to partners in partnership returns, many small business owners take a salary and pay payroll taxes. Do not assume there is no owner's salary with partnerships just because it is not clearly shown. Guaranteed payments can be treated as salary when shown for partnerships. Technically guaranteed payments is a distribution.
- **Accounts payable and accounts receivable agings.** These are helpful to understand cash flow and working capital for both cash and accrual accounting methods when available. Sometimes with accrual-based accounting, you will find old receivables that are uncollectable and not written off. Similar but rarer are old accounts payable that were expensed but never paid and will never be paid. Depending on the details, these can call for adjustment.
- **Questionnaires.** Standards bodies require management interviews. Questionnaires provide consistency and an

efficient way to start or do a management interview. These will be covered in greater detail in the next section.

These documents provide the information to determine cash flows and make adjustments so the comparables and the subject company are using comparable measures for cash flow. The data will also be valuable in assessing the quality of the company as it compares to the comparables under the market method. The income method uses the same processes to adjust cash flows.

OTHER DOCUMENTS FOR DETERMINING ENTERPRISE VALUE

Enterprise value is the value of the company itself. It is equal to the value of a 100% interest in the stock or assets of the company.

- **Top 10 client list.** This provides the analyst with a better understanding of customer concentrations. If the business has strong repeat customers, generating the list over 3–5 years to show consistency of customers is also strong evidence of continuing relationships. Continuing relationships are evidence of better-run companies in many industries.
- **Real estate lease.** Many businesses have advantages due to locations, low lease rates, or special build-outs, making the lease assignability and extensions a key to value. While often the lease assignment or extension will be assumed, for many purposes, issues surrounding the lease term and assignability can greatly diminish value. The lease should be reviewed to see:
  - What is the term of the lease?
  - Are there extensions or options to continue at the will of the tenant?
  - If close to the termination date, have notices been given?

- How is rent determined at an extension
  - a continuation of the historic rent increases?
  - a larger automatic increase?
  - an appraisal or other negotiation with no cap?
- Is the lease assignable?
- What is the history of the landlord with assignable or more so, unassignable leases?

    Lease terms need to be reviewed. In one mall lease, the business had agreed to give 10% of the sales price (not equity after debt) to the landlord. In another retail lease, rent went from $100,000 per year to $150,000 at the extension. Other landlords are known to not cooperate with assignments, no matter what the lease says. These are difficult matters that greatly impact business value for businesses with advantages due to location or rate.

    Finally, is the company subject to percentage rent? These are common in malls and high end retail locations. In those cases, ask if the landlord has performed an audit or if the client prepared an excess revenue worksheet to calculate additional rent.

- **Franchise agreements.** Transferability, including franchise transfer fees, can greatly impact value. More and more franchises are charging almost as much to transfer between owners as to start a new unit. Another wild card is the cost to upgrade facilities at the time of transfer. Upgrades can sap the value of many smaller franchise operations like sub-shops. Further ongoing fees should be checked against the financials to ensure they are consistent with the documents. Sometimes the old fees are not consistent with new fees. Finally, franchisors often have rights of first refusal and approval rights at time of sale. These too can impact value as they add time and sometimes reduce buyers. I have seen these rights exercised very late in the sale process. Do not assume the franchisor will not buy-in the unit without investigation.

- **Other contracts.** If the firm relies on one or two contracts for either supply or customers, these should be obtained. Time periods that the agreements remain in place need to be noted. This can be particularly important with government contractors and construction contractors. It is very important to know the type of contract, how long it extends, extension options, and terms, or if the contract was based on an owner status, such as disabled veteran or other.
- **Employment agreements.** Employment agreements of shareholder officers, key management, and perhaps other employees can contain non-competes and other restrictive covenants. Frequently the officer may be required to sell his or her shares of stock if employment terminates.
- **Lending documents.** Larger loans can contain loan covenants that specify requirements that the business has to meet. If the business does not meet them, interest rates can increase or the loan may be called. Also, in some industries like construction, be aware that short-term lines of credit may be called in recessions when they may be needed the most. (Early in my career as a homebuilder, I was given this advice about bankers. This advice has never failed me, "A banker is someone who gives you an umbrella and when it starts to rain, they ask for it back." Remember that for yourself and your clients.)
- **Equipment leases and financing agreements.** For many small businesses these payments can be substantial. They often also tend to slip past the request for all liabilities. Double-check if these exist and are properly shown on the financials. Even if they are not required to be shown on the financials, make sure they are in the cash flows.
- **Work In Process or Work In Progress (WIP) schedules.** For contractors and some large item manufacturers, work in process is an inventory category and the schedule is an effective tool for measuring job progress, backlog, profitability, and the like. Comparing WIP schedules over time can be quite useful to see trends.

- **Bid waterfall.** Organized contractors maintain data on prior bids and bids outstanding, along with a ranking of future likelihood based on past results with the contracting company and type of work. Often they will not provide it in sales situations out of fear of misleading the valuator as relationships and markets can change quickly. But, when available, they provide insight into the possible future.
- **Contract backlog.** Evidence of future work is an important indicator of value.

Most of the remainder of the documents on the list relate to valuing interests which constitute less than 100% interest in the company and will be discussed in Chapter 9, Valuing Partial Interests in a Business.

Add-Back Documents

Creating an apples-to-apples cash flow is a major component of doing a business valuation. Here we will list a few documents that may be required to verify add-backs. In general, if the valuation is a calculation, for internal use, and is not for dispute purposes "taking the seller at his word" is often acceptable. Do properly document the level of documentation and examination you are performing in your engagement agreement letter and report. Make your level of examination clear in the report also, just in case the report is given to a third party. Clarity is a valuator's best defense.

This list is assuming there is not a situation requiring forensic accounting-type work which is not covered in this book. Do note that the American Institute of Certified Public Accountants (AICPA) Statement on Standards for Forensic Services No. 1 becomes effective for engagements accepted on or after January 1, 2020. If an engagement is for litigation or investigation purposes, review and comply with the new standards.

- **Salary related.** W-2s for owners, if not shown on the tax return. W-2s for managers and family members, as applicable. Payroll reports for year to date as necessary.

- **Other family benefits.** If family members work at the business, develop a chart of titles, tasks, hours worked. Obtain 1099s or W-2s. Make reasonable estimates of the true economic value of the work performed and the profit distribution portion. A sample of an analysis of family benefits is shown in Table 4.1.

- **Auto expenses.** If the business really is not reliant on transportation, often the shown auto expense can just be added back. If the business does have delivery or other transportation expenses, then an understanding of how they are assessed is necessary. Verification documents will vary but could include credit card payments and statements, mileage information, number of vehicles, and who uses them. Document what is said and use reason and judgment. In general, few people will argue that an owner-used company car is worth $5,000–$7,000 or so between gas, maintenance, insurance, and so on. Sometimes it is reasonable to plug a figure like that if the accountant left the expenses in the tax return. Again, depending on the purpose, in some cases, if a "personal" auto is owned by the business, the cost of the auto and depreciation should also be removed from the balance sheet.

- **Debt payments, including auto loans.** Take care to check that loan principal is not being added back. Many owners and untrained bookkeepers do not understand that principal is not an expense in financial statements. Usually, but not always, if an outside accountant is used for tax returns, they will have corrected this. As a final check, when material, obtain the lender's payoff statement (sometimes the remaining balance is shown on the payment statement) for the loan and tie into the balance sheet.

- **Meals and entertainment, travel, etc.** Usually add back 50–100%, depending on the fact pattern. Rarely is additional support necessary unless amounts are very large or it is a divorce or litigation situation requiring forensic work.

TABLE 4.1 Sample Family Add-back Chart

Name	Relation	Title	Salary	Employer Payroll Tax	Auto	Health Ins	401(K)	Other	Total Benefit	Estimated Labor Value	EBITDA Adjustment	SDE Adjustment
Mary Smith		Owner	$100,000	$8,000	$10,000	$20,000	$5,000	$10,000	$153,000	$150,000	$3,000	$153,000
Sam Smith	Spouse	Bookkeeper	$50,000	$4,000	$10,000		$2,500	$5,000	$71,500	$20,000	$51,500	$51,500
Tammy Smith	Daughter	Labor	$45,000	$3,600	$5,000		$2,200		$55,800	$12,000	$43,800	$43,800
Theo Smith	Son	Driver	$65,000	$5,200			$3,000		$73,200	$50,000	$23,200	$23,200
Notes: EBITDA Add-Back											$121,500	
SDE Add Back (Includes all of Mary's compensation unless already added back elsewhere)												$271,500

It was reported by Mary Smith that:
Sam Smith works on Saturday putting the books together. Payroll is done by an outside service.
Tammy Smith is at college four hours away and works about 3–4 months per year.
Theo Smith graduated college last year and does a variety of things. It is hoped he will stay.

Notes:
This is viewing all benefits as part of compensation. Often each benefit will be added back and just salary adjusted.
Estimated Labor Value Calculations–pull data from Census or other source along with local knowledge
Mary Smith - This $3,000 adjustment would only be made for EBITDA. Using SDE, her entire compensation is an add-back.
Sam Smith - 8 hours a week times $40 per hour times 52 = $20,000.
Tammy Smith - 8 hours a day $16 per hour 90 days per year = $12,000
Theo Smith - Maybe the most difficult as it is unclear what his role really is. Likely to depend on starting pay scale in industry.

- **Health insurance.** Obtain payment statements to verify total monthly payment. Ask what percentage is paid by the company. Verify that it was not removed from the statements you are using as a basis for the valuation. Health insurance is complex and changing and treatment on tax returns for owners varies over years and entity types.
- **Credit card statements.** Generally, the statement must be examined. For most businesses, Victoria's Secret is an add-back. Home Depot for a contractor would be difficult unless delivery tickets or work order to personal home or office, and so on.
- **Vacation home, other personal items, children's schooling, mistress, etc.** Not getting into morality, the mistress's apartment in New York City is probably an add-back.

QUESTIONNAIRES AND MANAGEMENT INTERVIEWS

Questionnaires and management interviews are where the valuator really learns what is under the hood of the business. I refer to many of these factors as "soft" factors. Soft factors tie into motivations, culture, attitude and can be difficult to understand and quantify.

The financial information is a type of score. It indicates success or failure financially. The ability to quickly obtain clear financial information is also an indication of organization and effective business processes. Certainly, the old adage that "success breeds success" applies, yet the continuation of success into an uncertain future depends on many factors including soft factors. Those internal factors are learned by asking questions and listening to understand how the company really works.

Every valuator tends to use their own questionnaire. Several different forms and formats are provided on the website for this book. There is always a conflict between the amount of information the valuator would like to obtain and what the small business owner is willing and able to provide. In many cases, if you ask for too much, you end up getting nothing. Remember at all times, businesses are people, processes, and profits.

Does the business have a culture of: "forever and continuous improvement" or "resiliency in the face of problems"? These two factors often are the biggest indicators of future success or failure. They are also cultural matters that may be hard to quantify.

For small businesses, the following seem to be the major areas of emphasis:

- Company history, including start date, dates of ownership changes, timeline of major changes in products, services, business policy that made a difference
- Business culture, mission statements, employee handbooks[1]
- Current industry, products and services, unique niches
- Competitors and changes in market
- Sales and marketing methods
- Customer, supplier, referrer or other concentration
- Bid or sales waterfalls, backlog
- Licenses, permits, bonding issues
- Contingent liabilities not on the books, disgruntled former employees, union pension liabilities, customer complaints
- Organizational structure chart and key people. Number of full-time and part-time people at supervisory and production levels. Time with the company and likelihood of staying in future. This is often supplemented by a website or resumes if they exist.
- Human resource issues, union, unemployment and workers compensation, insurance matters, lawsuits, compensation and raise policies, benefit package
- Are key people independent contractors or employees? How is this impacted by employment tax law? Is this normal in the industry or a reason to be concerned?
- Processes and systems used in all areas of the business
- Are there commodity pricing risks or other "uncontrollable" parts of the revenue/expense chain?

- Intellectual property, trademarks (often very little and it is relatively unprotected)
- Accounting policies, cash, accrual or tax basis, attitude to personal expenses, cash handling processes
- Owner and owner's family personal benefits and add-backs
- Organization type and tax status. State tax issues, particularly if multi-state.
- SWOT analysis: Strengths, Weaknesses, Opportunities, and Threats
- Overall assessment of the last few years and some years in the future.

In every instance, the history and policies of the company are important. But, the fact is, the most important thing is what the foreseeable future is going to look like. How are these policies, people, processes, and so on going to impact the company over the next few years?

These items need to be reviewed against the following screen:

- Does this business have a defensible market position?
    - "Working harder" businesses or "trains run on time," namely, we out-hustle the competition can be very good businesses. They tend to be very dependent on culture and/or the owner/manager as a hustle and work ethic is a human resource. For this reason, they often have lower multiples. This can particularly be the case with businesses which often have HR/personnel issues, like restaurants, auto repair shops and the like.
    - Sticky businesses with continuing income streams like service mechanical companies, software as a service, and other recurring income streams often receive a premium.
- Are there customer concentrations or supplier concentrations? What is being done or can be done to reduce these risks?
- Does the company have systems in place?

- Quality systems are "when average people get extraordinary results every time." Use this as the standard to determine systems. One indicator is if there are, "lots of reasons why things are not working," generally, their systems do not work.
- Are proper systems in place to control cash, inventories, production, including production of services?
- Is the sales and marketing process stable or growing the business? Is it all based on the owner or a single salesperson?
- Who are the people running the systems?
  - Even quality systems need trained qualified people. How does the company obtain, retain, train people?
  - Are there key people in place? What are the tenure and likely future for these people?
  - Are they subcontractors, contractors, or employees?
  - Is the culture a "can-do" culture or other?
- Does the owner have the ability to continue growing and adopting or is the owner reaching their maximum capacity and/or interest?
- Does the company have other sources of resiliency that will allow it to survive as business continues to change?
- How does this fit within the industry and economic outlook?
- How does the company fare against "the Amazon effect," namely, ever-changing technology? (Although it seems to the author that Amazon is just a modern Sears Catalogue company.) These changes have been very detrimental to newspapers, taxis, retailers, distributors without a service component. It was recently reported that phone apps have started to replace some advertising premiums.

Again, will the people, processes, and profits in place promote the growth or retraction of cash flows for the business in the foreseeable future?

Questions that may be helpful for major important areas in most companies include:

Product/service

- What are the products or services provided by the company?
- Does it serve a very narrow niche or is it a broad base?
- Does the company have systems to improve the products and services?
- Is there an ability to change the products and services?
- What does the company do so well that the market allows them to make a profit?

History of the firm

- What is the story?
- How long has the business run substantially as it does today?[2]
- What need was being met?
- Have the primary services or products changed?
- What does the chain of ownership look like?
- Does the firm have a history of litigation, labor problems, and other risk indicators?

Systems

Quality systems are when ordinary people get exceptional results—every time.

Richard V. Caruso

Businesses have many systems, most of which are rarely thought about but each of which is necessary for the company. In each case, how does the company document these systems (usually orally in small businesses) and train the people who run them? Understanding this is essential to understanding the resiliency of the company. Figure 4.1 is a list of systems that exist in a typical business.

Product and Service-Related
Product development
Cost estimating
Bidding
Purchasing / buying
Contract negotiation / administration
Testing

Accounting
General Ledger
Accounts Payable
Accounts Receivable
Payroll
Job cost / Product sales & gross margin
Tax preparation
Regulatory requirement data collection

Sales and Marketing
Advertising placement and evaluation
Lead collection / CRM or other tracking
Website
Events, other marketing
Sales
Order taking
Delivery

Production
Receipt / storage
Production / processing
Quality control
Packaging
Delivery

Human Resources
Hiring
Compensation
Review
Promotion / Release

FIGURE 4.1   Systems in a Typical Business

Sales and Marketing

In small companies these are often combined. How are new customers attracted? Advertising, word of mouth, commission, independent contractor, salespeople? Some companies and industries are very sales-oriented, such as mortgages and specialty products. Others such as institutional food service and many distribution companies are very customer service-oriented.

How does the business retain and attract customers? Is the pipeline managed or is it more haphazard?

People

The value of most businesses goes home every night. Even most commodity businesses require service. Service requires people. Many small and very small businesses are labor suppliers for larger businesses.

How does the business attract, obtain, retain, train people? What do the results look like? Some industries and businesses have constant turn-over. Others are quite stable. How does the company compare to the industry?

Is there a culture of forever and continuous improvement?

This really gets down to the culture. Is the culture open, caring, can-do? How does this tie into results and how will it facilitate or hobble the future plans for the business? Employee energy along with a can-do attitude has gotten many companies through tough times and eventually into high profits. This can be a key factor.

Key management team. All employees are important in small and very small businesses. As the businesses grow, the management team becomes more important. Often in small businesses, the "management team" will be an administrator who handles purchases, a bookkeeper accounts receivable/accounts payable (A/R A/P) clerk and a salesperson or two.

It is important to know the age, health, and likely retirement of the management team. Often management teams are about the same age as the owner. If they are all retiring when the owner does, this can be a problem. For instance, a family business consisting of three brothers, one wife, and son, who are the management team of a small mechanical contractor, will have a problem as four of the five managers intend to retire within a year or two of each other.

Is there an up-and-coming "star" in the management team? Sometimes small companies sell for a premium because they have extremely talented sales or technical talent that is staying.

The likelihood of the management team staying with a successful business at a sale is a major factor in the value. Marketability even of a 100% interest is greatly reduced if there is no transition team staying with the company.

Facilities and Equipment

Facilities and equipment generally form a straightforward category. It is the stuff used by the people and systems to produce or distribute the goods and services. Important factors to consider are:

- Age and remaining life on equipment
- Capacity of equipment – if capacity is reached, what are the upgrade costs?
- Maintenance costs and maintenance practices to extend equipment life
- Possible obsolescence of equipment, particularly before leases or loans are up.

As an example, if the company has five trucks and they are varied in age and mileage, that should not cause an adjustment. If the company has five brand new trucks that could cause a small upward drift in value but probably not nearly enough to pay off the loans if the trucks were financed. If the company trucks all need replacement, that will lower value.

Facilities, particularly real estate, can affect a company in several ways and need to be investigated. Some companies have very favorable locations. Convenience stores, gas stations, and the like require long-term leases or owning the real estate to maintain value. They are clearly location-dependent. Others, while less clear, gain significant advantage by facilities location, such as some construction companies with yards close to major cities cutting transportation costs and driver labor, and companies with under market lease rates locked in. Some companies have an unusual build-out that would be costly to reproduce, such as bowling centers.

At the other extreme are companies that have long-term leases that a buyer would want to extinguish. Industrial, distribution, and service operations often consolidate locations to reduce overhead.

Example

> *A restoration (due to fire damage) dry cleaner was told at a retail dry cleaning conference that he needed a long-term lease to create value so he went home and locked one in. What he did not realize is the conference was mainly for location-dependent retail dry cleaners. His prospective buyers were industrial and had significant synergies if they could close his plant. Therefore, in his case, the long-term lease hurt his value.*

These changes may or may not be synergistic. Use of these facts will depend on the overall fact pattern, standard of value, and purpose.

Technology

Technology is affecting every business differently but it is affecting every business. A few pointers on different things seen in different businesses:

- **Software.** The movement to the Cloud is making the transfer of software at closing simpler. New issues are constant updates, security, backup, and what happens when the Cloud goes down or is locked up for "ransom"?

- ERP (Enterprise Resource Planning) software can help small businesses by providing a framework and standardization.
- Quickbooks is a mixed bag. It has simplified accounting but has also made it much easier to do things wrong.
- Does the company have a somewhat unified system or many separate systems?
- Is there an industry standard and a strong reason to use the standard? For instance, larger government contractors tend to use Delteck ERP and accounting software. If used by the subject company, this will allow for simpler integration of the company when sold.
- **Integration with suppliers and customers.** Larger customers and suppliers now require working through their systems. How does that affect the company?
- **The Amazon effect.** Is there something on the horizon that will change the whole industry or supply chain or customer relationships for the industry? What is the prognosis for the industry for the foreseeable future?
- **Obsolescence.** At various times new equipment that is cheaper to buy and use has come out that replaces earlier versions, causing substantial losses to companies. An example is CAT scan machines in radiologists' offices around 2010. New equipment came out and lowered reimbursement rates for CAT scans below the cost of operating two-year-old CAT scan equipment that cost $1,000,000 each with five-year payment plans. Needless to say, this created substantial one-time losses for those businesses.

Concentrations

Concentrations kill. Concentrations are the main reason why small businesses are so much riskier than larger businesses. A large customer or supplier or other concentration can cause major disruption and bankruptcy when relationships end. Small and very small businesses have all sorts of concentrations. Some almost by definition, others by choice. Many concentrations are unavoidable at least for periods of time.

- **Customer concentrations.** Industries where larger jobs are common, such as construction or software writing, are rife with this. Quality companies show a history of starting new jobs and relationships as old ones end. This greatly increases risk. Finally, there are small consultants and construction subcontractors who may only have one customer. In some small markets there may only be one or two primary customers. Great risk.
- **Product concentration.** Small companies may only have one or a few primary products putting them at risk of change of the product, supply chain, and so on.
- **Supplier concentrations.** Sometimes the company only has one or two suppliers for critical goods. Or perhaps the company is essentially a sales agent for one company. Can the supply be replaced quickly and cost effectively?
- **Referral concentrations.** In some cases, the company may have many customers but they only come from a few defined sources. Internet sales can come this way. For instance, if key words are used as a primary marketing means and they become too expensive. Or the engineering firm that has many customers but they all come from two or three architectural firm referrals. This can be harder to learn about and adjust for but can add just as much risk to the equation.
- **Key people concentration.** Almost impossible to avoid in small business. However, it greatly increases risk vs. a department of people with similar skill sets. Look for non-competes or non-solicits and/or employee contracts from/with key salespeople and top management. These do provide some protection from key people leaving immediately with other staff and customers.
- **Commodities concentration risk.** Transportation companies gain and lose profitability with fuel costs. Shippers that

focus on one product carry risk if the product price or desirability changes. Lumber yards, concrete suppliers, junk yards selling scrap metal may have commodity price and sometimes availability issues.

Site Visits

Site visits are an underutilized tool. Site visits are expensive and sometimes just not feasible. But a site visit can tell the valuator a great deal about the company. Particularly when the company is in full operation, the look and feel of the company can provide a greater sense of underlying company behavior than many days of financial analysis.

Preparing for the Site Visit. Often site visits are broken down into three parts. Meet and greet, the tour, and technical questions. Prior to the site visit, whenever possible, all financials should have been reviewed. The company information should be compiled and reviewed. Often a first draft work product may have been developed. From this work, general and specific questions can be developed for the visit.

Things to look for:

- Where is the business located?
  - Are there logistical or permit reasons for the location?
  - Would this place make employees and customers feel good?
  - Is it clean and safe?
- Entering the business
  - Is the appearance clean and organized?
  - If a company/industry that receives people at their offices, are the reception area and greeting proper?
- Tour
  - Again, is there a logical organization?
  - Are things clean and organized?
  - What is the feel or "energy" of the management and staff?

- Are equipment and means of production current?
- Is the equipment maintained?
- Is inventory adequate and safe?
- What is utilization of the equipment and space?
- Questions
  - Ask technical questions
  - Did anyone else participate besides the owner?
  - Does there appear to be management depth?
  - Overall, how did the visit go?

One sign of organization is if companies can get backup and detail in a reasonable timeframe. If every request requires building a spreadsheet from scratch, the company probably does not have proper organization in place (or you are asking for unimportant information).

Take notes through the interview. Remember nonverbal cues and look and feel and energy in a room often can say more about a company than questions and answers.

Skipping the Site Visit. Many businesses do not require a site visit to value them fairly. When performing a conclusion of value, if this step is not taken, it must be noted in the report. Small engineering firms, accounting firms, other firms located in offices may not require a visit. A franchise that must follow standards may not require a visit.

In the modern world many elements of a site visit can be duplicated. Google maps can show the location and street views for most businesses. Many retail businesses have pictures of inside the shop and many reviews. Menus, price lists, and other information can be listed on the website. Yelp, Facebook, and Google will often have rankings and references. These certainly tell you something.

Questions and answers can be handled over the phone or using a video service like Zoom. The main thing that is missing is being able to gauge the energy of the firm. Happy people and good energy somehow solve many problems that come up in business. Combine that with earnings and you have a powerful combination.

Ranking Strengths and Weaknesses

It is important to take the time to review the critical strengths and weaknesses of the business. Some businesses and certain industries are driven by different skill sets than others. Does this business have those skill sets? That would be a clear strength. A second way of looking at it is: What are the one or two critical factors that allow this company to compete? For example:

- Does it import parts for a low cost?
- Does it have strong goodwill with customers?
- Does the company have IT that creates efficiencies?
- Is the culture strong?

Weaknesses come from concentrations and limitations of all sorts:

- Is the business dependent on the owner/personal goodwill?
- Is the business dependent on other key personnel?
- Does the company have supplier or customer concentrations?[3]
- Is technology changing supply or sales chains?

Of note: What are the strengths?

- One or two people's brilliance may indicate transferability issues. If the key to success is that the team works harder, that can wear out over time or change when leadership changes. These are important strengths but may not give maximum value. If the strengths are more protectable, such as true trade secrets, or lower production costs, integrated and sticky systems with customers, then the strengths often create more value.

Typical strengths and weaknesses are shown in Figure 4.2.

In most instances the analyst will select two to five strengths and the same range of weaknesses. These should be weighted heavily later in the process when selecting the multiplier or

Possible Strengths	Possible Weaknesses
High revenues	Low revenues
Gross profit margin	Low gross margin
Profit margin	Low profit margin
Low cost suppliers	High costs
Market leader products	Generic products
Supply contracts	Unstable supply
Franchise name & relationship	No name
Relationships with	No relationships / unproven
Customer agreements	
Technology	Industry technology threats
Equipment	Worn equipment
Patents, licenses, etc.	
Limited competition	Easy entry / lots of competition
Trained workforce	No available talent
Managers, others with upside / long careers	Old management close to retirement
Sales system	Owner salesperson or sales in spite of self
Manufacturing system	Too much personal goodwill
Location	Concentrations of any type
Non-solicits, non-competes	Problems with staff / contractors
Positive enthusiasm, energy	Lawsuits
Barriers to entry	

FIGURE 4.2   Possible Strengths and Weaknesses

capitalization rate. The analyst can also provide strengths and weaknesses in each section of the business description.

Another way of presenting company strengths and weaknesses is shown in Figure 4.3 which is at the top of the next page.

DEAL KILLERS

The name is a bit of cliché but the following are items that can quickly reduce value and need to be investigated. Often they only last a year or two and in many cases they are eventually resolved. Yet, during the time they exist, they may cast a blight over the company and significantly reduce value.

- **State tax issues.** Very small companies may not have state sales, employment, and income tax issues in multiple states.

Strengths / Weakness Factors	Comments	Increase or Decrease
Profitability		
History of Growth / Stability		
Concentrations		
Owner Transition		
Systems		
Key People		
Workforce		
Location		
Equipment		
Goodwill / Customer Relationships		
Goodwill / Supplier Relationships		
Other Risks / Opportunities		

FIGURE 4.3 Company Strengths and Weaknesses

But with the spread of virtual workers and the ability to sell over the internet, many more companies are facing potential penalties and taxes from multiple states. The *Wayfair* case[4] has expanded the definition for having a nexus in the state. Once a company has a nexus in a state, it can be sued and taxed by the state. Many small business owners do not realize or choose to ignore nexus issues and the related sales tax, income tax, and payroll tax issues. If they are not addressed, they can become significant when penalties and interest are included and reduce value. Transaction due diligence over this issue has become heightened in recent years.

- **Lawsuits.** Lawsuits happen to companies. The pall they cast is usually much greater than the actual risk. Nonetheless while lawsuits are proceeding, particularly those for large dollar amounts that may not be fully insured, value is often reduced and marketability is affected.

- **Inability to extend or renew real estate lease.** Location-dependent businesses that cannot get lease extensions or assignments lose significant value until the problem can be resolved. Sometimes it cannot be resolved as the landlord wants to take over the business, take the profit from the transaction for himself, or change the use of the property.
- **Licensing issues.** Many businesses rely on licenses to perform their operations. If these are in jeopardy or become non-transferable, value can quickly diminish. While bars and restaurants losing their liquor licenses is common, this issue extends to many businesses with many levels of permits. Water discharge permits, zoning and occupancy permits including grandfathering restrictions, hazardous waste permits, professional licenses of all types, interstate and intrastate hauling road permits, bridge over-weight truck permits.[5] The list is long.
- **Government regulation/certifications.** Beyond licensing issues many small and very small businesses provide goods and services to various governmental entities. These governmental entities often have guidelines to promote small business, women's, veterans, minority participation, and other groups in their communities. These certifications can greatly increase the revenues of the business but in many cases those revenues and contracts can only be assumed by companies or owners who can obtain similar certifications. Since the classifications and certifications are generally for disadvantaged groups, it is logical that in many cases this will reduce the marketability of the company verses companies in the same industry without classifications. An extreme example of this is the 8(a) Disadvantaged Certification. Under that certification, certain qualifying minorities and disadvantaged people are able to obtain contracts at advantageous rates. But, the certification only lasts nine years with three additional years to complete contracts.[6] The statistics for companies staying in business at "graduation" from the program are terrible. It is reported

that two years after graduation, 90% of the companies are out of business. This is something that must be factored into a valuation of an eight-year old 8(a) company.

- **Internal disputes.** Internal disputes between owners is a major source of disruption and loss of value for small and very small businesses. Many companies are formed without proper documentation and thought as to the long-term relationships between owners. When situations change, there is no guidance or rules and a stalemate can ensure. Worse yet, one partner leaves with all or part of the business. Larger businesses have the momentum to survive these conflicts. They also have rules and agreements in place. The lack of proper documentation in the form of buy-sell agreements, operating agreements, employment agreements and the like can reduce the value of a business beyond the reduction in current operating results.

- **Consistent downward financials.** Small and very small businesses generally do not have forecasts, as stated before. They do not have trained financial people who can build forecasts and, more importantly, make a case for forecasts that show results different from the recent past. They also often just have limited markets and services and products, reducing their ability to change course. For this reason, consistent downward financial results produce very low prices. Exactly how this is translated into value is always up for discussion.

- **Poor balance sheet.** Weak balance sheets that indicate little long-term earnings (no income, no retained earnings, few distributions) weaken the valuation. For many small and very small businesses no or a weak balance sheet in the traditional sense may not hurt the value. But evidence that the company has never been profitable, or was marginally profitable shown in the equity section of the balance sheet can hurt the value or maybe right-size the value of a business that is showing a sudden surge in profitability. Some of the smartest business people the author has ever known spend most of their time examining the balance sheet when looking to acquire companies. That alone is something to think about.

- **Key employee agreements.** Signed employment agreements with non-solicits for customers and employees and non-competes can add value. Stay agreements that provide a bonus for staying a year or two years after a transaction or owner disability may also be viewed favorably.

EXTERNAL FACTORS AFFECTING THE COMPANY VALUE

The company operates in an environment with many factors beyond its control that are going to influence results in the foreseeable future. In this section we will review a few of those factors.

Key important factors to focus on from the economic and industry data are: does the background that the business operates in support growth or will it create challenges to growth? If the external future appears to create challenges, is it reasonable to believe this company will survive and at some point prosper?

In addition, consider how these external factors affect your subject company in ways that may vary from the comparison company set. This could be comparables for market methods or buildup data used for income methods.

The Economy

For small and very small businesses the impact of the economy on cyclical industries is underestimated in the short run. Many industries are tied into the economic cycle. All types of engineering firms, contractors, home-builders, appliance shops, moving companies, furniture stores, and the list goes on. A few small firms are well diversified and perhaps have a large component of service work but many will have two

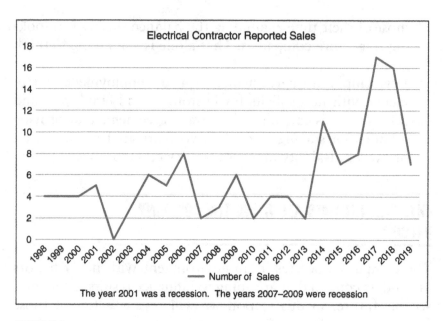

FIGURE 4.4   Electrical Contractor Sales by Year

or three breakeven/hopefully small loss years and then five to seven good years as part of the economic cycle. Very small companies in cyclical industries that carry a lot of debt often do not survive the downturn. Figure 4.4 provides the number of electrical contractor transactions shown in DealStats between 1998 and 2019. While certainly not conclusive, it appears that there are significantly less transactions in the years following the start of a recession (year 2001 had a recession and between the end of 2007 through early 2009 was a recession). This is very difficult to factor into a company value properly.

The most difficult part of evaluating the economy is that most people are pretty optimistic, particularly when things are going well. Obviously economic cycles are such that the best economic times come before the downturn. When times are really, really good, we "should" be downgrading our valuations because bad times are around the corner. For some reason as humans, we have a hard time doing that. It is always safer to look to the last few years rather than really honestly look at the future. Plus, how do we really know? By the way, it's not just valuation specialists, it's also the economists we need to rely on for this information.[7]

Having spent most of my life on the East Coast in Maryland, it was hard to understand just how much the local economy can impact a business. In Maryland, the local economy is really the regional economy, including much of the Federal government, and it is huge.

Recently having spent time in a ski resort town of 20,000 people in Colorado, which is 45 minutes from the next town (which has 2,000 people) and over 3 hours away from a major city, Denver, it has become clear in some instances how the local economy can be quite different from the regional one. In these cases, when that local economy is really the entire market, best efforts should be made to understand the primary drivers of the really local, local economy and evaluate them too.

Economic Data

Economic data can come from many sources and levels. International, national, regional, and, in some areas, local can all have an impact. There are many economic reporting bodies. A major one is the Federal Reserve. The Federal Reserve Market Committee regularly provides updates on the international and national economic outlook. The Beige Books provide an anecdotal-type analysis of the Federal Reserve districts. The Federal Reserve of Philadelphia publishes the *Livingston Survey* in June and December. Therein they provide their estimate of the maximum, mean (average), and minimum forecast of the growth of the economy for the next ten years. Finally, FRED, Economic Research from the Federal Reserve Bank of St. Louis has an amazing assortment of information, data, and even a downloadable mobile app because we all need instant economic data.

Economic data from international, to national, to regional and even local can be purchased from many sources, including BVR and ValuSource among others.

Industry Information

Industry information is available from a number of sources, including IBIS World, First Research, Hoover's Online, Value Line, and Current Industrial Reports from the U.S. Census, trade associations, and industry groups.

Industry information is the best source of data concerning the future of the industry. Is the industry growing or contracting related to the economy as a whole? Is the industry consolidated or fractured? What are expected changes in the industry? If major changes are expected, does it appear that the company being valued is in a position to benefit or lose out from the changes? Often suggested interview questions and areas of focus are provided.

Many major trade associations report economic data and indicators for their industry. Much of this must be purchased but often some indicators are available on the websites and blog posts and the like. Examples are the National Association of Realtors Economists' Outlook. One of the indices is Pending Home Sales Index.[8] Many people believe four months of downward pending home sales is a signal of a recession in twelve to eighteen months. At the time of writing the book, it fell from June of 2018 until December of 2018. It then recovered through July of 2019. We will see if it indicates the next recession.

Another example is the National Restaurant Association data. This information can be quite useful when valuing restaurants or restaurant-related suppliers and service companies.[9]

Sometimes local associations and boards may have indicative data. For example, real estate listings and sales data are available for many markets and are a leading indicator for many housing-related cyclical businesses.

The Amazon Effect

The Amazon effect is a term for the relentless rate of change primarily due to technology. How is the service and supply chain changing? If change is occurring in the company's industry, how will the company withstand and gain from it—or perhaps it will not.

Remember Moto Photos. If you are under 40, you probably do not. Amazing little businesses that printed pictures in kiosks located in shopping center parking lots with 35% profit (that is not a misprint) margins. Digital photos and phones quickly ended that business.

Industry data and parties to the business valuation are most likely to provide information on technology change. Careful questioning is the best way to reveal these issues.

The Amazon effect has had devastating consequences for many retailers. Yet large well-located convenience stores with gas have thrived. Small wholesalers have been decimated yet ones that provide repair and consulting services can carve out a niche and prosper. Be sure to understand how the company being valued is dealing with technological change.

FINANCIAL ANALYSIS

Financial analysis is important for determining how the business being valued ranks compared to businesses in general and more particularly comparable businesses. For small and very small businesses, which are the focus of this book, financial analysis may be of limited usefulness due to poor or incomplete bookkeeping of the subject company. However, it should be looked at for what it is worth.

One of the most important features of financial analysis is the trends. While attempts to compare a company to comparables is useful, paying attention to clear trends is essential. If clear trends exist, they will indicate if the company is improving or heading for trouble. Remember, the past is evaluated to form an opinion about the foreseeable future.

Limitations

A concern about all small business comparable data is that business brokers believe that only the top 50% of most small businesses are saleable. Therefore, how does data from a broad cross-section of companies get compared to market data which is compiled from saleable companies? Even more perplexing is how this fact compares when using the income method, which cannot really be tied into any referenceable small business data. When using the income method, we are comparing the subject company data to public companies. Quite a stretch for most small companies.

Comparable data has not had any adjusting entries made. Therefore, when comparing comparable data to adjusted data, remember that the adjusted data results are not as highly ranked as may appear. (A result that appears to be equal to a 70% or better comparable may be more of a 50% comparable, but it is impossible to know the exact ranking.)

Newer versions of market data comparable sale information usually contain data on some key ratios. This allows comparison of the company being valued to "typical companies" in RMA (Risk Management Associates) or other sources and to the actual comparables. But, caution must be taken when assuming correlations between key ratios and multipliers. This will be reviewed further in the Market Data sections.

Common Size Statements

Common size financial statements convert financial statements to ratios as opposed to dollars. For instance, if revenues are $100 and the cost of goods sold is $65, then the common size cost of goods sold is 65% (65/100). This ratio and other ratios calculated using this methodology can facilitate easy comparisons across companies.

Common size income statements are quite useful for comparing profitability and, depending on the level of data, for comparing the cost of goods sold and sometimes major expenses, such as rent. Major cost and profitability trends indicate if the business is becoming more efficient, more profitable, or if results are creeping away. Often with small and very small businesses the common size ratios change over time and a review of the trends will be more useful than the comparison to commensurate data.

While common size comparisons are important, the analyst must also evaluate the dollars on the statements independently. Both ratios and raw numbers can raise questions and provide reason for further query. An example of a common size balance sheet is shown in Figure 4.5 and a common size income statement is shown in Figure 4.6.

Balance sheet common size statements are harder to compare. Many small companies do not properly maintain

	RMA	Adjusted 2018	Historic 2018	Historic 2017	Historic 2016	Historic 2015
Cash & Equivalents	12.30	1.69	44.65	28.36	44.59	64.66
Accounts Receivable	31.90	29.45	12.38	64.38	49.36	28.71
Inventory	2.20	0.00	0.00	0.00	0.00	0.00
Other Current Assets	5.20	0.00	11.65	0.00	0.39	0.00
Total Current Assets	51.60	31.14	68.68	92.73	94.34	93.37
Fixed Assets Net	39.60	68.86	28.95	6.31	5.57	6.21
Intangibles Net	3.10	0.00	0.00	0.00	0.00	0.00
Other Non-Current Assets	5.70	0.00	2.36	0.96	0.09	0.42
Total Assets	100.00	100.00	100.00	100.00	100.00	100.00
Accounts Payable	12.30	0.00	0.65	11.14	6.43	24.26
Short-Term Notes Payable	6.50	0.00	0.00	0.00	4.17	5.39
Current Maturity LT Debt	6.50	0.00	0.00	0.00	0.00	0.00
Other Current Liabilities	8.30	0.00	3.74	1.63	3.02	3.12
Total Current Liabilities	33.60	0.00	4.40	12.77	13.62	32.77
Long-Term Debt	20.50	0.00	0.00	0.00	3.52	9.53
Other Non-Current Liabilities	3.60	0.00	0.00	81.54	53.32	33.88
Total Liabilities	57.70	0.00	4.40	94.30	70.46	76.19
Total Equity	42.40	100.00	95.60	5.70	29.54	23.81
Total Liabilities & Equity	100.10	100.00	100.00	100.00	100.00	100.00

FIGURE 4.5 Sample Common Size Historic Balance Sheet

	RMA	Dec 2018	Dec 2017	Dec 2016	Dec 2015
Revenue	100.00	100.00	100.00	100.00	100.00
Cost of Goods	69.00	72.51	78.24	64.32	72.37
Gross Profit	31.00	27.49	21.76	35.68	27.63
Operating Expenses	24.30	17.53	17.26	13.99	12.77
Operating Profit	6.70	9.96	4.51	21.69	14.85
Other Income/(Expense) Net	−0.50	0.70	0.00	0.24	0.00
Pre-Tax Profit	6.20	10.66	4.51	21.93	14.85

Notes: ANNUAL STATEMENT STUDIES, (TM) RMA THE RISK MANAGEMENT ASSOCIATION, (TM) and the RMA Logo are trademarks of the Risk Management Association. RMA owns the copyright in the ANNUAL STATEMENT STUDIES(TM) data. The data is used under license from RMA.

FIGURE 4.6   Sample Common Size Historic Income Statement
Source: Risk Management Association, Philadelphia, PA 2018

their balance sheets. This is most pronounced in restaurants and cash-based retail and other smaller operations. In many cases even if the statement is accurate, the owner moves money interchangeably between personal and business accounts and does not expect the business to be self-supporting without an occasional infusion. In fact, due to the taxation of undistributed income for pass-through entities, some owners distribute all profits every year and then re-invest if they must. Therefore, cash accounts may be artificially low on year-end balance sheets which are usually used for comparison. There can be similar issues with the recognition of receipt of receivables and overpayment of payables for cash basis businesses at year-end. If the company being valued "manages" earnings for tax purposes, request a balance sheet and the related payables and receivable aging for another more typical month just to see what "typical" balances look like.

Common size balance sheets should be compared if the statements are reasonable and include accruals but in many instances little or no weight will be applied as the trends may not be reliable.

Ratio Analysis

Most ratios are a comparison of a balance sheet account to an income statement account. Therefore, most ratios will be of little value or impossible to calculate if the balance sheet is not reasonably accurate. When accurate statements are available, ratio analysis can be quite indicative of strengths and weaknesses.

Huge numbers of ratios exist. Some industries rely on certain ratios. Common ratios that are useful for business valuation are shown below. This is by no means all ratios but they are highly indicative and use high-level data that may be available even with small businesses. The following are the most common important ratios:

- **Current ratio.** The current ratio is a liquidity ratio that measures a firm's ability to pay its short-term liabilities with current assets. The formula is:

  Current assets/Current liabilities = Current ratio

  Current assets are cash, accounts receivable, inventory, other current assets. Current liabilities are accounts payable and other current liabilities.

  The higher the ratio, the more cash available (and presumably the higher the level of liquidity) for payment of current liabilities. A higher figure is good, yet at some point cash should be put to other uses.
- **Quick ratio or acid test ratio** is a liquidity ratio which measures the ability of a company to use its quick assets to pay current liabilities. It excludes inventories that may not be easily converted into cash. The formula is:

  Quick assets/Current liabilities = Quick ratio

  Quick assets are cash and accounts receivable. Current liabilities are accounts payable and other current liabilities.

  The higher the ratio, the more cash available for payment of current liabilities. Again, a higher figure is good yet at some point cash should be put to other uses.

Days receivables outstanding or days sales outstanding is a measure of the rate of collection of accounts receivable. The formula is:

Accounts receivable/average sales per day.

Average sales per day formula is annual sales/365

In general, a smaller number of days outstanding shows good accounts receivable management. But, at some point perhaps the extension of more credit would result in more sales.

- **Inventory turn** is a ratio showing how efficiently a company is using its inventory. The formula is:

sales/average inventory

· Average inventory = (beginning inventory

+ inventory purchases) − ending inventory)/2

In general, higher inventory turn shows efficient inventory management. This can be offset if there are inventory shortages that reduce sales.

- **Debt to equity** is the ratio of total debt divided by total equity. It is a measure of leverage. The formula is:

total debt/total equity = debt to equity ratio

Note: suppose the debt = $40,000 and the equity = $60,000. The debt/equity ratio is 66.667%. Now divide this ratio into the number 1 and this results in a 1.5 relationship. Therefore, $40,000 times 1.5 = $60,000. This is very helpful when the relationship is provided and not the ratio.

In general, the lower the debt to equity ratio, the less debt and the safer the company is.

- **Return on investment** (ROI) is a measure of overall financial performance. ROI shows the ratio of profit or loss made in a year to the total investment. It is a measure of return/income.

The formula is:

Return on Investment

= (Net Profit/Total Investment) * 100

- Total investment is the total capital structure of debt and equity. Investors clearly prefer higher returns on investment.
- **Return on equity** is a measure of financial performance. Equity is total assets – total liabilities so it is also called return on net assets. The formula is

net profits for the year/average shareholder equity.

Again, investors clearly prefer higher returns on equity. More common financial ratios are shown in Figure 4.7.

Liquidity Ratios	
Current Ratio	Current assets/current liabilities
Quick Ratio	Quick Assets / current liablities
	Quick assets are cash and accounts receivable
Accounts Receivable Turnover	Revenue / Accounts Receivable; Note this assumes all sales are on credit. For some companies Sales on Credit would be substituted for Revenue.
Average Collection Period	365 / Average Receivable Turnover
Inventory Turnover	Cost of Goods Sold / Average Inventory for the Year
Days Sales Inventory	365/ Inventory Turnover
Leverage Ratio	
Debt to Equity	Total liabilities / Total Stockholders Equity
Coverage Ratios	
Times Interest Earned	Earnings Before Interest and Taxes / Interest Expense
Operating Ratio	
Return on Equity	Net Income after Taxes / Average Shareholders Equity
Expense to Revenue Ratios	
Gross Margin	Gross Profit / Net Sales
% Depreciation, Amortization / Revenue	
% Officers Comp / Revenues	
Profit Margin	Profit / Net Sales

FIGURE 4.7 Common Financial Ratios

Sources of Common Size and Ratio Data

Always ask your client if they have access to an industry period-ical or association that tracks financial data and ratios. Often these have a cost associated with them. These are often the most useful when available at a reasonable price.

- **RMA data.** The RMA (Risk Management Association) compiles data sent to banks. Some formats of the data show the number of tax returns, compilations, reviewed statements and audits. For smaller businesses, the data is heavily weighted to compilations and tax returns. Most of these financials are prepared on a tax basis and most owners have a bias to lower taxable income wherever possible. Therefore, while this is one of the best sources of data, it has limitations due to the origin of the data.
- **Integra.** Integra has data sources that represent the finan-cial performance of 4.5 million privately held businesses in over 900 industries. It includes an income statement, bal-ance sheet, cash flow analysis and over 60 financial ratios. They pull data from 32 different proprietary and govern-ment data sources.
- **BizMiner.** BizMiner (https://www.bizminer.com/) reports receiving over a billion sourced data points from 15 million business operations. BizMiner can be searched by NAICS, size, and a radius from an address. BizMiner has many uses, including a ranking system based on the results of a review of the financial information.
- **Industry data.** Many industry associations have outstanding data. But accessing the data can be expensive. Certainly, if the firm being evaluated has quality data and if the level of the valuation and purpose support it, this can be the best data. In many cases the industry data must be purchased year by year. Examples of industry associations with outstanding data include the Electrical Contractors Association, the Associated Building Contractors, the

National Association of Homebuilders, and the National Restaurant Association.

- **SEC, census, government and government-related sources.** Edgar Online, https://www.census.gov/, OSHA, and others can call provide useful data.

NOTES

1. A saying I have found helpful but do not know to whom to attribute is, "Company culture statements are just words on the wall until the management is willing to fire someone for not complying". Something to think about when assessing the soft factors of a company.
2. Recently I evaluated a 10-year-old firm that had changed so substantially that the owner only would allow 2.5 years of data to be reviewed. Results were very good but it was valued as a start-up, not an established company.
3. Tariffs and changing international relations have added new risks to importers.
4. *South Dakota v. Wayfair, Inc.* No. 17-494. https://www.supreme court.gov/opinions/17pdf/17-494_j4el.pdf
5. That was a real contingency on a recent transaction. The buyer wanted to run larger trucks to the facility and the only route in and out had a small bridge with weight limits limiting truck size. The permit was obtained.
6. *See* https://www.targetgov.com/government-contracting-institute/ myths-realities-of-8a-certification-golden-ticket-or-not/
7. *See* https://www.bloomberg.com/news/articles/2019-03-28/econo mists-are-actually-terrible-at-forecasting-recessions
8. *See* https://www.nar.realtor/blogs/economists-outlook?page=1
9. *See* https://restaurant.org/research/economy/snapshots

CHAPTER 5

Normalization of Cash Flows

Any cash flow that is measured in business can be used to compare the company being valued to the comparison set. These can include revenues, gross profit margin, operating income, after tax profit, and others. The most common comparison sets for small and very small businesses are revenues, earnings before interest, taxes, depreciation, or amortization (EBITDA), and seller's discretionary earnings (SDE).

NORMALIZATION OF FINANCIAL INFORMATION

Financial statements must be adjusted in order to create comparable information. Every business owner, bookkeeper, and accountant keeps financial records differently. Yet the basis for estimating a value is to compare THIS company's facts, circumstances, records and results with OTHER companies. Through comparison, the analyst estimates a value. Therefore, it is important to convert the financial information provided into comparable data. Basically, ensuring apples to apples comparisons. This process is described as normalizing or adjusting the financial records.

This chapter addresses adjustments made specifically for use in valuing various cash flows and not cleaning up the financial data. Adjustments to locate more workable starting point financial statements are covered later in Chapter 11, Accounting Issues with Small and Very Small Businesses.

The primary categories of normalization adjustments are comparability adjustments, non-operating or nonrecurring adjustments, and discretionary adjustments. Comparability adjustments are made so the information is comparable to guideline companies, comparative ratio information, and the selected valuation method. Non-operating or nonrecurring adjustments are one-time or highly infrequent events that skew the cash flow. Discretionary adjustments are owner expenses and expenditures that the new owner may or may not have to make. They are at the discretion of the owner.

Comparability Adjustments

These are made to make the financial statements comparable. The first step is to make clear corrections to the provided financial information. As discussed elsewhere, these may include re-categorizing information, adjusting from cash basis to accrual, updating balance sheets and the like. Again, see Chapter 11 for details on those.

Often the internal financials will be presented in a different format than the tax returns. Consistency means that an attempt should be made to adjust the statements so they are comparable and consistent. A common item is cost of goods sold (COGS). Many businesses' internal financials will not show COGS broken down but the tax accountant will regroup expenses into a COGS expense. For comparison purposes internally and in many cases for comparison to industry data, it may make sense to make that adjustment so all years have the same format.

Once the statements are in an acceptable condition, the next step is to make comparability adjustments to create uniformity in how the cash flow is measured.

ESTIMATING THE CASH FLOW

REVENUES

Revenues are used for the cash flow because they are easy to see and agree upon. Unfortunately, revenue does not indicate profitability or the ability of the business to generate distributable cash flows. Still, as will be shown later, revenues at times, can be a useful measure for value.

Usually there is little discussion about revenues. One exception is companies with a high "Other Income" category. For instance, a liquor store with high lottery sales. Lottery sales are very low margin but they bring people into the store and are easy sales. In some cases, it may make sense to move other income lottery sales to revenues. Particularly if the location otherwise has high gross margins. Again, this is a professional judgment situation based on all facts and assumptions.

Another exception occurs when some companies perform sales functions similar to those of brokers. In these cases, some companies might book the entire "sale price" of the sold goods and their fee revenues with a cost of goods sold for the cost of performance of the work. Other companies might just book the net portion of the total cost of services that they retain as revenues. (An example is freight forwarders.) This can legitimately relate to the party that is taking the credit risk of non-payment and other business terms. Just be aware that it will make the revenue method even more unreliable and it will skew all ratio and common size statement analysis.

There can also be large differences in revenues under the cash and accrual methods of accounting. These are covered more in Chapter 11.

EBITDA

By adjusting earnings to add-back interest, taxes, depreciation, and amortization (EBITDA), the EBITDA cash flow can be estimated. "Cash flow" alone is often the seller's discretionary

Sample Earnings Before Interest, Taxes, Depreciation, Amortization (EBITDA)
Date

1	Net Profit		$1,000,000
2	Add Backs		
3	Income Taxes		$200,000
4	Interest		$10,000
5	Depreciation		$30,000
6	Amortization		$0
7			
8	Officers Salary		
9	Add: Original Amount	$400,000	
10	Deduct: Market Rate Labor	$200,000	
11			$200,000
12	Add: Benefit Package	$50,000	
13	Deduct: Market Rate Benefits	$35,000	
14			$15,000
15			
16	Legal One Time Expense		$35,000
17			
18	EBITDA		$1,490,000
19			

NOTES by Line

3   For C corporations that pay tax

10   Assumed, should be researched and supported

12   Benefits can include family members on payroll above labor rate, health insurance, life insurance, auto, travel, etc.

Often the Officer's/Owner's Salary is adjusted to include benefits and then all benefits are added back.

13   Assumed, may be harder to research.

14   One-time expenses can include litigation or loss of lawsuit, loss from closed operations or investment, etc.

These are typical EBITDA-type add-backs and adjustments.

FIGURE 5.1   Example of EBITDA Add Back Calculations

earnings particularly for smaller businesses. These expense items are added together because they can be quite variable among companies and because they are often not actual cash expenses in the year they are taken. EBITDA is considered to be a measure of the distributable cash flow of the business.

These expenses for income statement purposes are added-back or adjusted for financial analysis and valuation purposes. Let's examine each item.

- **Interest.** Interest is the expense for the payment for the use of money that has been loaned to the business. When the loan is paid off, the interest commitment ends. Different owners are going to have different levels of debt and interest expense. Debt levels can be determined by the owner. The next owner may have no debt. If they do take on debt, they will pay their own interest and we want to eliminate the risk of double counting interest. Therefore, interest is added back.

- **Taxes.** In this case, taxes refer to income taxes. Again, in different situations, different businesses and owners will have different tax situations and outcomes. Most small and very small businesses do not pay income taxes at the business entity level because they are pass-through entities (S corporations, partnerships and most LLCs). If they are C corporations, the income taxes should be added back in this instance. Some states and cities do not recognize pass-through entities. Make sure those income taxes are added back.

- **Depreciation.** This is the expensing of the historic cost of capital assets. Capital assets are assets such as trucks, equipment, and buildings that are utilized over several accounting periods. Depreciation is not a use of cash. The actual payment of cash is separate and may have been made at the purchase or, if a loan was taken out, it is the principal payment of the loan. It is an accrual accounting adjustment. Therefore, depreciation is added back. It needs to be recognized that the loan principal is repaid out of earnings or net income. This is a below the profit line payment—not an expense. Many small business owners and their bookkeepers make this entry wrong on their internal books.

- **Amortization.** This is the same thing as depreciation except it applies to intangible assets. This generally shows up if a business was purchased as an asset sale. It also is the write-off over time of startup costs such as attorney's fees prior to operations of the business. Amortization also is added back as it is not a cash expense when it is being taken.

Officers' Compensation. For EBITDA adjustments it is assumed that the company being valued is fully managed. Therefore, EBITDA does not include any payment for management to operate the company. EBITDA is a return to owners as investors. Necessary calculations to adjust owners' compensation will be discussed in Discretionary Adjustments below.

An example of EBITDA add-back calculations is shown in Figure 5.1.

Seller's Discretionary Earnings (SDE)

For most small and very small businesses, SDE or seller's discretionary earnings is an easier way to estimate cash flow. SDE is EBITDA plus all the ways one owner makes money. Therefore, EBITDA plus all the owner's discretionary expenses such as owner's salary, the company payroll taxes on the owner's salary, unearned salary to family members, expenses to the business that are personal benefits like the owner's family health insurance, life insurance, personal auto expenses, and so forth. Owners can be quite creative and have a long list of discretionary adjustments.

An example of how to calculate SDE is shown in Figure 5.2.

Like the EBITDA adjustments, the applicable expenses are added back. A few examples.

- **Owner's salary.** The owner can determine his or her own salary. Often the amount of salary versus profit is based on tax considerations not the economic value of the work performed by the owner.

1	Net Profit		$50,000
2			
3	Officer's Compensation		$125,000
4	Officer's Benefits		
5	Employer Taxes on Salary		$10,000
6	Auto		$5,000
7	Health Insurance		$23,000
8	401 K		$10,000
9	Conference		$7,500
10	Meals & Entertainment		$2,000
11	Credit Card Charges in COGS		$5,000
12	Family cell phones		$3,600
13	Lawn equipment purchases		$15,000
14	Interest		$400
15	Depreciation		$5,000
16	Amortization		$3,000
17	Rent Adjustment		
18	Rent on Financials	70000	
19	Market Rent	−50000	$20,000
20			
21	One-Time Adjustment		$20,000
22			
23	Seller's Discretionary Earnings		$304,500

Note: These are typical SDE-type add-backs.

FIGURE 5.2 Seller's Discretionary Earnings (SDE) Add-back Chart

- **Health insurance.** For the owner and the owner's family. A direct benefit.
- **401K, pension, profit sharing,** and so forth for the owner.
- **Auto expenses.** The automobile use of the owner and family. One company reviewed had five automobiles on the books. One for each family member. Only one family member worked at the business. A rather substantial add-back.

Anything on the add-back chart and more may be personal benefits to the owner. Be aware this can be garbage in, garbage out. Some owners and valuators stretch personal benefit beyond what a second analyst might view as reasonable. A little variance between analyst views is normal but credibility is lost when add-backs are not tenable.

More on Discretionary Adjustments

Discretionary adjustments are adjustments for expenditures by the company made at the discretion of the owner. The owner chooses the expense and usually it is for the owner's benefit.

Owner's compensation. Owners can pay themselves whatever they choose within the bounds of IRS rulings. But the economic value of their labor can be estimated. The economic value is what reasonable third parties would pay to have the services performed. In many instances valuators need to estimate the economic value of the work and separate it from profit distributions.

When estimating SDE from the income statement and supporting documents, the salary of one owner is included. In most instances this means it is "added back" and not expensed for this calculation. In effect, the single owner salary is part of this particular cash flow. The theory is most small owner-operated businesses have one owner, so that is the standard.[1]

The same type of analysis is performed when EBITDA is being used as the cash flow. The difference, for EBITDA, is the assumption that the company's salary expense plus officer's compensation covers the cost of full management. Namely, the owner is an investor, not an owner operator.

Back to calculating SDE, in situations with multiple owner operators, the economic value of additional owners is estimated and any excess value or profit is added back. For instance, XYZ Corp. has two owners. Bob owns 60% and takes a salary of $125,000. He works full-time and is doing high-level project management/owner work. His co-owner Sara owns 40%. Sara is paid $75,000 for which she keeps the books 8 hours a week and has another job the other four days a week. Her economic value to the business may be estimated as follows.

Example

8 hours times $35 hour for an internal bookkeeper = $280 times 52 weeks = $14,560. $75,000 salary less $15,000 economic value = $60,000. Therefore, approximately $60,000 ($75,000 less $15,000 rounded) should be deducted from expenses and added to the operating income.

This will increase the estimated profit and SDE. In many small businesses the second owner may be underpaid. Frequently it will come out that a spouse works almost full-time for a nominal sum or no payment at all. This too should be adjusted. Children, friends, and other family members can all fall into this category.

While not shown above, assuming the payments were made through payroll, there will also be the company portion of the payroll tax (8% is a reasonable proxy up to a salary of approximately \$132,900 (for 2019) and then above that 1.5% continues for Medicare with no cap).

To calculate EBITDA, the company being valued is to be fully operational with ALL salaries necessary for it to stand alone being paid. Essentially under the EBITDA cash flow calculation, the owner's compensation should always be adjusted to the true economic value.

A commonsense approach to estimating the economic value is to look at the size of the company and determine if it were to be purchased by a larger company, what the owner's likely role would be. Sometimes this is a chief salesperson, sometimes it is a plant manager, sometimes a project manager, or perhaps a high-level technical expert. While the position could be a CEO or CFO for most small companies, the owner would become a plant or sales manager cog in the wheel and have a more specified role. This role can then be assessed through free web services (not recommended but it is free), the Census data (also free but much easier to access through subscription services), industry surveys for some industries, compensation databases, and pure estimating. For very low level estimates of value, a reasonable figure can be assumed and used.[2]

Sources of Compensation Data

- **Free websites.** Every website differs. The data often can be sliced for quite detailed job descriptions and localized for area. The issue is how the data is obtained. Some require providing information on your current job to get data for your next job. It is difficult to impossible to verify methodology and validity of data. Some sites are: https://www.payscale.com/, https://www.salary.com/, https://www.glassdoor.com/Salaries/know-your-worth .htm.

- **Census data.** The data is often limited but for small and very small businesses, this is often the best data available. High-level jobs may only have information up to the mean salary or no data at all. While data comes from government surveys, it is primarily self-reporting and subject to error. Since it is collected by a Federal agency under most rules of evidence, it is admissible. While it has limitations, for many small businesses where the owner really is more of a plant manager or project manager or other defined role, the data is a useful starting point. See www.bls.gov/oes/tables.htm
- **Industry survey data.** Many industries have associations or peer groups that collect financial data, including fairly detailed compensation data from members. Often this will include both base salaries along with detailed benefit information. While this data is suspect in that it rarely would meet sampling standards for true statistical purposes (usually it is voluntary), it is often very thorough and useful for estimating comparable company compensation ranges.
- **RC reports.** This is one of several services that provide comprehensive salary assessments. Michael Gregory has indicated from his own experience that this service has been used successfully with IRS consistently.[3] It is an unbiased data-derived source that has been scrubbed to accurately and objectively determine reasonable compensation for closely held businesses. See https://rcreports.com/

Other Discretionary Adjustments

Discretionary adjustments cover all the owner benefits that are being claimed as business expenses by the owner. In most cases discretionary adjustments can be pretty straightforward. A long list of potential add-backs, provided by Ron Rudich, CPA, ABV, is shown in Figure 5.3.

Type

Wages at Market Rates (W-2 Salary)
Payroll Taxes (both FICA & Medicare)
Perquisites:
   401K
   Defined Benefit Plan
   Country Club
   Excess Vacations
   Household expenses
   Children school expenses
   Insurance (Non-Compete)
   Insurance (Life for Owner)
   Insurance (Personal Auto)
   Vehicles (company cars)
   etc.
Rent (to market rates if property owned by owner)
Capital Gains and Losses
Contributions (this is taken on the Owner's personal return)
Extraordinary one-time (non-recurring occurrence) Items
   Employee Lawsuit for wrongful termination
   Product Liability
   Contingent Liability Lawsuit
   One-time miscellaneous expense
    recognized installment sale
    restructuring charges
    research for a patent, trademark, etc.
    preparation of a letter of intent
Prepayments on a cash basis of accounting
Excess Attorney's & Accounting Fees
   to defend an IRS audit
   any litigation like wrongful termination
   Merger & Acquisition research
Miscellaneous Income (maybe)
   Non-Recurring income
Miscellaneous Expenses (maybe)
   Non-Recurring expense
Discontinued Operations
   Both the revenue and corresponding expenses
Excess Bonus and Accelerated Depeciation
   consider the useful life of the asset
In some cases Amortization (Goodwill)
Salary paid to an individual who doesn't work in the business
as well as the related payroll taxes and perquisites, if any
   Related Party consideration

FIGURE 5.3   Normalization Adjustments

Rent expense if different from market rates
Personal expenses paid by management that are non-operating
by nature (i.e.; expenses for a second home, vacation trips,
non-titled assets, such as a speedboat, etc.)
LIFO Inventory in the Balance Sheet
Restate to FIFO the beginning and ending inventory within
the income statement (cost of goods sold)
Travel per-diem rates in excess of IRS safe-harbor rates for
lodging, and meals and incidentals
GAAP (generally accepted accounting principles) Adjustments
Deferred taxes receivable
Deferred taxes payable
Prepaid Expenses (possibly because it will end up in RE)
Prepaid Revenue (possibly because it will end up in RE)
Other Tax Entries

Notes: I thank Ron Rudich for this thorough list.

FIGURE 5.3   *Continued*

A big issue is, what type of back-up should be required for discretionary adjustments? Again, what is the level of the work (opinion or calculation)? For opinions, particularly opinions subject to cross-examination or for third party use, a higher level of work is recommended. For calculations that are internal (the users are the owners), a lower standard may be acceptable. Certainly, highly unusual or very large add-backs should be reviewed more thoroughly. Let's work through some examples: Starting with the simple ones.

- A small school with $600,000 of revenues and $100,000 of SDE that does not have an internal bus service. The two owners have $2,500 each of auto expenses for a total of $5,000. The $5,000 clearly shows on the tax returns as auto expense. Outside of having an engagement to perform forensics, this is sufficient to show as an auto expense add-back.
- Take the same situation but there is no auto expense shown on the tax return. At that point, an understanding of where the expense is recorded in the accounting system, along with verification of where the tax accountant put it on the tax

return, is in order. Many tax accountants move some personal expenses from expenses to distributions without the owner ever really knowing. It is important to not add back something that was not deducted. Frequently the small business owners and bookkeepers do not realize what the tax accountant did.

- Take the same situation but now the auto expense claimed is $40,000 for the two owners. Assume $20,000 is shown on the return for auto expenses. At that point whether it is on the return or not, it is a material amount for the school business described here and needs to be backed up with documentation, for example, accounting system entries and details as to exactly who was paid. Verify where the tax accountant put the deduction in the tax return. Often, when researched, the very large entries will be for the purchase price of the asset or will include principal and interest. While interest is usually added back (make sure it is not counted twice), loan principal properly is paid out of earnings and not deductible. If loan principal was wrongly deducted on the tax return, then it can be added back. (In that case, also adjust the debt on the balance sheet.)

Let's look at something more complex:

- An owner claims that credit card expenses were for business-related personal use.
- In most cases the credit card statements will need to be reviewed.
- For most businesses, if the charges are for Victoria's Secret, the determination is easy. It's an add-back. Again, make sure it traces through to the tax return. If outside accountants are used, it is often placed in distributions.
- Say the company is a contractor and $20,000 of the $60,000 of charges are from Home Depot. Verify where it is on the tax return. Often companies like construction contractors that carry a cost of goods sold put many

personal expenses there. Since it is a huge account with many entries, tax accountants are less likely to find the entries and adjust for them. Verify that the statements were paid by the business. Then each statement must be reviewed. The statement charges will probably need to be tied to purchase orders or receipts specifying what was purchased. A pool table delivered to the home address of the owner is going to fall on the side of an add-back most of the time. (Yes, you can order almost anything through Home Depot online.) Lumber delivered to a job site is not an add-back. Lumber delivered to the home or a home office is more difficult. At some point add-backs cannot be seen and verified and what cannot be seen and verified cannot be added back.

Cumulative Effect of Discretionary Add-Backs

As one final thought, if each add-back is small but the total add-backs are very material, make sure verifications and documentation are sufficient for the total adjustment. For example, a company with $1,000,000 revenues and breakeven profits is claiming $200,000 of add-backs increasing SDE. One expense category held about $120,000 of the add-backs. The rest was in 10 categories as small charges. In a case like this, barring unusual circumstances or a VERY low-level calculation engagement for internal use, everything should be verified closely.

Cash

There is no good way to deal with unreported cash. In many industries the use of credit and debit cards has greatly reduced cash transactions but this is still an issue. Liquor stores, dry cleaners, restaurants, small service providers, distributors selling to small contractors and the like may all have cash transactions.

I have been told by more than one business brokerage client that there is a much larger "cash" economy than I could imagine. In some industries, I'm told, the cash customers even refuse to pay state sales tax.

Sometimes cash transactions will show up where it is least expected.

Example

An example is the suburban indoor lacrosse and soccer center with all reported revenues from leagues and parties, which are paid for mainly with checks and cards. Yet, the "restaurant league" turned out to be $15 a head, cash only, pick-up soccer league starting at 10:00 p.m. every night when the restaurants closed. At some point it was reported that a lot of people liked the restaurant league. The restaurant league was not on the books.

Most main street business brokers who deal with cash businesses will tell you that the biggest problem with cash businesses is that cash is not only received but it is spent. Therefore, if you can verify the cash coming in (which for smaller businesses sometimes can be done), you may not be able to verify if it becomes profit or is spent on expenses.

In some industries, large portions of the workforce may not be on the reported books and records. In addition, some owners have reported using completely different suppliers for what they believe may be cash transactions than for other transactions so the supplier invoices and statements cannot be traced. In effect, the company has no visible records of the sale or the expenses.

Of course, this is the case until you show up and the seller wants a high value, or the buyer wants to verify information received, or until a partner or spouse who is "surprised" to find out about cash transactions wants a complete accounting. For example, a counseling service that took cash payments from non-insurance customers consistently showed small losses. Yet by reviewing patient time records and eventually admission under deposition, the owner admitted to approximately $75,000 per year of unrecorded "distributions."

Without getting into full forensics, which is beyond this book, some suggestions are:

- Some traditional cash industries can be estimated by looking at key commodities or supplies and comparing gross margins. For instance, in coin laundries, you can verify the price on the washing machine. You can also verify the amount of water used by the machines. Finally, you can compare revenues to the water bill. Has anyone ever just let the water run? Probably, but this is an industry rule of thumb.
- At small restaurants and single location retailers, you can sit and watch the cash register. Remember to watch the back door for expenses. Of course, collusion in cash businesses is easy, so figure you need to watch at least two weeks (many a bar had the best week ever during a watch period) or more. Of course, there is no fail-safe way to verify these revenues or expenses.
- When valuing hotels and motels, consider analyzing how many times sheets are being laundered. Some locations may have an hourly or day rate that is predominately paid in cash.
- Often the "no records" business will have years of cash register receipts if they think it is to their benefit. It has been reported that owners had copies of every dollar coming in the door. Second sets of books do tend to exist in these situations if the owner wants you to see them. Tying into sales documents, ratio analysis of key supplies, and other procedures can be used to test to a degree. It's just hard to know if they are true.
- If you know cash is involved but are unable to verify details, sometimes the market method—revenue basis can be used.

	Reported	Estimated Unreported	Adjusted Total	% Variance	Formula
Revenues	$900,000	$50,000	$950,000	5.26	$50,000/($900,000+$50,000)
Profit	$50,000	$50,000	$100,000	50.00	$50,000/($50,000+$50,000)
Estimated Unreported Cash	$50,000				

Note: If there is evidence of unreported cash along with some evidence of earnings, then the revenue method may be more accurate Revenues are 5% from actual yet cash flow has a 50% variance.

FIGURE 5.4 Cash Flow vs Revenues % Missing

If it reasonably appears that the business is profitable under the thought that if they are hiding 10–20% (or whatever amount), they have probably hidden 75% or more of SDE but a smaller percentage of revenues. Therefore, the revenue method is likely to be more accurate in those situations where little can be proven. Figure 5.4 shows an analysis of the ratio difference of missing cash to the revenue verses SDE cash flows.

- If you or your client wants or needs some level of true confidentiality, then a forensic person (if not you) should be hired by an attorney who is doing the work for the purpose of litigation and dispute. Kovel agreements are when an attorney hires an accountant to fully understand a situation. The lawyer's confidentiality will then extend to the accountant. Recognize that anyone who files a tax document related to the business or owner will not have any confidentiality protection from the IRS or state tax authorities.

- If these matters are getting into the area of possible tax evasion or tax fraud, review how to best protect yourself and your client with an attorney (or an attorney for each of you as you have separate interests). Make sure you do not cross the line and end up participating in a fraud situation. Good intentions without careful guidance can result in loss of licenses and much worse.

As a final thought or warning on cash.

- An old-time business broker told the story of when he was selling a waterfront seafood restaurant. They had grown comfortable with the buyers and pulled out the second set of books. At that point the buyer pulled guns and badges. Yes, the buyer was the IRS. This had happened five years before I was told the story by the broker and you could still see the fear on his face.

Real Estate Owned

If the owner or a related entity owns the real estate used by the business, then the rent needs to be reviewed. In addition, if there are other major assets leased to the company owned by related parties, they will need a similar review. For instance, in some cases, the owner may own an equipment leasing company and rent or lease assets to the company being valued.

In these situations, sellers may subsidize or overcharge themselves for rent based on their tax, mortgage payment, and business philosophies but they generally want to sell the real estate at market or receive market rent once they sell the business. Therefore, for opinions of value and for higher quality estimates, real estate should generally be appraised by a real estate appraiser if it is a material component of value.

Business value is determined based on market rent. An exception to that is if there is a long-term lease protecting the savings. Still, it must be remembered that "rent deals" can change with bankruptcies, foreclosures, real estate sales, future business sales, and sometimes just impossible landlords. Many a small retail business won the rent court case against the landlord to then have the lease terminated at the end of the lease period. Who won the lawsuit is questionable as certainly the business lost value when it lost the lease.

Typically for small businesses, if an outside real estate appraiser is appraising the real estate, that value can be used for our valuation purposes.[4] Sometimes the real estate appraisal estimates market rent for the property. Sometimes the appraiser just finds a sales value based on comparables. Most small businesses occupy real estate with a rent capitalization rate between 6% for a restaurant in a fashionable shopping district or mall to about 11–12% for industrial property in an undesirable neighborhood.

Example

For instance, if the real estate appraiser says a 2-acre parcel with 1 acre being used as a yard and a 10,000 SF building has a value of $1,000,000, a typical capitalization rate for that might be 9%, so the business should pay $90,000 of market rent. If the business was paying $120,000 in rent maybe to get money to the owner outside of self-employment taxes, then there would be a $30,000 add-back. If the owner was charging $50,000 in rent because that is what the mortgage was, and the owner never bothered to increase the rent, the adjustment would be an increase of $40,000 added to the expenses.

If there is not a current real estate appraisal, market rent may be estimated by looking at Loop-Net, a commercial real estate listing service. If you have access, Co-Star, who owns Loop-Net, has wonderful real estate sale and leasing data. But, it is expensive and generally only maintained by larger real estate brokerage firms and real estate appraisers. If working from Loop-Net, remember those are asking prices. In most cases it is reasonable to assume a long-term lease of a reasonable size block of space may be 5–15% below the asking price. Try to find three or more comparables and estimate from there.

In many markets this rent would be Net Net Net (aka NNN or Triple Net Lease) if industrial or small retail, so assuming the business was paying all maintenance charges and utilities, there would be no further adjustments. Commercial rents generally have two components. Rent and Additional Rent.

Included in additional rent are common area maintenance charges (also known as CAM charges). Property taxes above a base amount or all property taxes may also flow through above the assessed rent. These tend to show up in larger complexes with shared expenses for things like parking lot maintenance. Different property types will be assessed differently in different geographic markets so you need to find out the local practices.

NON-OPERATING AND ONE-TIME ADJUSTMENTS

Non-operating adjustments are adjustments to remove items that are not required to run the business. A typical non-operating expense is a boat or vacation home used for "entertainment" or other questionable purposes.

A more complex non-operating adjustment is for past events that will not reoccur in the future. For instance, the company has shut down a location that was a drain. If the location is not going to re-open, then the location results can be added back or in effect removed when calculating cash flows that are to be used to estimate future cash flows. This is because business valuation is forward-looking. Valuation professionals and real-world buyers are trying to understand what is going to happen in the next several future periods.

Remember these one-time adjustments can also lower cash flow. For instance, if a change in a safety regulation causes a bubble in the sales of related safety gear that is not be expected to be repeated. In that case the bubble amount should be estimated and removed.

When making adjustments removing this type of loss, consideration must be given to contributions to overhead and operating results. Namely, make sure that the closed unit was not contributing to overhead even if it was not generating a bottom line profit. In addition, remove the unit from all prior years so the data is truly comparable across the review period.

Figure 5.5 shows how to perform a simple contribution analysis. Contribution analysis is a very powerful analysis that can be used to compare customers, products, performance of managers, and more to understand profitability and opportunity. Contribution analysis is used to estimate the profitability of parts of the business.[5] In some cases, it makes economic sense to keep unprofitable parts of a business if they contribute to overhead, allowing other parts to be more profitable. In most cases in the longer run, the company strategy should be to replace the low margin work with high margin work and increase overall profitability.

			Year 1	Year 2	% Changes
	Division 1 - All Smaller Clients				
1	Revenues		$500	$500	0.00%
2	COGS - Variable 30%		$150	$150	0.00%
3	Gross Profits	(1-2)	$350	$350	0.00%
4					
	Division 2 - Big Builder Client				
5	Revenues		$500	$0	-100.00%
6	COGS - Variable 50%		$250	$0	-100.00%
7	Gross Profits	(5-6)	$250	$0	-100.00%
8					
9	Total Gross Profits	(3+7)	$600	$350	-41.67%
10					
11	Fixed Expenses				
12	Rent		$100	$100	0.00%
13	Equipment		$150	$150	0.00%
	Semi-Variable				
14	Admin		$100	$80	-20.00%
15	Fixed and Semi Variable	(12+13+14)	$350	$330	-5.71%
16					
17	Profit	(9-15)	$250	$20	-92.00%

Note: The Company was evaluating what the loss of Division 2 - the one large client would do to overall profitability.

FIGURE 5.5 Contribution Analysis to Overhead and Profit

Example

This example is a true situation of a sediment control contractor (they put in silt fencing and other devices to control water run-off from construction sites) that had many small clients (Division 1) and a one major homebuilder client (Division 2). The contractor had been told that he would receive a one-time "haircut" or nonpayment of $200,000 in accounts receivable by the large client. He used this analysis to determine whether to sue the client or take his licks and keep working. He decided to keep working due to the huge loss of earnings. Fortunately, it did turn out that this was a one-time loss.

Another typical non-operating adjustment is the gain or loss from the sale of equipment. If this is an unusual event for the company and involves a material amount of money, then the gain or loss should be removed. If it is a nominal amount of money or the company is frequently selling equipment, then perhaps this should be left alone. Of course, in that case, the timing of the frequent sales would need to be examined to verify that the equipment sales and cash flow arising from it can continue into the future.

One-Time Adjustments. The typical one-time adjustment is high legal costs related to an unusual lawsuit. Of course, if there is a lawsuit every year, this is no longer unusual. For instance, a real estate developer that wants to add back expenses related to a development that did not go forward. This seems like a normal operating risk in that industry and would not be added back. Another example of a one-time expense is the cost to move a large warehouse or plant. This is a one-time expense particularly if a long-term lease has been obtained so the company should not have to move in the foreseeable future. Examples of one-time adjustments are shown in Figure 5.6.

Unusual legal fees
Unusual legal settlements
Net loss from closed operations
Loss from loss of key person
Loss due to systems change over
Loss due to moving
Fire loss
Flood / other casualty
Commodity pricing / availability issues

Note: While less often mentioned at least by owners/management, these one-time losses can also be one-time gains. For instance, when a owner has a large insurance loss recovery.

FIGURE 5.6   Possible One-Time Adjustments

Process for Working with Add-Backs

In summary, the process for working with add-backs is as follows:

- Verify that the proposed add-back fits the category definition. Care should be taken to review the fact pattern with one-time and non-operating adjustments.
- Verify that the add-back is shown on the tax return or financial statement being used as base financials.
- Appropriately document the add-back for the ultimate report based on the user (internal vs. third party), the materiality of the adjustment to overall cash flow being measured and whether a calculation or opinion is being issued.
- If the cumulative effect of the add-backs are large and material, consider providing a higher level of review.
- If add-backs are starting to look like tax evasion or tax fraud, give notice to your client about your concern and if they want you to document it. A phone call might be a way to start. If they want you to proceed, make sure you have

a clear email chain or other documentation that you gave them notice and they told you to proceed. Unlike Canada, in the US, there is no duty to report to authorities, particularly if you are not the tax preparer. Do recognize that certain state courts are required to report evidence of tax evasion, and certainly Federal agencies may report it. Err on the side of caution and check with your attorney if you are giving any type of advice that might be seen as assisting or participating in the fraud prior to issuing your work.

- For full report opinions, clearly specify the level of work performed to verify add-backs and provide assumptions made. For other levels of reports, compare your reporting level to the materiality of the adjustment(s). Report appropriately. Err on the side of caution to protect yourself.

Protect yourself—business brokers regularly state that they have not verified data and do not make representations or warranties. If well trained, they also do not make projections beyond straight line annualization. In business valuation, valuators should only be liable to our client and any stated users. But, if at all possible, make the level of your work clear even to unintended potential "users." They often do not understand these distinctions and while valuators should not be liable (a court is not a consistent place though) for misuse of the work, no one wants unauthorized users to be harmed if avoidable. Finally, carry errors and omissions insurance just in case.

NOTES

1. A true but theoretical extreme was five family members who owned and daily operated a HVAC company and thought all of their salaries should be part of SDE.
2. J. Hitchner, S. Pratt, and J. Fishman, *A Consensus View: Q&A Guide to Financial Valuation* (New Jersey: VPS, 2016), p. 48, has more detail on these excess compensation analyses.

3. Michael Gregory, ASA, CVA, PE, was in charge of Engineering (that is valuation) for the IRS and handles many IRS matters. *See* https://www.mikegreg.com/

4. SSVS 100 .20 You must clearly note the appraiser and the level of responsibility being assumed by the valuator.

5. Forms of contribution analysis can be used to review profitability of products, services, jobs, employee utilization, etc. This is an extremely valuable and underutilized management tool.

CHAPTER 6

Market Approaches

The market method is a comparative method to estimate business value. Actual reported business sales are compared to the subject company's to estimate a value. The concept of market value is:

Expected Future Cash Flow × Multiplier = Value (Price)

Cash flows used for business valuation are future cash flows. Future expectations drive price and value. This is similar to the fact that the public stock markets often move 18 months ahead of predicted economic change. While the past is studied in detail it is to better understand the future.

In the market method one or more cash flows are used as a proxy for the comparison. Frequently used cash flows include revenues, gross profit, profits, seller's discretionary earnings (SDE), and earnings before interest, taxation, depreciation, and amortization (EBITDA). A multiplier of cash flow will be applied against a cash flow to estimate a value.

Like most simple things, simplicity masks complexity. Let's be clear, the market method using revenues as a cash flow at the rule of thumb level is very simple. However, when carefully applied to properly adjusted cash flows, that are thoughtfully related to appropriate comparables at the opinion of value level, it is quite complex.

Interestingly, in business valuation, the use of the market method is looked down upon by many practitioners. This makes little sense. As a contrast, in real estate valuation, ignoring the market method would be unimaginable. While there are many issues with the market method, refusing to recognize and use the market method is like throwing the baby out with the bath water.

For small businesses, which are the subject of this book, the market method is the absolute best method available in most cases. The main reasons why the market method should be favored with small and very small businesses are:

- It is the only method that can empirically relate actual results (sales) to valuation findings.
- Twenty years ago, small business administration (SBA) financing was relatively new, so much of the data was from before the advent of an organized source of financing. Organized financing has brought stability and a level of predictability to the market.
- Twenty years ago, databases were very incomplete and the market method was much more rule of thumb-based. That is no longer the case.
- In addition, the database providers (particularly Business Valuation Resources (BVR) with DealStats) have been improving their collection and verification methods. The amount of data available nowadays is quite impressive. The data is quite useful when analyzed skillfully.

OBJECTIONS TO THE MARKET METHOD

The major objection to the market method is the quality of the data. All methods have data collection and comparison issues. The issues with the market method are easier to understand than those with the income method. The fact that valuators can understand the issues means they can adjust for them. The income method's apparent simplicity means there is no ability to adjust that can be tied into data.

The difficulty in evaluating soft data[1] is pervasive in business valuation and exists in both income and market methods. Today's comparable data for key ratios, gross margins, and profitability measures for the market method is more analytical than guessing a specific company premium.

A real estate-related analogy for the income method and valuing very small businesses would be valuing suburban single family homes (very small) starting with downtown office buildings (i.e., major public corporations) and then working down in structure, size, and location. Sure, you can do it, but is that really the preferred method?

The major problem for all business valuations is seeing what is coming (the future) or what actually exists (soft data) in the subject company. To use another sports analogy, look at a basketball team. One star player being hurt will change a season for a team. Small business is the same. One or two star players, often the owner, a material customer, or a material supplier, can change everything. No one knows how to fully account for this. But, in the market method, often very high cash flowing businesses (on a percentage basis) will have lower multipliers than low cash flowing businesses. Perhaps this is a partial accounting for the fact that small business can be star player-driven. See the plotted cash flow multipliers in Figure 6.1. They were plotted based on profitability shown across the bottom based on SDE versus multiplier shown along the left side. As profitability increases, the multiplier drops. Not an intuitive outcome but a frequent one.

Another issue with market data is we cannot know everything going on around the comparable business. In fact, we are blind to many important facts. For instance, say we are valuing a local hardware store. Clearly there is a huge variation in value if a Home Depot is being built a mile away from this store versus a hardware store in a very small town an hour from a Home Depot. We cannot see those types of issues in the market method

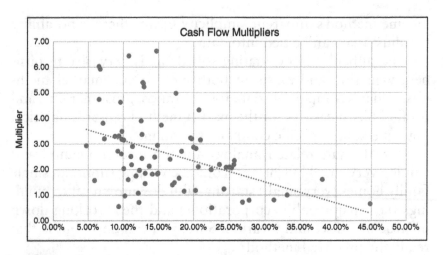

FIGURE 6.1 Cash Flow Multiplier by Profitability

comparable data. Of course, we cannot see them in the income method investment alternatives data either.[2]

A concern with market data is comparables only show sold businesses. There is no data on the 75% of small businesses that did not sell. Determining when a small business is salable and therefore has value can be difficult particularly with high goodwill personal service businesses. A common complaint with market data is that we only see one year's results in the comparable data. This is a legitimate issue. Of course, we do not know anything really about the aggregated income method investment alternatives data over time either. It's just "in there."

There also are issues knowing what assets are included in the business sale and what assets were retained by the seller. This applies to both stock sales and asset sales. This issue, while not completely solvable, is covered extensively in this chapter.

There is no use pretending that small business market data can be "cleaned up" and adjusted on an individual comparable basis for these types of data issues. We do not know what we do not know. But, aggregate data can be "cleaned up" and reviewed and analyzed to take into account issues like those above. Aggregate data parsed properly often becomes quite comparable. Remember, there probably are reasons for a lot of the outlier data shown in the market method (perhaps it is the Home Depot next door). Is the subject business you are valuing an outlier? If it truly is, make the adjustment and the explanation.

WEIGHTING THE CASH FLOW

In the market method the normalized cash flow as developed in Chapter 5 from each year reviewed is used to estimate a cash flow figure. The final selected cash flow should represent cash flows in the foreseeable future. Growth beyond the selected cash flows is provided in a properly selected multiplier.

To estimate the cash flow figure for the market method for small and very small businesses, typically three years plus a year to date column will be analyzed. Five years can be analyzed but for most small businesses five years is a long time and the business is likely to be very different than in the current year.[3] Remember, a key factor is we are reviewing the past to forecast the future.

Weighting the cash flow is the process of taking the multi-year data and combining it to come up with the single cash flow number for our basic market method equation. The formula is:

Expected Future Cash Flow × Multiplier = Estimate of Value

Each year's estimated cash flow is now weighted to come up with a selected cash flow for the formula. The simplest method is to weight each year's cash flow evenly. This, along with other common methods, is shown in Figure 6.2.

Another common method is to weight the years so as to place more weight on the current years and less on the past years. If three years' data and a year to date column is being used, the weighting might be 4 in the estimated current year,

Year	2020	2019	2018	2017	Calculated
SDE Annual Cash Flow	$40,000	$60,000	$80,000	$100,000	Cash Flow
Weighting Methods					
Average Weighting	1	1	1	1	
As Weighted	$40,000	$60,000	$80,000	$100,000	**$70,000**
Weighting Current Years	4	3	2	1	
As Weighted	$160,000	$180,000	$160,000	$100,000	**$60,000**
Weighting Early Years	1	2	3	4	
As Weighted	$40,000	$120,000	$240,000	$400,000	**$80,000**
Weighting Current Year Only	1				
As Weighted	$40,000	$0	$0	$0	**$40,000**

An example showing the power of weighting. Weighting will vary with the fact pattern behind the numbers.

FIGURE 6.2   Examples of Weighting A Cash Flow – Market Method

three times the last full year, two times the year before that, one time the year before that. These numbers would be added and then divided by 10 (4 + 3 + 2 + 1 = 10). An example of this is shown in Figure 6.2.

Outside other considerations, in general the following rules should be used:[4]

- Cash flow is consistently increasing: typically the last year's cash flow will best reflect the future cash flows. If the cash flow growth is small, then perhaps the weighted average explained above is to be used.
- Cash flow is consistently decreasing: typically the last year's cash flow will best reflect the future cash flows. If the cash flow drop is small, then perhaps the weighted average explained above is to be used.
- Cash flow is up and down: typically an average of the years will be used. A weighted average may be used depending on the fact pattern.

- Next year is considered to be like the best or worst year even if that is not the last year, select the best or worst year.

The key is to be able to reasonably justify the cash flow weighting selected. Correctly selecting cash flow is an important part of the Art of Business Valuation. Remember to ask yourself, "Does this make sense?"

The above statements imply that there is not a reason why the cash flow is going to change in the near future. For instance, if cash flows have been consistently increasing but a major competitor opened up in the last three months and is hurting revenues, then determining a fair selected cash flow may be more complex.

It should also be noted that market method data used for comparables is only the data of the year of the sale or the prior year data. Therefore, market multiples are calculated from current results, not a weighted average result. This is a problem with the model but a small problem compared to other available models.

THE MARKET METHOD: ESTIMATING THE MULTIPLIER

The second component of the market method is the multiplier. Multipliers for very small and small businesses can be developed from several different methods:

- The simplest way to develop a multiplier is to use a rule of thumb.[5]
- Development of a multiplier from specific comparable transactions.
- Development of a multiplier from private company guideline comparable data.
- Development of a multiplier from public company guideline data. That will not be addressed here as it is more effective for larger companies.[6]

Standard of Value for Market Comparables

Market comparables are based on market sales. In general, market sales are the highest bidder. In theory, the highest bidder may have market synergies not available to the typical hypothetical buyer. This can raise the issue of what is the standard of value of market data. Most small and very small businesses often do not have synergistic buyers (they often are too small for a larger synergistic buyer to underwrite) or else most buyers are synergistic. For instance, retail stores and restaurants tend to be purchased by individuals who do not have synergies. Small accounting firms tend to be purchased by accountants. Most buyers fall in that category. As discussed earlier, if most buyers are synergistic, then that is fair market value. Therefore, both situations support a fair market value standard.[7] This is important when comparing the comparisons to the subject company. In most cases the multiplier should not require adjustment for standard of value matters. But, there are always exceptions.

Rules of Thumb

Many rules of thumb are used in business brokerage and investment banking to estimate the value of small businesses. These rules of thumb can be reasonably accurate for average profitability businesses. *The Business Reference Guide* by Tom West, published by Business Brokerage Press, is a great source of rules of thumb. https://businessbrokeragepress.com/ This book is updated every year. Most business brokers buy a new version of the book every year or two or have access to the online version.

A few examples of rules of thumb:

- Accounting firms sell for 1 times revenue.
- Portable toilet firms sell for $1,100 times the number of toilets in the field (i.e., 100 units times $1,100 = $110,000).
- Sub-shops and small restaurants sell for 35% of revenue.

The two most versatile rules of thumb are that small and very small businesses sell for 1.5 to 2.5 times SDE and 3 to 4 times EBITDA. These two rules of thumb are remarkably useful and usually not completely accurate.

Using the median or mean multiplier developed from raw market data sorted at the North American Industrial Classification System (NAICS) or the Standard Industrial Classification (SIC) code level is similar to using a rule of thumb unless the subject company really exhibits average characteristics and results.

For very low level estimates, rules of thumb can be applied to the cash flow being measured. Often rules of thumb will be used to check if the calculated figure seems reasonable. Rules of thumb are NOT a business valuation method but they can be useful as a sanity check or for "quick and dirty" guides to possible value.

Developing a Multiplier from Available Market Data

There are two primary ways to develop a multiplier from available market data for small business valuation: the specific comparable method and the private company guideline method.

For small and very small business valuation the specific comparable data method is very difficult to reliably apply because there are too many unknowns for each submitted transaction. The Home Depot distance to a small hardware store is just one example. While extensive financial data may have been collected from the last year, little else is known about the company, the local economy, the seller or the buyer. Even if the financial data is a relative match, these other factors which are almost impossible to verify may have greatly impacted the final price. For this reason, specific comparables (at least two or three in total) are an unreliable method when used alone.

An exception to this can exist if the valuator actually knows enough local comparables. This is rare in general and very rare outside gas stations, restaurants, and bars or other highly active markets. But it does happen. In those cases, an analysis of both soft factors and financial factors should be performed, compared to, and used with guideline data as explained below.

The private company guideline method takes multiple comparables which are used to develop multiplier ranges. The available data points are then further assessed and reviewed in the aggregate in order to develop the multiplier. This methodology will be further developed in the remainder of this chapter.

Review of Available Market Data

There are several sources of small business sale market data. Each service has different parameters. It is important to understand the key definitions for cash flows like seller's discretionary earnings (SDEs) used in the database as they may vary. But, also understand that the contributors of data to the database may not fully understand the definitions when they submit them. In most cases the small and very small business comparables are being submitted by business brokers who receive free access in return for the submission. In addition, most submissions are not complete. Due to the huge amount of data being collected, most submitters do not have all the data. Again, just like the companies being valued, many of the smaller businesses being sold did not have the data either. In fairness to the market data databases, they do reach out and take strides to ensure their data is correct. It's just a somewhat impossible task.

Major market data providers are DealStats (www .bvmarketdata) from Business Valuation Resources which was formerly known as Pratts Stats, ValuSource Market Comps,[8] formerly the IBA database (www.bvdataworld.com), Bizcomps, and DoneDeals. For larger businesses, there is Capital IQ and FactSet.

For small and very small businesses the ValuSource /IBA database and Bizcomps are useful. However, DealStats has the most complete and through database at the time of this writing. https://www.bvresources.com/

Each database collects and parses the data differently. Techniques will be reviewed to parse the data to make it more useful for valuation purposes.[9] These techniques will be shown with DealStats data. The techniques will work with all databases that have sufficient data.

Clearly the closer the subject company is to the comparable companies in terms of primary metrics used to value the company, presumably the more reliable the analysis will be.

THE MARKET METHOD: SELECTING THE COMPANY INDUSTRY

The first issue is determining the subject company industry. Two coding systems are maintained in the United States:

1. The North American Industry Classification System (NAICS). This code system is used by Federal statistical agencies in classifying business establishments. It was developed to allow comparability throughout North America by the Office of Management and Budget (OMB) along with Canadian and Mexican participants. It was intended to replace the Standard Industrial Classification code system (SIC) although it has not done that. For more information, see https://www.census.gov/eos/www/naics/.
2. The SIC System (https://www.osha.gov/pls/imis/sicsearch .html) was last updated in 1987 and is still used by the Department of Labor, particularly the Occupational Safety and Health Administration (OSHA).

Both systems are used and are sufficient. Often, for older industrial and manufacturing industries, there may be more detail in SIC codes. For newer industries, such as information technology, there is more choice in NAICS codes. The NAICS code system will be primarily used throughout this book.

Both systems provide key word searches. Analysts can also Google a word string such as NAICS Code Electrician and obtain the code. When this search was performed, the NAICS code 238210 came up. Coincidently the SIC code 1731 also came up just below the NAICS code. This code is the starting point for any search.

The concept is to generate hopefully 10–30 or more comparable sale transactions when the search is complete. In most instances the next sort is by revenues. Generally small businesses increase in value, all other things being equal, as their revenues increase. A likely reason for this is a business with revenues under $750,000 is not only owner-operated but likely owner-worked,. namely, the difference between "making the sandwiches or overseeing them being made." Because of this, when there are enough comparables, it is important to have the minimum size be somewhat close to the actual revenue stream size. For instance, a restaurant with $1,000,000 of revenues might have a minimum revenue stream of $750,000. On the same basis because there are always more smaller comparables than larger comparables, usually the high end of the search will have a larger gap. Therefore, perhaps the high end will make sense at $1,500,000. Within reason, it is helpful to have the median revenue somewhat near the average or selected weighted revenues.

SORTING THE INDUSTRY DATA SET BY CASH FLOW

The next sort is by an indication of profitability. In most cases, SDE is the most accurate indication of cash flow (hence profitability for valuation purposes) to use for valuing businesses up to about $2,000,000–$3,000,000 in revenues. Thereafter, EBITDA tends to become more accurate. The reason SDE is more accurate with smaller businesses is because estimating a replacement salary for the owner is almost impossible for small businesses with small cash flows. Yet those businesses sell.

Figure 6.3 shows the relationship between EBITDA and SDE and total value with very small businesses. Note that EBITDA

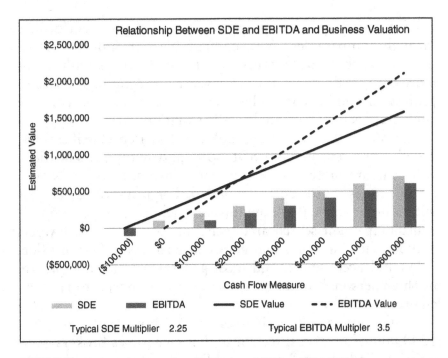

FIGURE 6.3 Relationship Between EBITDA and SDE and Total Value

cannot result in a value (there is no positive EBITDA) for many very small owner-operated businesses where the owner basically earns a salary. Yet there are many of those businesses and many do sell.

Once the sort by revenues is complete, assuming that the business being valued is profitable, select an SDE or EBITDA number as a minimum cash flow. Often a minimum cash flow of 5% of revenues, if using SDE, is reasonable. Eliminating very low cash flow comparables helps eliminate huge multipliers. For instance, a business with revenues of $2,000,000 with cash flow of $2,000 sells for $100,000. That is a cash flow multiplier of 50. It is also nonsense unless you have a similar business in terms of revenues and profitability.

Of course, for some low cash flow (even unprofitable), high revenue businesses such as restaurants, convenience stores, and auto repair shops, there are enough comparables that the analyst can search out potential value for poor performers through comparables. With comparable rich industry classifications such as restaurants, this might leave us with 25 or more comparables. An honest assessment using high levels of professional judgment of the subject company along with the comparables may help analyze the situation.

If you need more comparables in less rich classifications, broaden the revenue and SDE sorts and many classifications will generate more than 10. In some instances, other NAICS or SIC codes will need to be added. For instance, a business with a high personal goodwill issue, such as an expert witness consultant might search architects, interior designers, lawyers and/or other high personal goodwill businesses. (As an aside, CPAs and accountants and most general practice doctors are not high personal goodwill businesses for this purpose in today's environment.)[10]

With very small businesses, often those with less than $500,000 of revenues, recognize that sometimes brokers overestimate "add-backs" inflating SDE. Be cautious if the SDE just seems too high even for an owner who is doing the work. In addition, brokers will tell you that companies with SDE below $75,000 are usually difficult to price (and therefore they may be difficult for valuators to value) because most buyers at some point will just take a job. The sale often becomes more driven by assets (including licenses), start-up cost, location, or emotion driven rather than cash flow.

ANALYSIS OF SORTED DATA SET

One of the problems of the databases are that they tell us the various multipliers and other statistics by percentile but they do not tell us how those multipliers relate to profitability. Just reading the data it is easy to assume that a 75% percentile multiplier of 3.1 should be applied to a company that looks like it is in the 75th% percentile of performance. Yet, for us to know this accurately, we must chart the results against profitability, as shown in Figure 6.4.[11]

Limited Service Restaurants			NAICS	722513	
SDE	$100,000 and up		This is an appropriate search for a profitable		
Revenues	$800,000 to $1,400,000		limited service restaurant		

(This is a partial table. There were many more comparables.)

MVICPrice	NetSales	SDE	SDE / Rev %	Rev Mult	Cash Flow Mult
$175,000	$1,264,915	$59,665	4.72%	0.14	2.93
$80,000	$865,752	$51,177	5.91%	0.09	1.56
$450,000	$1,147,162	$74,657	6.51%	0.39	6.03
$275,000	$889,777	$58,054	6.52%	0.31	4.74
$510,000	$1,288,504	$86,087	6.68%	0.40	5.92
$265,000	$981,282	$69,618	7.09%	0.27	3.81
$190,000	$815,000	$59,293	7.28%	0.23	3.20
$290,000	$1,000,000	$88,000	8.80%	0.29	3.30
$200,000	$799,590	$73,692	9.22%	0.25	2.71
$75,000	$1,463,757	$136,916	9.35%	0.05	0.55
$320,000	$1,031,276	$96,588	9.37%	0.31	3.31
$450,000	$1,017,155	$97,380	9.57%	0.44	4.62
$330,000	$1,300,765	$126,644	9.74%	0.25	2.61
$410,000	$1,317,704	$128,969	9.79%	0.31	3.18
$284,800	$831,175	$81,588	9.82%	0.34	3.49
$279,130	$878,322	$88,623	10.09%	0.32	3.15
$180,000	$878,322	$88,623	10.09%	0.20	2.03
$80,000	$807,580	$82,877	10.26%	0.10	0.97
$130,000	$757,294	$81,320	10.74%	0.17	1.60
$695,000	$1,000,374	$108,000	10.80%	0.69	6.44
$250,000	$900,000	$100,000	11.11%	0.28	2.50
$275,000	$1,124,311	$126,129	11.22%	0.24	2.18
$255,000	$774,618	$87,852	11.34%	0.33	2.90
$180,000	$872,168	$103,315	11.85%	0.21	1.74
$190,000	$1,462,526	$177,820	12.16%	0.13	1.07
$65,000	$750,689	$92,033	12.26%	0.09	0.71
$256,935	$1,063,908	$131,129	12.33%	0.24	1.96
$540,000	$1,104,746	$138,722	12.56%	0.49	3.89
$247,971	$805,091	$102,033	12.67%	0.31	2.43
$400,000	$936,933	$118,860	12.69%	0.43	3.37
$800,000	$1,159,507	$148,254	12.79%	0.69	5.40
$800,000	$1,159,507	$149,218	12.87%	0.69	5.36
$610,000	$901,094	$116,765	12.96%	0.68	5.22
$163,500	$861,306	$112,963	13.12%	0.19	1.45
$225,000	$926,577	$121,776	13.14%	0.24	1.85
$290,000	$997,430	$136,567	13.69%	0.29	2.12
$340,000	$1,326,823	$187,414	14.13%	0.26	1.81
$310,000	$865,000	$125,000	14.45%	0.36	2.48
$996,000	$1,022,584	$150,331	14.70%	0.97	6.63

FIGURE 6.4 Revenue and Cash Flow Multipliers by Profitability

Limited Service Restaurants		NAICS	722513		
SDE	$100,000 and up	This is an appropriate search for a profitable			
Revenues	$800,000 to $1,400,000	limited service restaurant			
(This is a partial table. There were many more comparables.)					

MVICPrice	NetSales	SDE	SDE / Rev %	Rev Mult	Cash Flow Mult
$375,000	$1,385,770	$205,709	14.84%	0.27	1.82
$600,000	$1,374,000	$204,000	14.85%	0.44	2.94
$395,000	$1,433,138	$214,022	14.93%	0.28	1.85
$600,000	$1,046,666	$160,927	15.38%	0.57	3.73
$575,000	$1,443,771	$240,259	16.64%	0.40	2.39
$350,000	$1,473,257	$250,308	16.99%	0.24	1.40
$222,000	$867,654	$149,973	17.28%	0.26	1.48
$860,000	$989,683	$172,926	17.47%	0.87	4.97
$260,000	$875,000	$157,000	17.94%	0.30	1.66
$570,000	$1,151,522	$210,553	18.28%	0.49	2.71
$230,000	$1,076,364	$201,059	18.68%	0.21	1.14
$595,000	$940,203	$184,093	19.58%	0.63	3.23
$475,000	$752,709	$148,502	19.73%	0.63	3.20
$430,000	$750,000	$150,000	20.00%	0.57	2.87
$250,000	$1,046,563	$212,192	20.28%	0.24	1.18
$650,000	$1,134,499	$230,821	20.35%	0.57	2.82
$560,000	$1,290,615	$266,653	20.66%	0.43	2.10
$710,000	$791,270	$164,233	20.76%	0.90	4.32
$625,000	$945,072	$198,084	20.96%	0.66	3.16
$525,000	$1,174,614	$263,738	22.45%	0.45	1.99
$140,000	$1,237,643	$279,009	22.54%	0.11	0.50
$450,000	$872,245	$205,958	23.61%	0.52	2.18
$300,000	$1,000,000	$242,570	24.26%	0.30	1.24
$385,000	$755,139	$185,344	24.54%	0.51	2.08
$395,000	$756,111	$189,177	25.02%	0.52	2.09
$415,000	$796,841	$201,764	25.32%	0.52	2.06
$615,000	$1,100,000	$282,100	25.65%	0.56	2.18
$625,000	$1,041,831	$267,890	25.71%	0.60	2.33
$225,000	$1,168,731	$313,936	26.86%	0.19	0.72
$175,000	$796,859	$221,422	27.79%	0.22	0.79
$200,000	$800,000	$250,000	31.25%	0.25	0.80
$250,000	$760,000	$251,656	33.11%	0.33	0.99
$599,000	$981,058	$373,442	38.07%	0.61	1.60
$270,000	$922,905	$413,971	44.86%	0.29	0.65

FIGURE 6.4 *Continued*

Unless the subject company is truly a median company, this next step is essential. Using SDE as a guide to profitability, take the comparables and chart SDE, Revenues, and Sales Price in adjacent columns for each comparable across a row. For each row in the next column divide SDE by Revenues to get a profitability percentage measure. Repeat this but divide MVIC or Sales Price by Revenues to get a revenue multiplier and in the next column divide MVIC or Sales Price by SDE to get a cash flow multiplier. Each of these comparables will form a list. Take the list and chart it as shown in Figure 6.4. (Again, you can Google how to do most of these steps in Excel if you are not familiar with Excel and get very clear instructions. The website for this book has Excel files with the formulas built in although adjustments must be made every time a new chart is produced.) The same process can be performed with EBITDA for larger businesses. In some cases, both cash flows or even other cash flows are charted. A partial table used to create the graphs is shown in Figure 6.5.

Usually the revenue multipliers increase as the profitability percentage increases. Sometimes the cash flow multiplier is stable across all the profitability measures but usually the cash flow multipliers decrease as the profitability percentages increase. This seems counter-intuitive but is fairly consistent across most small and very small business comparable charts. It is important to perform this for similarly sized companies if enough data exists to allow that. Remember if the owner is performing direct services, the SDE is likely to be much higher due to small size than when the owner is managing the workforce. Generally, managing the workforce is more desirable by buyers.

If database data is limited or if your company may be an outlier or sometimes because things just do not seem to fit, it may make sense to query the database several times with different sort patterns (revenue size, industry codes, SDE or EBITDA, start dates for data, key terms such as "franchise" when a franchise). Often this will help the analyst better understand the data and how it might relate to the subject company.

At this point, look at the comparable data including key ratio metrics that indicate a well-run shop and profitability. (Comparable data and ratio analysis was discussed in

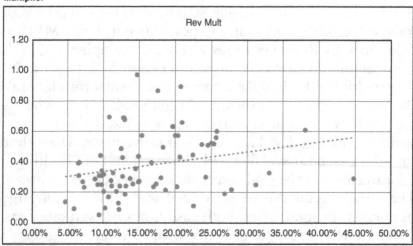

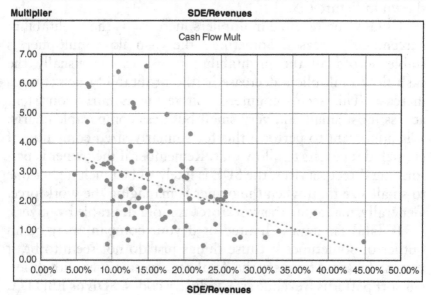

FIGURE 6.5   Graphing Revenue and Cash Flow Multipliers by Profitability

Chapter 4.) Gross margins, while rarely calculated exactly the same way in two companies, can often be an indicator of how well the company is managed. Other metrics to look at include inventory turn, rent, labor costs, and unadjusted profit.[12]

If using DealStats, open the Insight tab. Each valuator will review the compiled data differently. The distribution of transactions to multiplier is useful for seeing how the multipliers are really distributed. This can help the valuator understand if there is a broad dispersion in multipliers or measures or if it is very concentrated. Regression analysis, covered below, also provides insight on dispersion.

SELECT BY TRANSACTION TYPE OR NOT?

Proper reporting of transaction data includes reporting on whether the transaction was a stock sale or an asset sale. There is an assumption among many users of the data (IF data is properly reported, according to the specifications for reporting data) that asset sales prices do not include current balance sheet accounts and all liabilities. Carefully read how the database you are using addresses balance sheet assets.

It is assumed for stock sales that the assets on the balance sheet are conveyed as part of the reported price. But, among the business brokers that report small transactions to the databases, the distinction in assets included in the transaction as part of an asset sale or stock sale does not exist. Assets can be distributed out prior to a stock sale and in limited cases may be included in the price of an asset sale. Therefore, for very small businesses (generally, those with revenues under $5 million, sometimes up to revenues of $10 million), there is likely to be little distinction between asset sales and stock sales in the data. Based on observation in many valuations, this issue is more apparent with SDE cash flow than with EBITDA. This makes sense as SDE is generally a better cash flow to use for the smallest transactions which are likely reported by less experienced brokers and, because of the very small size, have less reliable financial data.

In many cases, it makes sense to review how many transactions are stock sales and how many are asset sales. For small and very small businesses, often most transactions will be asset sales, simplifying this matter.

One day, someone will study this issue for very small businesses. For larger businesses the reported data may be very different. In general, those brokers are much more sophisticated.[13] Therefore, when valuing very small businesses, there may be no need to separate stock sales from asset sales.

SELECTING THE MULTIPLIER

Clearly the multiplier and the final cash flow estimate are the most visible components of a market valuation. Changes in those two factors are going to materially change the estimated value found. Therefore, careful thought and professional judgment apply to estimate the final selected multiplier. For an Opinion of Value with a full report, an explanation of the process used to choose the multiplier and other important factors should be provided. For lower standards and different levels of reports, the level of logic provided may vary. Figure 6.5

Soft Factor Analysis

In Chapter 4, Assessing the Subject Company, the topic of understanding and assessing the soft and financial factors of a business was addressed. Now this understanding needs to be applied to select or adjust the selected multiplier. Selection of the multiplier, like selection of the cash flow, is the true Art of Business Valuation. Primary considerations may be:

- Trend of cash flows including revenues and measures of profitability
- Management structure and size of company
- Concentrations or unusual risks or reduction of risk

- Clarity of comparables
- Any known local market comparables (reported or not)
- Comparability of subject company to comparables
- Profitability charting and comparison to subject
- Timing of economic cycle
- Industry trends
- Any material factor not included above.

How to Present Soft Factor Analysis

There are three main methods of presenting "soft" analysis.

1. The percentage or direct weighting method.
2. The major factors method.
3. The list method.

Figure 6.6 demonstrates these methods.

In the percentage or direct weighting method, attempts are made to put a numerical value on the importance of specific considerations, then come up with a value to calculate the multiplier or to increase or decrease it. This is an attempt to take the subjective and make it objective. *It is still subjective.*

This method is more commonly used by business brokers to develop a multiplier than by business valuators.

The pros and cons of this method are the same. Namely, by creating the perception of exactness where there really is not any, the analysis can be picked apart by reviewers or litigators. Of course, the precision also allows the applied logic to be very clear. Many people like thinking that soft factors can be turned into rigid calculable numbers. Perhaps artificial intelligence will be able to do so in the future but it cannot be done at this time. So, if clear logic is important and the review is going to be reasonable (perhaps for internal management planning purposes), then this may be best way to present the factors.

Direct Weighting

The median Seller's Districtionary Earnings was: 2.5
This had been adjusted by the following factors

Factor	Explanation	Adjustment
Cash Flow Trend	Cash flow has been steadily increasing	0.5
Management	Overreliance on owner. Limited management for size company	−0.25
Economy	The economy is late in the recovery. Forecasts for downturn in 18 months are becoming common.	−0.5
Industry	The industry has strong long-term growth trends.	0.25
Location Risk	Overall the location is good. There is the risk of new competitors entering the market.	−0.25
Total Adjustments		−0.25
Adjusted Seller's Discretionary Earnings		2.25

Major Factors

Median Seller's Discretionary Earnings: 2.5

        Factors that Raise Seller's Discretionary Earnings
                      Cash flow trend
                      Industry

        Factors that Lower Seller's Discretionary Earnings
                      Overreliance on owner
                      Economy, risk of downturn
                      Risk of new competitors

Adjusted Seller's Discretionary Earnings   2.25

List Method

Notes: Based on the following factors, cash flow trends, industry, overreliance on owner, risk of economic recession, risk of new competitors, along with a review of the provided comparative data, I am selecting a Seller's Discretionary Earnings (SDE) of 2.25

FIGURE 6.6   Direct Weighting, Major Factors, and List Method Example

Cash Flow	Multiplier	Indicated Value
$200,000	2.8	$560,000

FIGURE 6.7 Calculating the Indicated Market Value

The major factors method lists the major factors considered along with the analysis and the reasons, but does not attempt to mathematically calculate a multiplier or adjustment to the multiplier. In many cases this is a good methodology to use as the logic is clear but the somewhat unsupportable level of detail is not present.

The list method is to just list the factors with no analysis. A basic statement such as "Based on the following factors A, B, and C, reviewed in my professional opinion, the multiplier is 3." Depending on how this is presented, this is generally viewed as sufficient.

Calculating the Indicated Value

Once the cash flow is estimated and a multiplier selected, calculating the indicated value is simple math. See Figure 6.7.

ADJUSTMENTS TO THE CALCULATED INDICATION OF MARKET METHOD VALUE

The market method estimates the cash flow value of the company. Adjustments may be necessary to finalize the enterprise's value based on balance sheet accounts, as compared to assumptions about the balance sheet account treatment in the comparables.

Most transaction databases assume that asset sales are reported with current asset balance sheet accounts and all liabilities being "retained" by the seller. The theory is that the business needs the equipment necessary to produce the cash flow but financial accounts are brought by the buyer and prior liabilities are paid for by the seller. This forms a cut-off generally on the closing date. Even with very small businesses, since inventory has little value outside the business and is needed by the business, inventory (a current asset) is traditionally taken at lower cost or market value and sometimes added to the value found.

As previously mentioned, stock sales, in theory, are reported with conveyed assets included. But, with small and very small transactions, it is not safe to assume that means that working capital or inventory has been conveyed or that reported values are correct for valuation purposes. Even the "transaction" balance sheets created as part of the sale transaction are usually negotiated for tax purposes and may not reflect market values (often due to accelerated depreciation recapture, hard assets may be valued closer to liquidation value). Therefore, usually they are not representative of the market value of assets being conveyed for valuation purposes. Because of this, be cautious about placing too much weight on listed asset values in the comparable databases for small businesses.

These assumptions will be further discussed below. Much of the discussion centers around how business brokers see the situation and what often happens in transactions. This is relevant because they are reporting the transactions. Valuators must understand what is really clear in the provided data and what may be fuzzy or not clear in reported transactions.

An example of a market method calculation with balance sheet adjustments is shown in Figure 6.8. Further explanation follows.

Inventory

The value of inventory is often added to the value found, based on cash flow for small businesses when using the market method.

According to some transaction databases, the value of good and usable inventory is not included in the price.[14] For very

Selected SDE		$100,000	
Multiplier		1.5	
Indication of Value		$150,000	If estimating a 'price', use this figure

Plus Current Assets			Usually the balance sheet adjustments will be shown
Cash	$25,000		on their own table and the Net amount (17,000 here)
Accounts Receivable	$10,000		will be carried to a calculation of value table
Inventory	$7,000		Note that inventory may or may not be included in this
Total Current Assets	$42,000		calculation. If inventory was in base price/value it
			would not be included here. This is a judgment call
Liabilities			and with small businesses often depends on the
Accounts Payable	$5,000		industry and database
Long-Term Debt	$20,000		
Total Liabilities	$25,000		
			Net Current Assets = Total Current Assets − Total Liabilities
Net Current Assets		$17,000	If estimating price, you may want to note that net assets are usually retained by the seller.
Indication of Value		$167,000	If estimating 100% equity value, use this figure

FIGURE 6.8 Market Method with Balance Sheet Adjustments

small businesses, this is often the case. As businesses grow, adding inventory varies.

From working both as a business broker and valuator, this rule of thumb appears to be a reasonable starting point for business valuation:

- When inventory turn is under 30–60 days, often all good and usable inventory will be added to the price. The theory is this is reasonably close to a cash equivalent at this point and can be liquidated rapidly.
- Inventory turn is 60–180 days, 50% of good and usable inventory (often a little higher percentage at 60 days and lower at 180) will be added to the price.
- Inventory turn is over 180 days. At this point, inventory is similar to a capital investment and is quite illiquid. Under the market method, the multiple might be tweaked up a little due to the inventory but generally the inventory will not be added to the price. This was much more common in the pre-Amazon days when retailers such as hobby shops, fabric

stores, and the like carried deep inventories and offset low inventory turns with higher mark-ups. This has become less common but occasionally still exists.

- Finally, for smaller businesses, if the SDE multiplier is above 2.5–3 before adding reasonable inventory, apply a high level of professional judgment to make sure a reasonable return can be made on the total investment. (For instance, a liquor store with a multiplier of 4 is likely to have at least some inventory in the multiplier. From there, the analyst needs to look at the facts of the case.)

In sale situations, when a price is involved, inventory will often be negotiated. Often what is found is that 20–30% of the inventory turns rapidly and the remainder has very slow sell-through. Depending on all the other factors in the business, sometimes a portion of the inventory will be added to the price or the multiple may be increased to compensate for the quick selling inventory.

Remember the ultimate test—does this value make sense? Namely, don't allow computations with correct math to override the Art of Business Valuation. At some point an acceptable cash flow return cannot be made on additional inventory purchases. If the entire huge inventory is really required to run the business, then the business may not be saleable at all. This has been the demise of many small hobby shops and specialty stores. They cannot compete against the seemingly unlimited inventory on the internet. In those cases, the going concern assumption needs to be revisited and liquidation value seriously considered.

Working Capital Adjustment

Another area that comes up as businesses become larger is working capital. Again, the databases state that working capital is not conveyed in asset sales and generally is conveyed in stock sales as part of the definitions, yet for larger "very small" businesses (over $1,500,000 or more in value in most cases), this is not consistently the case, according to business brokers. Again, how do we as valuators work with this fact?

Applying Working Capital in the Valuation (Market Method)

The ultimate question is, should a business requiring a large amount of working capital (many subcontractors, suppliers, service companies for very large companies, etc.) include the working capital in the market method value estimated from cash flow or should all or a significant portion of the required working capital be added to the value?

Talking to business brokers who generate the data, experience seems to be that, under $2,000,000–$3,000,000 in revenues often equating to under $1,000,000 in price, typically the working capital will be added to the purchase price. Namely, for very small business sales, the seller in the transaction keeps the working capital (working capital here is defined as current assets other than inventory already addressed less all liabilities) and it is reported that way to the database services.

Therefore, when using the market method, valuators will add the net current asset value less inventory over liabilities to the cash flow value found. This is because in the base transactions, the seller kept those assets and therefore benefitted from them. Many small business owners are quite conservative and keep substantial current assets and little debt on their balance sheets so this adjustment can be significant. Finally, these transactions tend to be smaller and are frequently reported on an SDE basis. Over $10,000,000 of revenues and $5,000,000 in price, the sellers almost always convey reasonable working capital in the price. Coincidently these transactions are generally reported on an EBITDA basis.

Under the market method for companies with revenues between $2,000,000 and $10,000,000, there appears to be no consistent answer as to the impact of balance sheet accounts to the final value found. Only these observations:

- If the company is a retailer or other business that is usually paid at the time of service, this is really a moot point. It is likely not material to the value found.
- The better the economy, the more accounts receivable tend *not* to be conveyed.

- Consistent with this is the more active the lending market, the less accounts receivable tend to be conveyed. (Hence, the availability of affordable lines of credit.)
- Larger, more sophisticated buyers on larger deals (approximately $1 million EBITDA up) tend to demand working capital as part of the transaction.
- Consistent with this, EBITDA market method multipliers which are used in "larger" small business transactions appear to include more working capital (often accounts receivables) in the value than SDE multiplier methods.

In all methods, clearly excess working capital is an excess asset. A simple method for estimating working capital when necessary is shown in Chapter 11, Accounting Issues with Small and Very Small Businesses.

As stated with inventory, this discussion must be tempered by common sense and the recognition that there must be a return to all buyers under all standards of value that makes economic sense. Valuation is based on rational assumptions even if not every underlying market price is rational.

Example

Construction subcontracting companies often work for general contractors who are notoriously slow payers. 60–90-day old receivables are common. Poorly managed subcontractors and almost all subcontractors in severe downturns require more accounts receivable than a typically leveraged buyer can support. At those valuation dates these companies are likely worth their liquidation value after adjusting for warranty work. That is assuming they can collect the receivables once their clients realize they are liquidating.

STATISTICS AND THE MARKET METHOD

It is often proposed that a sensitivity analysis can be used to determine if the correct variables and assumptions are being considered and used in a valuation. The assumption is that the financial and statistical analysis[15] can be used to determine which variables will most impact a valuation. There are two major problems with this assumption. First, many soft variables, such as the economy, have major impacts on valuation yet cannot easily be turned into a comparable number.

For cyclical businesses, that is a tremendous determinant of future results, yet economists and valuators do not really know how to predict the next recession or what the severity will be in the local, regional, or national economy in which the subject company operates.

Other examples of risk due to change that is difficult to evaluate with statistics include key people, changing technology, interest rates, tax changes, availability of financing for operations and expansion, and new or more aggressive competitors. These are often far bigger factors in the future of the subject firm than small variations of cash flow, capitalization rates, multipliers, known taxes, etc.

Second, even where this is not a problem, statistics can only be used to show correlation, namely, association, but not causation. The big risk is the human mind usually assumes causation where there are simply associations. However, that is often not the case.

A prime example of this is the coefficient of variation (CV) which is used to determine how reliable a comparable measure of value may be. Often the lowest CV value will be for the revenue cash flow indicator. Yet it is common knowledge that revenues alone are not enough to sell or create value in a business. Remember, the databases have revenues of businesses that SOLD and, in a high percentage of cases, that were profitable. We have no data on all the businesses that could not sell (which are estimated to be up to 75% or more of small and very small businesses). If an analyst applies the revenue multiplier to a very low profitability or no profitability business because it appears to be the most reliable indicator based on the CV value, the value found is highly likely to be wrong.

Therefore, use statistics with caution. They "support" or do not support a multiplier or other measure used IF the measure has causation (or perhaps correlation is enough if there are other strong, related causation factors) but they do not "prove" anything. In fact, in the hands of the inexperienced, they may do more harm than good.

Remember the USPAP Standards:

USPAP STANDARDS Rule 9-5 Comment, The value conclusion is the result of the appraiser's judgment and not necessarily the result of a mathematical process. (2018-2019 USPAP)

And, always, ask "Does this make sense?"

With that caveat in place we will briefly cover statistics and the market method.

Calculating Statistics as an Indicator on Market Method Comparables

Statistics is a huge topic. Only a very small sliver of the world of statistics required to better understand market data is covered here. Two main statistical measures will be touched upon: regression analysis[16] and the coefficient of variation.

Regression Analysis. At the highest level, regression analysis is the measure of the association between one variable (the dependent variable) and another variable (the independent variable). Usually this is formulated as an equation where the independent variables may be used to estimate a value of the dependent variables. Again, statistics does not investigate the "cause" of the correlation, only that there is a correlation.

The regression equation of a line is shown as:

$$Y = mX + b$$

Y = dependent variable, which will be assigned to business sales price, more formally called the market value of invested capital.

X = independent variable, which will be assigned to the cash flow used measure, which may be revenues, gross margin, profit, SDE, EBIT or EBITDA.

m = samples or data points of the independent variable (otherwise known as a factor).

b = is the intercept or null variable. It is where the value found is equal to 0 which may be a positive or negative number.

What regression analysis does is show whether the selected metric (say, SDE to price) provides cogent or correlated results.

Regression analysis shows relationship trends, again SDE to price for example, to known ratios to establish a variance to a trend line. The trend line is the "line" which approximates the most centrist location to all the points being compared. In theory, the closer the result (or point) is to the trend line, the more reliable the point becomes. In a "perfect" correlation, all points would be on the trend line.

Therefore, regression analysis determines how similar the data points are. It is presumed (but, as already discussed, that presumption may be false) that the data is more useful and more accurate as it becomes more similar. As the data points become more similar, it is said they are more correlated.

What low correlations really mean is that the multiplier may vary more from the trend line. Therefore, professional judgment in the selection of the multiplier becomes more important with low correlations. If there are enough data points, it may still be supportable. In the alternative, high correlations in most cases require less judgment since the multiplier of a reasonably typical company should be near the trend line.

The regression technique used here is R-square or the coefficient of determination. R-square yields results from 0.0–1.0. The closer to 1.0, the more uniform and highly correlated the data. See Figure 6.9 for an example of the calculation using Excel.

SDE X	Price Y	Y/X Metric	
100	301.1	3.011	Highest
700	1800	2.571	
120	300	2.500	
240.5	600	2.495	
195	482	2.472	
396	950	2.399	
175	395	2.257	
225.5	455.5	2.020	
350	600	1.714	
390	650	1.667	
220	350.8	1.595	
325	500	1.538	
525	800	1.524	
500	450	0.900	Lowest
		2.047	Mean (Average)
		2.139	Median (Mid-point)

SUMMARY OUTPUT

Regression Statistics	
Multiple R	0.822152037
R Square	0.675933972 → This shows that the data is more reliable than not (over .50)
Adjusted R Square	0.648928469
Standard Error	229.5878857
Observations	14

ANOVA

	df	SS	MS	F	Significance F
Regression	1	1319319.407	1319319	25.02949	0.000307788
Residual	12	632527.167	52710.6		
Total	13	1951846.574			

	Coefficients	Standard Error	t Stat	P-value	Lower 95%	Upper 95%	Lower 95.0%	Upper 95.0%
Intercept	23.43082946	133.5260971	0.175478	0.863631	-267.4975441	314.359203	-267.4975441	314.359203
X Variable 1	1.861579648	0.372096526	5.002948	0.000308	1.050850963	2.672308332	1.050850963	2.672308332

X Variable is the angle of the line graph generated. It can be viewed as the base "multiplier"

The Intercept is where the nul variable (essentially 0 value would cross through the 0 value of the Y axis of the graph chart.

FIGURE 6.9 Calculating the Regression Metric

In theory, an analyst could take the X variable as calculated, in this case 1.852, and multiply it by the SDE, then add the intercept of $29,480 to come up with price. Therefore, if the SDE were $100,000, price would be $185,200 + $29,480 = $214,700 (rounded). This is not suggested as that level of correlation between the data and the subject company is unlikely.

Again, what this indicates is how closely correlated the data is. If it can be demonstrated that there is causation between the variables (SDE vs. business price in this case) and then if it is used properly, it can increase confidence that the data is useful. It does not show that it is correct.

A low correlation indicates that the value found may be quite far from the trend line. More weight will need to be placed on the assumptions, fact pattern, and soft factors to justify the multiplier selected as the possible range is much broader. Not surprisingly, often with smaller "cash" retail businesses, there is a low correlation to the reported financial data. A low correlation DOES NOT INDICATE THAT A MULTIPLIER IS RIGHT OR WRONG. Just that the correlation is low, therefore, that any selected multiplier is likely to be less supported solely by the financial data. A graph of the regression analysis results is shown in Figure 6.10.

Do not confuse charting the regression analysis with charting revenues and cash flow multipliers to profitability. They show very different measures.

Coefficient of Variation. The Coefficient of Variation (CV) is also known as the relative standard deviation and is a standard measure of dispersion. It is the ratio of the standard deviation to the mean. It is a dimensionless number. Dimensionless numbers are usually ratios, they are useful for comparison (another example is common size statements where ratios are compared across time and across different businesses).

- This is useful for comparing between data sets with different units or different means. That is why it is used to compare different business value to cash flow ratios.

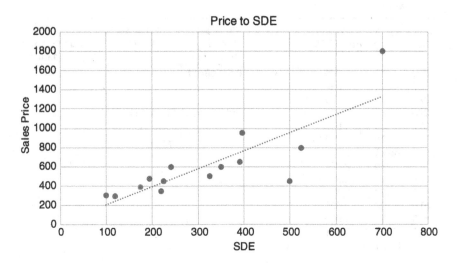

FIGURE 6.10 Regression Analysis Graph

- The CV becomes unreliable when the mean value is near zero as the coefficient is sensitive to small changes in the mean.[17] Revenue to price tends to have very low ratios and a low mean which may make the CV as calculated for them suspect for comparison purposes.
- The CV does NOT provide confidence intervals for the mean. A "low" CV does not ensure reliable data. *Only if it is reliable,* does it indicate how it might rank compared to other possible choices.

The CV is calculated by first calculating the standard deviation of the range of values, (in this case the range of, price/SDE) which is an Excel function =STDEV.P, and then dividing it by the average of the range of values. Figure 6.11 is an example of calculating the CV.

If you do not understand formulas in Excel, use Google, as excellent examples are online. A starting point Excel file is found on this book's website.

SDE X	Price Y	Y/X Price/SDE		Price/SDE Standard Deviation	Price/SDE Average	Price/SDE Coefficient of Variation
500	450	0.900	Lowest	0.55209411	2.047	26.97%
525	800	1.524				
325	500	1.538				
220	350.8	1.595		Std. Deviation/Average = CV		
390	650	1.667				
350	600	1.714				
225.5	455.5	2.020				
175	395	2.257				
396	950	2.399				
195	482	2.472				
240.5	600	2.495				
120	300	2.500				
700	1800	2.571				
100	301.1	3.011	Highest			
		2.047	Mean (Average)			
		2.139	Median (Mid-point)			

FIGURE 8.11   Calculation of the Coefficient of Variation

NOTES

1. Soft data, in this book, has to do with people and processes internally and industry and economic forecasting externally to the company. This was discussed in Chapter 4, Assessing the Subject Company.
2. In fact, in the income buildup approaches we are using the Home Depot as a basis for the comparison. Perhaps that is an even more difficult comparison.
3. Sometimes the argument about seeing the whole business cycle is made and that may be legitimate but that would require 7–11 years' data and 11 years is a long time in small business.
4. See J. Hitchner, S. Pratt, and J. Fishman, *A Consensus View: Q&A Guide to Financial Valuation* (Ventner, NJ: VPS, 2016), p. 42, has more detail on weighting cash flows for capitalization of earnings which is very similar.
5. Rules of thumb are technically not valuations.

6. *See* J. Hitchner, *Financial Valuation Applications and Models*, 3rd Edition (Hoboken, NJ: Wiley, 2011), p. 270 for how to apply public company guideline data

7. *BTR Dunlop Holdings, Inc. v. Commissioner*, 78 T.C.M. 797 (1999). Also see Chapter 3, Valuation Basics, section Standards of Value in this book.

8. At the time of publication ValuSource has announced that they are making a major upgrade to their market data, but it was not yet available.

9. For a detailed analysis, see Fred Hall's paper, "Analysis of Transactional Databases". Retrieved from http://www.affordablebusin essvaluations.com/Database_Analysis-Pratt_s_Stats__IBA__Bizc omps.pdf. Fred Hall has many excellent articles on market data. My view, based on years of business brokerage experience (which varies from Fred Hall's published work) is for small business broker transactions with values under $1–$2 million range, the detailed data is unreliable and does not justify further analysis beyond that explained in this book. Clearly this is a valid point of contention in the valuation community.

10. What is meant by this statement is the CPA's personal goodwill is conveyable personal goodwill. See Chapter 10, Goodwill and the Small Business.

11. Fred Hall, "Using Regression Analysis in the Market Approach," an "Around the Valuation World" webcast (NACVA, January, 2017). The suggested charting is the first step in data analysis.

12. *See* Chapter 4, the section Ratio Analysis. Remember per Tom West, it is estimated that 75% of very small businesses do not sell (those under $5 million revenues) and only 50% of small businesses (with $10 million revenues) sell. Therefore, for many uses, likely meaningful comparative data is often the 75th percentile.

13. *See* Fred Hall, "Analyzing Transactional Databases." Retrieved from https://quickreadbuzz.com/2018/01/10/analyzing-transactional-databases. He makes the assumption that the market data can be further parsed and more detailed data used. I believe inaccuracies are rampant and are better viewed lumped together and then professional judgment applied.

14. DealStats indicates that inventory is included. In BizComps, inventory is not included. In ValuSource, inventory is included. Common sense and professional judgment must be applied as reporting by data providers to the database services is inconsistent.

15. *See* https://scientificliteracymatters.com/2015/03/the-problem-with-statistical-evidence/; also https://ed.ted.com/lessons/how-statistics-can-be-misleading-mark-liddell

16. Fred Hall, "Use of Regression Analysis to Calculate Multipliers in the Market Approach," NACVA Program 13PBV0319. I agree with a first-level regression to show correlation. I do not agree with the concept of using multiple regressions to improve reliability.

17. National Institute of Standards and Technology. Retrieved from https://www.itl.nist.gov/div898/software/dataplot/refman2/auxillar/coefvari.htm

CHAPTER 7

Asset Approaches

The asset approaches look at the value of the assets of the company being valued. This is often used to determine a "floor value" which could otherwise be thought of as a "high liquidation value," when a company is not performing well and may face dissolution. In most cases, business valuators are not hired to determine the asset value of small or very small businesses. Therefore, a brief discussion will be given here for those cases when the asset method turns out to be all there is left with a small or very small company.

It is suggested that this chapter be reviewed along with the Balance Sheet sections of Chapter 11, Accounting Issues with Small and Very Small Businesses. Much of the material in these two chapters goes hand in hand.

A simple, but typical Balance Sheet Adjustment Worksheet is shown as Figure 7.1. Note that the first series of columns is an estimate of the current market value of the assets. The second series of columns is a further markdown to estimate the liquidation value of the assets. More on estimating for liquidation values is addressed below in the section Fixed Assets.

Date Preparer	Book Value	Market Val Adjustment	Market Value	Liquidation Adjustment	Liquidation Value
Current Assets					
1　Cash	$50,000		$50,000		$50,000
2　Accounts Receivable	$75,000	($25,000)	$50,000	($5,000)	$45,000
3　Inventory	$50,000	($10,000)	$40,000	($20,000)	$20,000
4　Other Current Assets	$0		$0		$0
Long-Term Assets			$0		$0
5　Loans	$0		$0		$0
6　Other Investments	$0		$0		$0
7　Buildings and Equipment	$250,000		$250,000	($25,000)	$225,000
8　Less: Accumulated Depreciation	($175,000)		($175,000)		($175,000)
9　Intangible Assets	$25,000	($15,000)	$10,000		$10,000
10　Less: Accumulated Amortization	($10,000)		($10,000)		($10,000)
11 Total Assets	$265,000	($50,000)	$215,000	($50,000)	$165,000
Liabilities and Shareholders Equity					
12　Accounts Payable	$50,000		$50,000	($20,000)	$30,000
13　Current Portion of Long-Term Debt	$20,000		$20,000		$20,000
14　Other Current Liabilities	$24,000		$24,000		$24,000
15　Long-Term Debt	$40,000		$40,000		$40,000
16　Other Long-Term Liabilities			$0		$0
17 Total Liabilities			$0		$0
Owners' Equity					
18　Capital Stock	$2,000		$2,000		$2,000
19　Other Paid in Capital	$18,000		$18,000		$18,000
20　Retained Earnings	$111,000	($50,000)	$61,000	($30,000)	$31,000
21　Less: Cost of Treasury Stock	$0		$0		$0
22 Total Liabilities and Stockholders' Equity	$265,000	($50,000)	$215,000	($50,000)	$165,000
23　Adjusted Asset Value (18+19+20)					
Book Value	$131,000	Market	$81,000	Liquidation	$51,000

NOTES
Line
  2 $25,000 of A/R was past 90 days and appears uncollectable for Market. Estimated 10% no pay if liquidated.
  3 $10,000 for mark-down of inventory past 2 years old. $20,000 or approx 50% cost is estimated liquidation valuation.
  7 Estimated further equipment write-down. Sometimes with accelerated depreciation or owned real estate there is a write-up.
  9 Intangible assets have no market value in this case and are written off.
  12 Accounts payable write down, unlikely to pay several service creditors if liquidated.
  20 Retained earnings reduced to keep balance sheet balanced,
  23 Equity accounts total the net asset value. (Lines 18–20)
    Orderly liquidation is assumed here.
    Under proper accrual accounting, income statement accounts will also need to be adjusted based on these changes.xs

FIGURE 7.1　Balance Sheet Adjustment Worksheet.

ARE ALL ASSETS AND LIABILITIES ON THE BALANCE SHEET?

The starting point for this analysis is to determine that the balance sheet is complete. Assets and liabilities may not have been put on the books because they were not required to be or because of an error. For instance, most leases in the past were not shown on balance sheets.[1] Also, as companies get into trouble, sometimes owners or employees will hide liabilities. In addition, there may be contingent liabilities, guarantees, and other obligations that may come into play particularly as a company approaches insolvency. Start by making sure you know what are the assets and liabilities of the firm.

Every Now and Then

Rarely, but occasionally, the asset method will produce a larger value than the income or market method. Some companies are very conservative and keep a lot of cash on hand. Others may have large receivables. An unusual example is when commodity prices are very high for a company that has commodities under contract or option. An example is homebuilders/speculative builders in strong markets who have substantial land holdings under option contracts. While the high valuations are unlikely to last, as of the valuation date, even after marketability discounts for "flipping" the land, this value could be above the long-term operating earnings value of the company.

CURRENT ASSETS UNDER THE ASSET METHOD

When reviewing current assets, cash is cash. But accounts receivable should be scrutinized for collectability. While accounts receivable should always be checked for collectability, often management of companies under pressure will avoid writing off uncollectable receivables as this will further lower profits. In that case the valuator may need to impose a cut-off such as 90 or 120 days for collectability. Yet, this is not always the case.

Construction contractors often have a 5% or 10% of the invoice amount retained by the customer. Retention is a warranty reserve. While exact timing of the release of the retention will vary by contract, it is usually paid on completion of the contractors' work or completion of the project. If the contractor has organized records breaking out retention, an analysis of historic retention collection can be performed. Some discounting may be in order to partially offset work required to obtain the release (unless this is already booked as a liability). In most cases, retentions are collected outside of disputes.

On a final note, failures to release retentions or pay on time by general contractors who have a history of doing so may be a tell-tale sign of impending financial problems. Beware, particularly if the general contractor is a major concentrated client with or without large sums outstanding. Factor this into the risk equation.

Some suppliers use the willingness to extend credit as a competitive advantage. In those cases, review the collections from prior years. One way to do this is to review the accounts receivable (A/R) schedules at the end of each quarter. Verify that the receivables are in fact being collected. An example of this was a direct mail house that did political campaigns. They collected at 105 days to give their clients the opportunity to collect from the mail campaign. They had a 98% payment rate. In cases like this, perhaps some discounting is in order but not a wholesale removal.

FIXED ASSETS

If a company is hard asset or real estate heavy and the value of the assets is likely to drive the value found, then it is important to rely upon equipment or real estate appraisers. If, like many small and very small companies, the asset value is nominal, then estimating an adjustment to market may be appropriate.

If doing a valuation for exit planning or for a transaction, find out what assets are going to remain with the conveyed company. Is the "new" vehicle being conveyed? Sometimes significant assets have been purchased since the last tax return and are not shown on the list provided. These should be adjusted in those cases.

In most cases, the balance sheet shows the purchase price and the depreciated value of the fixed assets. Proper valuation theory is that the assets should be marked to market to reflect what they are really worth at the valuation date. Marked to market is a term meaning adjusting the book asset value to a market price as of the valuation date.

There is usually more than one market price that can be the basis of the adjustment. Market values include:

- In place value, which is a value for a total assemblage of assets that may be higher than the individual assets. Often this may apply to a productive industrial operation where there are high set-up and fit-out costs.
- Fair market value assumes a reasonable period to trade and no compulsion. It is often viewed as dealership buy/sell-type pricing.

Liquidation values, which are a subcategory of asset value, include:

- Orderly liquidations, which assume a compulsion to sell but there is still some sales period.
- The forced liquidation value is the auction value with a set limited timeframe.

Always specify the standard of value you are using to restate assets in your business valuation.

For the typical small business with very little equipment, the valuator can review the equipment list. Often the best list is part of the depreciation schedule. Obtain an indication of wear such as mileage for vehicles and estimate an adjustment. Computers, office equipment, phone systems, and the like often have no resale value. Racking, fork lifts, trucks, and construction equipment have a value that decreases in recessions and increases when the economy is strong.

Excess assets under other methods should be treated as any other asset under this method as all assets are assumed to be sold off.

BUILT-IN GAINS

Built-in gains occur when a C corporation sells its assets. C corporations are income tax-paying entities separate from their owners. If a C corporation owns an asset and sells the asset at a profit, this results in a taxable event to the C corporation. Unfortunately, C corporations do not receive capital gains treatment either, so this tax will be at ordinary rates. This is less of a problem while the Tax Cuts and Jobs Act (TCJA) is in effect with the 21% corporate rate. However, real property depreciation (Section 1250) is recaptured at a 25% rate. Later, if the shareholders want to access the money personally, the distribution from the corporation to the shareholder is also a second taxable event.

The built-in gains effect can also happen if a C corporation accumulates large amounts of cash and does not distribute it. If a shareholder buys the C corporation to access the cash, the distribution of cash to the shareholder will be a taxable event.

For instance, if a C corporation is purchased, which has $1,000,000 of undistributed excess cash in it, the purchasing shareholder will only receive the after-tax amount. Assuming a personal tax rate of 15% on distributions, the $1,000,000 is worth $850,000 after federal tax. State tax may also be due. Would anyone pay $1,000,000 for that? Probably not.

Depending on the situation and the purpose and the standard of value, most valuation analysts will adjust or net out all or most of the built-in gains tax at the best estimated tax rate for the asset. A sample adjustment is provided in Figure 7.2.

CLIENT NAME
BUILT-IN CAPITAL GAINS CALCULATION
As of March 31, 2019

<u>State Tax Estimate</u>

Total Capital Gains	$1,550,000
Times the State Income Tax Rate - 6.00%	<u>**93,000**</u>
Net Capital Gains Before Federal Income Taxes (A)	1,457,000

<u>For the Federal Income Tax</u>

Real Property Depreciation (B)	$ 560,600
Times the Recapture Tax Rate	<u>25.00%</u>
Total Recapture Income Tax on Depreciation	<u>**140,150**</u>
Less: Accumulated Depreciation (B)	<u>560,600</u>
Net Capital Gains to be Taxed at Capital Gains Rate (A-B)	896,400
Times Federal Capital Gains Rate	<u>20.00%</u>
Total Capital Gains Income Tax	<u>**179,280**</u>
Total Federal Income Taxes	<u>**$ 319,430**</u>

Total Federal and State Capital Gains Taxes (State+Total Fed Tax)	412,430
Times the Control Partner's Equity Percentage	<u>100%</u>
CAPITAL GAINS TAX ATTRIBUTED TO THE CONTROL PARTNER	<u>**$ 412,430**</u>

Capital Gains Tax Divided by the Total Capital Gains	<u>**26.60839%**</u>

FIGURE 7.2   Built-in Gains Calculation
Source: Ron Rudich.

INTANGIBLE ASSETS

The primary problem with the asset method is estimating the value of intangible assets. For small and very small businesses, intangible assets are embedded in the indicated value and shown as goodwill. Goodwill for business valuation is the simple mathematical calculation of subtracting all identifiable tangible assets from the total found value of the business. That remainder is goodwill. Current goodwill cannot be calculated without using some sort of valuation method that measures an earnings stream which is why the asset method alone is not reliable for valuing profitable companies. Figure 7.3 shows a simple goodwill calculation.

Goodwill in small businesses and very small businesses is a catch-all for the intangible value. Personal goodwill is a further classification of goodwill that will be addressed later in Chapter 10. Generally, there is no useful purpose in trying to further define intangible assets (i.e., trade name, trademarks, value of customer list, value of supplier list, value of workforce, trade secrets) with small and very small businesses.

If an existing business was purchased as a going concern by the current owners, there may be a goodwill value on the books. While this may be significant for tax purposes, market goodwill in small and very small businesses will change regularly with the value found. The book value of goodwill should not be used as a goodwill estimate in current valuations.

But, in most cases other than certain licenses, such as liquor licenses or below market leases, where transferable, it is very hard to place a value on intangibles using an asset method. In many locations limited market data can be obtained for liquor licenses.

- For instance, in Maryland, in certain limited locations (by election district in certain cities and counties), liquor licenses have been reported to be worth over $250,000. In other counties in Maryland liquor licenses are easy to obtain and run with the location, therefore they have no real intangible value.
- In New Jersey, liquor licenses can be over $1,000,000. While these types of prices are somewhat rare, they certainly can change the valuation of a poorly performing restaurant, bar, or nightclub.

Calculating Goodwill:

Conclusion of Value 100%	$750,000
Less Tangible Assets (A+B below)	$275,000
Goodwill Value	$475,000

I have assumed book value is also market value
This may need to be adjusted as shown earlier.

Balance Sheet with goodwill shown.

Current Assets	
Cash	$50,000
Accounts Receivable	$150,000
Inventory	$30,000
Other Current Assets	$5,000
Total Current Assets (A)	$235,000
Fixed Assets	
Furniture and Fixtures	$20,000
Automobile	$50,000
Accumulated Depreciation	($30,000)
Total Fixed Assets (B)	$40,000
Intangible Assets	
Goodwill	$475,000
Amortization	$0
Total Assets	$750,000
Liabilities	
Current Liabilities	
Accounts Payable	$250,000
Long-Term Liabilities	
Auto Debt	$30,000
Total Liabilities	$280,000
Net Worth	$470,000
Total Liabilities and Net Worth	$750,000

FIGURE 7.3   Calculating Goodwill

Therefore, the asset method is used for companies when there is little profitability or related situations where continued profitability is questionable. It is very rare that small and very small companies have any intangible value when they are unprofitable, unless it comes from permits, licenses or transferable below market leases and advantageous contracts.

LIABILITIES

In general, there is an assumption that liabilities will be paid. When companies get into trouble, this is not always the case. In some cases, accounts payable, notes to private parties, and rarely, even notes to institutional type investors and banks are discounted. At some point, something is better than nothing. Estimating a discount rate on payables and debts is very difficult as there will rarely be history on such activity. Outside of bankruptcy where this is part of the process and a little more predictable, common sense, professional judgment, and a belief in management's plans (or a trustee or new management) are required.

Personal Guarantees

While perhaps beyond the "business" in business valuation, if a valuation is being performed to estimate the loss to an owner due to a failing business, it must be remembered that leases and loans may have personal guarantees and that those obligations may continue beyond the life of the business. Estimating what will be required to obtain a release can be quite complex. In addition, some owners have structured their finances to protect themselves from liability adding further complexity. I have been told that SBA loan losses are obligations to the United States Government and can even be offset against Social Security.

Owners' Equity

Owners' equity is the net worth of the business. Namely, it is the total of all the assets less all the liabilities. It is also the total of all the equity contributed plus all the earnings less all the distributions.

The adjusted net worth estimated to market value or a level of liquidation value is the calculated estimate of value under this method. Professional judgment needs to be used depending on the facts and standards as to how to use this estimate in the overall valuation.

NOTE

1. Accounting Standards Update (ASU) No. 2016-02 Leases (Topic 842) recognizes a right-of-use (ROU) asset and lease liability on the balance sheet for most leases. Implementation is now required for private companies for fiscal years beginning after December 15, 2022.

CHAPTER 8

Income Approaches

The income approach is the workhorse of the valuation profession. In the income approach, the estimated cash flow is divided by a capitalization rate in the capitalization of earnings method, or discount rate in the discounted cash flow method to estimate the value.[1] These are the two primary income methods.

The two primary income methods will be reviewed back and forth in steps throughout the chapter. This is because many of the steps have similarities and build on one another. We start with a discussion of some critical issues about the income method that only applies to very small businesses. Then we will look at estimating cash flows under the two approaches including tax affecting and other adjustments. Subsequently we will estimate a discount rate and follow with the further adjustments to estimate a capitalization rate. Next we will complete the capitalization of earnings estimate and then discuss a few variations of that method. Finally, we will complete the discounted cash flow estimate to determine the appraisal.

A complete calculation including estimating the cash flow, calculating the discount or capitalization rate, and then completing the estimates is shown in Figure 8.3 on p. 163 for the capitalization of earnings and in Figure 8.15 on p. 213 for the discounted cash flows method. Refer back to these frequently. In fact, if this material is new to you, it may be easiest to go to the website and review the related Excel files including look-ing at the formulas. Then print the files and make notes on the printout when going through this chapter.

The income method's main variance from the market method is that instead of a market multiplier determined from comparable transactions, a discount rate for forward-looking cash flows or capitalization rate applied to adjusted historic cash flows is determined by looking at the relative risk of this investment to other available investments to investors.

"There are three main components that need to be investi-gated to use the income approach:[2]

1. What is the cash flow and is it reliable and predictable?
2. How is the cash flow going to grow and how do we estimate a growth rate?
3. How risky is this investment compared to all other invest-ments available?"

An essential element in applying the income method is to make sure the income stream is properly aligned with the cal-culated discount rate.[3] "Apples to apples," while this seems simple, it often is not.

There are many different cash flows. Revenues, gross profit, EBITDA, EBIT, after-tax cash flow, net income, cash flow to equity, cash flow to invested capital, and so on. Each may call for a different estimated discount rate. The valuation will be wrong if an improper alignment between cash flow and dis-count rates is used.

Another issue related only to very small businesses is, are there really investors for this business?

WHO IS AN "INVESTOR"?

A primary difference between the market approach and the income approach is that the income approach is "value to the investor." This is often conveniently overlooked when valuing very small businesses.

For many small businesses, particularly those with less than $1,000,000 of earnings before interest, taxes, depreciation, and amortization (EBITDA), there is a limited "investor" market. There are mainly owner-operators; namely, people buying jobs hopefully with opportunity. Owner-operators can be considered investors but they need compensation. The mix of compensation for labor vs. return for investment is very murky and with very small businesses often inseparable. As a practical matter, this problem gets bigger as EBITDA or other cash flows get smaller. At $500,000 of EBITDA, there are almost no third-party investors other than family members and loved ones. These businesses and smaller businesses are typically purchased by owner/operators and financed using small business administration (SBA) loans.

What this creates for valuators who insist on using the income method for smaller businesses is either converting to seller's discretionary earnings (SDE) instead of after-tax cash flow or EBITDA. SDE cannot be tied into any method of estimating a capitalization or discount rate except maybe the guess method. (Or a back-door market method, but then it would be better to just be honest and do a proper market analysis.)

Or, valuators are presented with the unsupportable but true possibility that very small businesses have much lower discount rates than larger businesses. (Supply and demand could explain it, after all there are many more people who can afford a $100,000 value business than a $50,000,000 value business.) But, that goes against "common knowledge" and logic. See Figure 8.1 for an analysis of increasing discount rates necessary to value very small businesses.

To restate, as the cash flow goes below $500,000 EBITDA, it becomes very difficult to determine EBITDA, as it is hard to estimate the employment value of an owner-operator of a small enterprise. Yet this can have a very large effect on the value found.

SDE	$100,000	$200,000	$300,000	$400,000	$500,000	$600,000	$700,000	$800,000	$900,000	$1,000,000	$1,100,000
Reasonable Salary	$150,000	$150,000	$150,000	$150,000	$150,000	$150,000	$150,000	$150,000	$150,000	$150,000	$150,000
EBITDA	($50,000)	$50,000	$150,000	$250,000	$350,000	$450,000	$550,000	$650,000	$750,000	$850,000	$950,000
SDE Market Multiplier 2.5											
SDE Value Estimate	$250,000	$500,000	$750,000	$1,000,000	$1,250,000	$1,500,000	$1,750,000	$2,000,000	$2,250,000	$2,500,000	$2,750,000
Implied EBITDA Discount Rate (%)		10.00	20.00	25.00	28.00	30.00	31.43	32.50	33.33	34.00	34.55

Note:
This chart shows the "Implied" Discount rate as businesses get very small. Note how the rate drops precipitously.
While a simplification, this chart clearly shows problems with the model as business value drops below $2,000,000 and even more so under $1,000,000 of value.

FIGURE 8.1 Comparable "Required" Discount Rate After Tax Cash Flow Drops

Unlike large companies, there is limited data on the employment value of a leader of small businesses who works 55 + hours a week, rarely takes vacations, and also often has very high-level technical skills across the many situations that arise in a small business. He or she knows they are making $500,000 a year in total. They choose to grow their business by reinvesting some of this capital and are still well compensated, particularly compared to their other likely choices. But how much of that is for replaceable management and other measurable labor tasks versus how much is really profit for owning a business? How do we even define the job? Further, this theory is at least supported by the anecdotal common belief that, as businesses grow, usually three distinct skill sets and people are hired to replace what the owner has been doing: sales, finance/accounting, and operations.

Example

A company has $400,000 EBITDA before adjusting for the owner's compensation. If the replacement labor value adjustment of the owner is $100,000, that is going to produce a huge swing from finding the replacement value adjustment is $150,000. Valuators certainly can use professional judgment to assess the situation but clear data will never exist because owners pay themselves salary based on many different reasons often relating to tax advice provided. Assuming a 33% capitalization rate, this produces values of $900,000 with a $100,000 compensation figure ($300,000/.33) or $750,000 with a $150,000 compensation figure ($250,000/.33).[4] See Figure 8.2 for this and related calculations.

Clearly as EBITDAs and after-tax cash flows increase the risk of the error in estimating owner's compensation decreases. For one thing, as companies get larger, there may be more accurate data. Additionally, simply because the likely range of owner compensation becomes a smaller part of the overall cash flow, the risk of significant error in this adjustment drops.

Line												
1	SDE	$100,000	$200,000	$300,000	$400,000	$500,000	$600,000	$700,000	$800,000	$900,000	$1,000,000	$1,100,000
2	Reasonable Salary	$100,000	$100,000	$100,000	$100,000	$100,000	$100,000	$100,000	$100,000	$100,000	$100,000	$100,000
3	EBITDA	$0	$100,000	$200,000	$300,000	$400,000	$500,000	$600,000	$700,000	$800,000	$900,000	$1,000,000
4												
5	SDE Market Multiplier 2.5											
6	SDE Value Estimate	$250,000	$500,000	$750,000	$1,000,000	$1,250,000	$1,500,000	$1,750,000	$2,000,000	$2,250,000	$2,500,000	$2,750,000
7												
8	Implied EBITDA											
9	Discount Rate (%)		20.00	26.67	30.00	32.00	33.33	34.29	35.00	35.56	36.00	36.36
10												
11												
12	SDE	$100,000	$200,000	$300,000	$400,000	$500,000	$600,000	$700,000	$800,000	$900,000	$1,000,000	$1,100,000
13	Reasonable Salary	$150,000	$150,000	$150,000	$150,000	$150,000	$150,000	$150,000	$150,000	$150,000	$150,000	$150,000
14	EBITDA	($50,000)	$50,000	$150,000	$250,000	$350,000	$450,000	$550,000	$650,000	$750,000	$850,000	$950,000
15												
16	SDE Market Multiplier 2.5											
17	SDE Value Estimate	$250,000	$500,000	$750,000	$1,000,000	$1,250,000	$1,500,000	$1,750,000	$2,000,000	$2,250,000	$2,500,000	$2,750,000
18												
19	Implied EBITDA											
20	Discount Rate		10.00%	20.00%	25.00%	28.00%	30.00%	31.43%	32.50%	33.33%	34.00%	34.55%
21												
22	Discount Rate Variance		10.00%	6.67%	5.00%	4.00%	3.33%	2.86%	2.50%	2.22%	2.00%	1.82%
23												
24	Percentage Difference 20/22		100.00%	33.33%	20.00%	14.29%	11.11%	9.09%	7.69%	6.67%	5.88%	5.26%

Notes:

This chart shows the relationship between selecting replacement labor value and EBITDA with smaller businesses. Note not only the high implied discount rates (the bottom half of the chart is the same as Figure 8.1) but the large swing in implied discount rates at lower business values.

Replacement Salary is shown at $100,000 on the top chart and $150,000 on the lower chart. Discount Rate Variances are shown at the bottom.

At higher cash flows, SDE multipliers will be higher and become less likely to be the correct valuation multiplier. Yet, the problem illustrated at low values is very real.

FIGURE 8.2 Impact of Reasonable Compensation in Very Small Companies

Figure 8.2 shows the effect of the difference between $100,000 and $150,000 of reasonable compensation on the "required" implied capitalization rates as companies get very small.[5] The variance on the discount rate to find the likely correct value is huge. (I say this as small businesses DO sell on their SDE value. This is a fact.) Note how at higher values, (approximately $1,500,000 of value in this case), the variance created by a $50,000 salary difference becomes manageable.

As EBITDA and after-tax cash flows increase, the income method becomes more reliable. If adequate market data exists for small and very small businesses, the market method generally should be the preferred method. But, certainly, the income method is an important secondary method.

For this reason, once cash flow is over $500,000 SDE, the market method using EBITDA and the income methods should be more closely analyzed. (This is also a requirement of Valuation Standards for opinions of value, all valuation methods should be considered.)[6]

CASH FLOW FOR INCOME APPROACHES

Estimating the future cash flow is the first major component of the income method. The two main income methods are the discounted cash flow and the capitalization of earnings. The major difference in the two methods is how the future cash flows are forecast.

In the discounted cash flow method, a portion of the future, often three to ten years, is forecast. Growth is part of the forecast and can vary in each forecast year. This method is often used when early cash flows are going to vary significantly from future cash flows. A steady growth rate is then estimated to calculate the growth in the remaining cash flows used to perpetuity. Perpetuity is a 'long business period' that contemplates the highs and lows of operations over time. It is likely not to be the year-over-year growth in forecast periods.

The capitalization of earnings method is a shortcut to the discounted cash flow method. Past financial information is used to estimate a cash flow for the next period that is then divided by a capitalization rate. The capitalization rate is a discount rate that is further adjusted to incorporate a growth factor to reflect projected future growth. A calculation of cash flow, a calculation of the capitalization rate, and an estimate of value are shown below. Use Figure 8.3 as a map when reading the portions of the chapter on capitalization of earnings.

CAPITALIZATION OF EARNINGS METHOD

The capitalization of earnings method is a shorthand version of the discounted cash flow method.[7] Growth is calculated as an adjustment to the discount rate. A discount rate with a growth rate adjustment is a capitalization rate. (Said another way, the capitalization rate = discount rate – growth rate.) This capitalization rate is estimated and applied to adjusted past cash flows to calculate the effect of future cash flow growth.

Steady historic and likely steady future cash flow growth is the best situation for this model. That is because the valuator must select one growth rate for the future. Yet most small businesses do not have steady cash flow growth. Many cyclical businesses have more of a roller-coaster cash flow effect than steady long-term growth. Therefore, weighting or averaging a longer time period (perhaps five historical years) to estimate the growth rate is often reviewed. The found average rate is rarely directly used. Instead a rate to perpetuity must be estimated from this data. Growth rate can have a huge impact on the value found.

For instance, the value of a company with $1,000,000 of after-tax cash flow next year with a 20% discount rate and no growth is a 20% capitalization rate. This could well be the case

Line No.	Determination of After-Tax Cash Flow	Historic Year 3	Historic Year 2	Historic Year 1
1	Historic Adjusted Pretax Cash Flow	$609,900	$609,900	$609,900
2	Weighting	1	1	1
3	Weighted Average Cash Flow	$609,900		
4				
5	Deduct Average Depreciation/Amortization	$40,000		
6	Taxable Income	$569,900		
7	State Corporate Tax Rate	8%		
8	Estimated Tax	$45,592		
9	Subtotal	$524,308		
10	Estimated Federal Tax Rate	21%		
11	Estimated Federal Tax	$110,105		
12	Subtotal	$414,203		
13	Plus Depreciation/Amortization	$40,000		
14	Decrease (Increase) Working Capital	$0		
15	Decrease (Increase) Capital Expenditures	$0		
16	Decrease (Increase) Long-Term Debt	$0		
17	Selected After Tax Cash Flow	$454,203	$454,203	
18				
19				
20	**Calculation of the Capitalization Rate**			
21				
22	Cost of Equity			
23				
24	Risk-free Rate of Return	3.0%		
25	Common Stock Equity Risk Premium	6.0%		
26	Small Stock Risk Premium	5.4%		
27	Industry Risk Premium	3.7%		
28	Company Specific Premium	0.0%		
29	Total Cost of Equity	18.1%		
30	Less Sustainable Growth	3.0%		
31	Next Year Capitalization Rate	15.1%		
32	Current Year Capitalization Rate	14.7%		
33				
34	Selected Capitalization Rate	14.7%	14.7%	
35				
36	Estimated Value Capitalization of Earnings		$3,089,818.50	

Notes:

This Chart will be broken down and explained in detail.

Line No.

1 Historic Adjusted Pretax Cash flow is used.

Normalization adjustments will be made similar to those shown for the market method.

Weighting is performed similar to weighting in the market method.

5 Average depreciation/amortization is subtracted from the cash flow before taxes are adjusted.

32 Current Year Capitalization Rate - The analyst can either increase the cash flow to reflect next year's after growth earnings (Current Year earnings times 1 + long-term growth) or adjust the capitalization rate for the same amount. Namely take next year's capitalization rate and divide it by (1 + long-term growth) Per the Gordon Growth model theory the immediate next period's cash flow is applied against the capitalization rate.

36 Line 17/line 34

FIGURE 8.3 Complete Capitalization of Earnings Calculation

for a mature small business where cash flow is not even keeping up with the rate of inflation. If the same company has a 4% growth rate, then the capitalization rate (discount rate - growth rate) is 16%. Perhaps new management has recently demonstrated short-term growth which is believed likely to continue into the foreseeable future.

The difference in value found is $5,000,000 at 20% and $6,250,000 at 16%.[8] This shows the importance of estimating the growth rate correctly.

The underlying theory of the capitalization of earnings method is the Gordon Growth model or dividend discount model (DDM) as further explained in the next section.

The Gordon Growth Model

Variations of the Gordon Growth model are used to estimate a value of the future earnings stream of a company. It is the basis of many calculations in the income methods. It is the direct basis for the capitalization of earnings model and in estimating terminal value under the discounted cash flow model. A brief explanation follows.

The Gordon Growth model, also known as the dividend discount model (DDM), calculates the intrinsic value of a company's stock price. The stock value is calculated as the present value of all of the stocks' future dividends.

Stock value = expected annual dividend (cash flow)/(Investors'
rate of return − expected dividend growth rate)

Generalizing this to fit all business sales, the formula becomes

expected cash flow/asset value
= (required rate of return − expected growth rate)

For small businesses usually (but not always) instead of the dividend or distribution amount being used, the theoretical amount available for distribution (the distributable amount) is used. This figure is usually either EBITDA or EBIT or after-tax cash flow (essentially after-tax earnings plus depreciation and amortization) or somewhat improperly SDE.

This raises the issue of: how is reinvestment reflected in the model? The model assumes all reinvestment is at the perpetuity rate. In reality, as money is distributed, it often is spent or placed in safer investments that do not produce the same rate. This is an issue with the model as all models have problems. Again, professional judgment involves selecting the most useful models for our situation.

The Gordon Growth model accounts for the value of free cash flows that continue growing at an assumed constant rate in perpetuity.

Also, the projected free cash flow in the first year beyond the historic data (N+1) is used. This value is divided by the discount rate minus the assumed perpetuity growth rate:

$$T_0 = D_0/k - g$$

T_0 Value of future cash flows (Price)

D_0 Cash flows estimated for the next period of time

k Discount rate

g Growth rate

See

- The cash flow (CF) for the year after the historic data is adjusted to grow at the estimated growth rate.
- The discount rate for the last year of the discrete cash flows then has the growth rate subtracted from it to estimate the capitalization rate.
- CF is then divided by the capitalization rate to find the value in perpetuity

Using this formula as the basis for estimating a value requires determining a cash flow, a discount rate, and a growth rate. Details on these matters and determining forecast cash flows and related issues under the income method are covered in the rest of this chapter.

MORE CASH FLOW CONSIDERATIONS

As suggested above, the first step is to normalize cash flows usually to either a seller's discretionary earnings (SDE), or earnings before interest and taxes (EBIT), or earnings before interest, taxes, depreciation, and amortization (EBITDA), or the after-tax cash flow standard. Usually EBITDA or the after-tax cash flow is assumed to be distributable cash flow to investors or the equivalent for small business purposes.

Normalization adjustments to the cash flow will be made similar to those covered in Chapter 5, Normalization of the Cash Flows and Chapter 11, Accounting Issues with Small and Very Small Businesses.

Tax Affecting

In theory, buildup methods use after-tax cash flows because they are based on public companies which post after-tax earnings. When valuing a pass-through entity, valuators "tax affect" or make tax rate-based adjustments to maintain an equivalent cash flow basis (taxable to taxable) for the comparison.

Therefore, most valuators tax affect when using the income method to value very small tax pass-through entities.[9] They believe it is the best alignment of the subject company to comparable data. Many small businesses are pass-through entities avoiding the double taxation of C corporations. These pass-through entities historically had a lower total tax to the investor at the investor level than non-pass-through entities. There is some level of debate about the true extent of this pass-through tax advantage, particularly with the passage of the Tax Cuts and Jobs Act (TCJA). Even prior to the TCJA, the tax rate of public entities in different industries was rarely the posted 35% average rate stated for companies with $10 million and above of taxable income.

TCJA may have solved most of the big differences in taxes to the shareholder between C corporations and pass-through entities at the Federal level but in high tax states, there still appears to be advantages for pass-through entities (PTEs) overall. Finally, it is still unclear what Code Section 199A Qualified Business Income Deduction (QBI) really means in the application for taxation of pass-through entity owners.[10] More important, since it can depend on other income streams to the owner, how can we really make valid determinations as to what a buyer's tax benefits will be in our estimates?

There is a great debate on these topics at the time of writing of this book. It is beyond this book to go down every rabbit hole. Instead a reasonable methodology for use with small and very small businesses is going to be provided. Certainly, other methodologies may be used and there will be cases where this methodology is inappropriate but this should serve as a guide to work through these issues.

Factors to consider:

- Is this a valuation for the Internal Revenue Service (IRS)?
- Is the valuation standard fair value, investment value, or fair market value?
- Should state taxes be considered and deducted before the IRS rate?
- Do we have a reasonably reliable disposition date of the interests being valued?

IRS

The Tax Court has consistently found that when using the fair market value standard for PTEs, the cash flows should not be tax affected.[11] However, two recent cases have to give the

IRS pause. These are the *Estate of Aaron Jones*[12] and *Kress vs. United States*.[13] The IRS lost in both of these cases. What we don't know as of the writing of this book is if the IRS will acquiesce (i.e., accept them as law) with them or not. From a practical perspective it is unclear how the IRS will respond.

The historic IRS position has been that the future taxes of a hypothetical buyer are unknown. They cannot be known because different buyers will have different internal tax consequences depending on state taxes, loss carryforwards, whether the entity will remain private or become part of a public entity, etc. While this fails to deal with the issue of using two different income streams on different sides of the valuation equation, when valuing PTEs, it has been the IRS and Tax Court position at least until the *Estate of Aaron Jones*[14] case. For this reason, many advisors take heed to this and use non-tax-adjusted cash flows for estate or gift tax type purposes.[15]

Issues with Tax Affecting

Similar to past IRS arguments, under fair market value, it is hard to know exactly what a buyer's tax status will be and if tax benefits of the seller will accrue to a buyer.[16] This is made even more complex under the TCJA where a 20% qualified business income (QBI) deduction may be applied to a pass-through taxed business in certain industries that meet other income/wage limitations of the company and shareholders.

Qualification for these tax benefits are so complex as to almost be beyond many small and very small business tax advisors' ability to estimate future taxes, much less our ability as valuators to fully comprehend or adjust.

Below are some problems, not with the concept of tax adjusting, which conceptually is an easy "yes" we should, but by how much to adjust.

- When might the tax rates be changed again?
- The normalization process for calculating EBIT, EBITDA, and after-tax cash flows changes the tax status of many

owner benefits. Namely, they were expenses by the company and in some cases not recognized by the beneficiary, i.e., some auto expenses. After being recast, they are now taxed. This can be a substantial portion of small business cash flows in some situations.

- The interaction of 199A of the tax code with pass-through entities is still being digested by the tax community, making it difficult to compare. With this provision it may always be difficult to create cross-industry models. In fact, some buyers may lose QBI deductions for buying certain types of businesses. (For instance, investment banking and valuation have often been performed by the same companies. Investment banking qualifies for QBI but business valuation does not and could theoretically cause a disqualification for the overall entity.)
- The 199A provisions sunset end of 2025 meaning the value of the tax benefit drops every year.
- These results under TCJA may also vary with the income of the owner and possibly the spouse, if married and filing joint taxes. This is a much more pertinent issue with very small businesses. How do we know or account for that?
- Strictly for very small businesses: The inability to amortize the purchase price of C corporations that tend to be stock sales raises the cash flow necessary to successfully buy a business. This is a barrier to sale. Most very small business sales are leveraged buy-outs using SBA loans. If the purchase price cannot be amortized, all of the principal payments have to be "after-tax" dollars. While a 10-year loan does not line up perfectly with 15-year amortization, it does make a big difference. (Plot the cash flows yourself.) This can be a 15% +/- "penalty" or gross up in terms of earnings required to really make the payments.
- In some cases, this is offset by personal goodwill. But there is still likely to be a large portion of un-amortizable corporate purchase price. Fortunately with small and very small businesses, personal goodwill does tend to exist.
- Most industries do not pay the "stated" tax rate. How do we really know (or how can we calculate) the tax rate

being paid in the underlying public company data? Industry adjustment in the buildup methods is related to beta. Does that really mean we now have an implied industry tax rate in the buildup data?

- High state taxes vs. low state taxes can swing the analysis. Does the fact that the cash flow in Idaho with a 7.4% C corporation tax or Wyoming,[17] the state next door with no corporate income tax, mean pretax earnings are really worth 6–8% more than the adjacent state? How is that passed through in value? How would we prove it even if it is true?

- According to Nancy Fannon,[18] an expert on business valuation and taxation, research indicates that because a portion of the public company investor earnings stream is long-term capital gains and because much of the dividend-issuing stock is owned by investment companies that have different tax rates than individuals, the estimated implied tax rate on stock appreciation is 9% not the 20% capital gains rate. (I assume plus state taxes for high income earners.) Yet another big swing that an analyst may or may not agree with but could be difficult to explain.

- Daniel R. Van Fleet, ASA, another noted expert on taxation and business valuation, concludes because of TCJA, "that there are now three distinct types of business entities from a tax perspective: (1) C corps, (2) PTE service businesses, and (3) PTE nonservice businesses." He further concludes that C corps experienced the greatest increase in value, non-service PTEs continue to have benefits above C corps, but service PTEs' benefits have largely disappeared[19] as compared to C corporations.

- Using a tax effect calculator, the results vary dramatically with many plausible situations. How do we account for that? See Figure 8.5 on p. 174.

Something that is clear compared to larger companies:

- One thing that does simplify the analysis is that most small and very small companies are either purchased by pass-through entities or the buyer forms a new pass-through entity. It is very rare for a small or very small business to be purchased by a C corp. Therefore, the cash flows and perhaps tax benefits of buyers are likely to be similar to sellers. (Again, beware of service vs. non-service PTEs if that can be determined.)

- Prior to the TCJA, a study of data from Pratt's Stats (at the time, only small private company data was represented) found evidence of a PTE premium WHEN the buyer can take advantage of the pass-through benefits. This premium was estimated to be in the 15–24% range using varying methodologies.[20]

Some analysts may have clear answers to many of the above questions. Much of it does not appear to be knowable. Therefore, apply reason. Another situation for asking yourself: "Does this make sense?"

Suggested Tax Affecting Method for Small and Very Small Businesses

Based on the situation today, below may be one methodology to use. It is logical and supportable assuming a typical fact pattern. This area is in flux and lacks agreement. Use tax affecting or not according to your best judgment.

The first step is to tax affect the cash flows to the estimated corporate rate:

- Tax affect the found normalized cash flows.
- For guidance to the tax affect amount, assuming you are using an industry adjustment, look at the IRS statistics on corporate taxes by sector.
- Tax affect for the state tax rate. Again, most small businesses' income stream is often derived from one state. If it is derived from multiple states, a composite rate may be used. The first step is to tax affect the cash flows to the estimated corporate rate:[21]

Weighted Average Cash Flow	$500,000
Deduct Average Depreciation/Amortization	$40,000
Taxable Income	$460,000
State Corporate Tax Rate	8%
Estimated Tax	$36,800
Subtotal	$423,200
Estimated Federal Tax Rate	21%
Estimated Federal Tax	$88,872
Subtotal	$334,328
Plus Depreciation/Amortization	$40,000
After Tax Cash Flow	$374,328

Note: This estimate is before adjusting for working capital, long-term loans and capital investment

FIGURE 8.4 Tax Affecting for Capitalization of Earnings

An example of tax affecting to the corporate rate is shown in Figure 8.4.

- More details to think about when applying the above suggested adjustment are shown in https://www.treasury .gov/resource-center/tax-policy/tax-analysis/Documents/ Average-Effective-Tax-Rates-2016.pdf
- Here is average tax rates for individuals prior to TCJA: https://www.irs.gov/pub/irs-soi/14insprbultaxrateshares .pdf
- If they are not available or do not appear reasonable for your industry, use 21% for the corporate rate.[22]
- State taxes can be difficult, as they vary. (Forty-four states levy a corporate income tax from 2.5% in North Carolina to 12% in Iowa. Four states have a gross receipts tax instead of an income tax. Two states have no corporate income tax or gross receipts tax.)[23] Small and very small businesses tend to be in one state and pay that state's tax. In addition, some larger cities have their own taxes so if that is material, they should be added. If multiple state taxes are paid, use a figure based on a reasonable weighting as most taxes are based on profits derived from earnings in the state.[24]

- This should provide a reasonable adjustment to account for the corporate tax rate used in the buildup methods. Now the valuator must still adjust for differences between the buildup tax level and the pass-through entity tax level.

Adjust the discount rate or capitalization rate for the pass-through tax benefit (if any)

- Use the tax affect calculator below to develop a sense or range of options.
- Understand if the PTE is a service or non-service entity. This may require a detailed look-up. Many of the broad titles are misleading. For instance, it is widely stated that brokerage is under the service category. But real estate brokerage and business brokerage count as non-service. Architecture and engineering are in non-service but accounting is service.
- Non-service entities are likely to justify a reduction in discount or capitalization rate by 2% or 3% (example: 16% – 2% tax benefit = 14% cost of capital), a range based on Van Fleet's and Eric Barr and Peter L. Lohrey's findings.
- Use common sense and judgment.
- For small and very small businesses this may be like trying to perform surgery with a hatchet.

I find this simpler than trying to create a comprehensive formula. We are simply creating apples to apples with the cash flows, then adjusting for assumed advantages due to tax treatments where it appears they exist. This should also be much easier to explain to less sophisticated users and produce a reasonable result.

Use a tax affect calculator, such as the one in Figure 8.5, to approximately estimate the difference in after-tax cash flows between public C corporations and pass-through entities. Be sure to factor in both state and Federal taxes. In addition, remember the research that indicates a 9% paid tax rate on distributed cash flows from the public company earnings.[25]

	C Corp	S Corp
Income Before Corporate Tax	$100	$100
Corporate Tax Rate (State and Federal)	29.00%	0.00%
Available Earnings	$71	$100
Taxes At Personal Level	28.00%	43.00%
After Personal Level Tax Earnings	$51	$57
Premium per S Corp Model		11.50%

Assumed 21 % Federal Corporate Tax Rate plus 8% State
Assumed 20% Capital Gains plus 8% State
Assumed 35% individual plus 8% State

Notes:
*If research cited by Nancy Fannon is believed and the 28% C Corp personal tax is replaced with 9%,
  then there would be a -12% rounded premium.
*If the 9% is then plus the 8% State Tax, the premium is - 3%.

FIGURE 8.5   Tax Affect Converter Table

Use this with various scenarios to develop a sense of how your situation may play out. (A functional Excel file is on the related website.) Two scenarios are shown using a very simple tax affect converter table in Figure 8.5. Then use your best judgment.

This analysis may change as the current law is better understood, technology allows better tax estimates, and the tax law changes.

Adjusting Cash Flows for Working Capital, Capital Expenditures, and Debt under Capitalization of Earnings

The theory behind the income methods is that we are calculating the distributed cash flow to owners adjusted to compare to a public company and therefore after-tax data. In practice, particularly with the capitalization of earnings method for small businesses, distributable after-tax cash flow is often used. This can be justified because the undistributed cash flow is usually used in the business for expansion. This expansion, assuming it is profitable, increases future earnings power and often produces a higher growth rate than when the company distributes frequently. Remember, small and very small businesses have much less access to affordable capital. Because of their volatility, debt is often much more risky for them. So, retaining a portion of the distributable capital is usually neutral to a positive.

In some cases, if the cash needs during growth are high for two or three years, then phase out, it may be worth preparing a rough forecast as opposed to "jamming" that situation into the capitalization of earnings model. Again, this model works best with fairly consistent cash flows into the future.

Yet, in some circumstances, the best application of the model does include further adjustments to the distributable cash flow. These adjustments fall under the categories: increase or decrease in working capital, capital investment, and debt.

Because the method can only adjust all future cash flows (there is not a mechanism to change the cash flow year by year), the best that can be done when these factors are present is to estimate the current amount and then reasonably adjust the amount to a figure reasonable for use in perpetuity. This requires recognizing that early money and cash flow are much more valuable than later money. Because of the time value of money and the assumption of declining growth rates over time at typical capitalization rates for small and very small businesses, after about 40 years the present value contribution of earnings is near 0. See Figure 8.6.

Therefore, one factor in determining these adjustments for cash flow is how long the use of cash is likely to continue. Principal to pay off a new 10-year note might be shown at 50%, as it is to be allocated out over a reasonably long time early in the life of the projection. Perhaps a few larger mid-term equipment purchases would be allocated at 10% of the payment figure, if they are going to be reduced significantly after two or three years. Of course, if reinvestment is continuous, then the whole amount might be deducted from the cash flow. Again, this is an area for judgment and the capitalization of earnings model is used in these situations on a "best we can do" basis (Figure 8.7).

| Annual Cash Flow Amount | | | | | | $100,000 | | | |
| | | | | Capitalization Rate | | | | | |
Period	10.00%	15.00%	20.00%	25.00%	30.00%	35.00%	40.00%	45.00%	50.00%
1	$90,909	$86,957	$83,333	$80,000	$76,923	$74,074	$71,429	$68,966	$66,667
2	$82,645	$75,614	$69,444	$64,000	$59,172	$54,870	$51,020	$47,562	$44,444
3	$75,131	$65,752	$57,870	$51,200	$45,517	$40,644	$36,443	$32,802	$29,630
4	$68,301	$57,175	$48,225	$40,960	$35,013	$30,107	$26,031	$22,622	$19,753
5	$62,092	$49,718	$40,188	$32,768	$26,933	$22,301	$18,593	$15,601	$13,169
6	$56,447	$43,233	$33,490	$26,214	$20,718	$16,520	$13,281	$10,759	$8,779
7	$51,316	$37,594	$27,908	$20,972	$15,937	$12,237	$9,486	$7,420	$5,853
8	$46,651	$32,690	$23,257	$16,777	$12,259	$9,064	$6,776	$5,117	$3,902
9	$42,410	$28,426	$19,381	$13,422	$9,430	$6,714	$4,840	$3,529	$2,601
10	$38,554	$24,718	$16,151	$10,737	$7,254	$4,974	$3,457	$2,434	$1,734
11	$35,049	$21,494	$13,459	$8,590	$5,580	$3,684	$2,469	$1,679	$1,156
12	$31,863	$18,691	$11,216	$6,872	$4,292	$2,729	$1,764	$1,158	$771
13	$28,966	$16,253	$9,346	$5,498	$3,302	$2,021	$1,260	$798	$514
14	$26,333	$14,133	$7,789	$4,398	$2,540	$1,497	$900	$551	$343
15	$23,939	$12,289	$6,491	$3,518	$1,954	$1,109	$643	$380	$228
16	$21,763	$10,686	$5,409	$2,815	$1,503	$822	$459	$262	$152
17	$19,784	$9,293	$4,507	$2,252	$1,156	$609	$328	$181	$101
18	$17,986	$8,081	$3,756	$1,801	$889	$451	$234	$125	$68
19	$16,351	$7,027	$3,130	$1,441	$684	$334	$167	$86	$45
20	$14,864	$6,110	$2,608	$1,153	$526	$247	$120	$59	$30
21	$13,513	$5,313	$2,174	$922	$405	$183	$85	$41	$20
22	$12,285	$4,620	$1,811	$738	$311	$136	$61	$28	$13
23	$11,168	$4,017	$1,509	$590	$239	$101	$44	$19	$9
24	$10,153	$3,493	$1,258	$472	$184	$74	$31	$13	$6
25	$9,230	$3,038	$1,048	$378	$142	$55	$22	$9	$4
26	$8,391	$2,642	$874	$302	$109	$41	$16	$6	$3
27	$7,628	$2,297	$728	$242	$84	$30	$11	$4	$2
28	$6,934	$1,997	$607	$193	$65	$22	$8	$3	$1
29	$6,304	$1,737	$506	$155	$50	$17	$6	$2	$1
30	$5,731	$1,510	$421	$124	$38	$12	$4	$1	$1
31	$5,210	$1,313	$351	$99	$29	$9	$3	$1	$0
32	$4,736	$1,142	$293	$79	$23	$7	$2	$1	$0
33	$4,306	$993	$244	$63	$17	$5	$2	$0	$0
34	$3,914	$864	$203	$51	$13	$4	$1	$0	$0
35	$3,558	$751	$169	$41	$10	$3	$1	$0	$0
36	$3,235	$653	$141	$32	$8	$2	$1	$0	$0
37	$2,941	$568	$118	$26	$6	$2	$0	$0	$0
38	$2,673	$494	$98	$21	$5	$1	$0	$0	$0
39	$2,430	$429	$82	$17	$4	$1	$0	$0	$0
40	$2,209	$373	$68	$13	$3	$1	$0	$0	$0

FIGURE 8.6 Present Value Contribution over 40 Years

Increase or Decrease in Working Capital

A simple and usually sufficient formula for estimating working capital is provided in the balance sheet adjustments section in Chapter 11, Accounting Issues with Small and Very Small

Line No.	Determination of After-Tax Cash Flow	Historic Year 3	Historic Year 2	Historic Year 1
1	Historic Adjusted Pretax Cash Flow	$609,900	$609,900	$609,900
2	Weighting	1	1	1
3	Weighted Average Cash Flow	$609,900		
4				
5	Deduct Average Depreciation/Amortization	$40,000		
6	Taxable Income	$569,900		
7	State Corporate Tax Rate	8%		
8	Estimated Tax	$45,592		
9	Subtotal	$524,308		
10	Estimated Federal Taxe Rate	21%		
11	Estimated Federal Tax	$110,105		
12	Subtotal	$414,203		
13	Plus Depreciation/Amortization	$40,000		
14	Decrease (Increase) Working Capital	($30,000)		
15	Decrease (Increase) Capital Expenditures	$10,000		
16	Decrease (Increase) Long Term Debt	$0		
17	Selected After Tax Cash Flow	$434,203		
18				

Notes:
This Chart will be broken down and explained in detail.

Line No.
1. Historic Adjusted Pretax Cash Flow is adjusted pretax profits plus depreciation and amortization.
5. Average depreciaion/amortization is subtracted from hte cash flow before taxes are adjusted.
7. Estimated State Corporate Taxes.
10. Estimated Federal Corporate Taxes.
13. Depreciation and amortization is added back to cash flow.
14. Adjustment to Working Capital. Remember this is for each year to perpetuity, not next year.
15. Adjustment to Capital Expenditures each year to perpetuity.
16. Long-Term Debt adjustment each year to perpetuity.

FIGURE 8.7 Estimating the Cash Flows for Capitalization of Earnings

Businesses. If additional (or less) working capital is going to be required in the future, the question becomes how much working capital change is really required to tie into the assumption of perpetual growth at a fairly low but persistent rate. That figure can be tied to a rate of revenue growth and adjusted for perpetuity.

Finally, if the balance sheet shows excess assets on the valuation date, including excess working capital, this should be added to the final value found.

Capital Investment or Cap X

Some industries require constant capital investment in order to grow or even maintain operations. Trucking, excavation, some manufacturing lines that wear out equipment, and the like. Most small and very small businesses are using computer-based technology to enhance productivity and certainly many industrial machines have computer enhancements. But the cost and complexity of large-scale automated equipment have prevented large-scale implementation in small and very small businesses. Therefore, generally, most small and very small businesses, even in manufacturing, tend to do repairs, refurbishing, or assembly as opposed to heavy manufacturing. These businesses, similar to service providers, tend to have lesser capital investment compared to revenues and other cash flows.

If capital investment is a material factor and a requirement for the company's cash flow to continue, then it should be estimated and put into the cash flow calculation. Note that depreciation, whether accelerated or not, is often not a reasonable assumption for long-term capital investment in most cases. Some businesses have major investments from time to time. These are not always predictable. Estimating the timing of these investments may be difficult.

Example

When valuing a medical practice, large sums are spent on expensive diagnostic equipment along with the computers to operate them. The practice may not expend additional Cap X for many years until the equipment is either paid off or the equipment has become obsolete.

In all cases with similar fact patterns and material capital investments, an estimate of likely or reasonable future investment needs to be made.

Increases and Decreases of Debt

Debt can be used for growth capital or to get "cash out" of an investment. If the debt is undertaken with the intent to get cash out of an investment, the discounted cash flow method will be superior, as this is almost always a one-time event, at least in the foreseeable future.

When a company carries material amounts of debt, it is important to align the cash flows with the discount/capitalization rate. Cash flow to equity (after the payment of all debt in the capital structure) can vary dramatically from cash flow to total invested capital. This is magnified by the fact that these are cash flows to perpetuity.

Most small businesses do not carry significant debt indefinitely into the future. When they do, it is often in the form of lines of credit against invoices or inventory, or equipment debt where the equipment is regularly replaced. Some small and very small companies do carry receivables lines and while they are short-term debt in name, the small companies often treat the line as long-term debt. These callable lines are not reduced but a long-term feature of the capital structure and should be treated as long-term debt.

Long-term debt may also be handled by not adjusting the cash flow (assuming EBITDA cash flow is being used) and reducing the value found by the debt similar to the treatment under the market method. This is often a reasonable treatment if the purpose is to determine equity value in a sale. In instances where the standard is more a value to the holder and the debt is continuing, a cash flow adjustment for principal payments may be the best solution to address the debt. Note these variations in treatment can result in large fluctuations in value if not performed thoughtfully.

Next we will review estimating cash flows under the discounted cash flow method. If you wish to continue reviewing the capitalization of earnings method, skip down to "Calculating a Discount or Cap. Rate".

CASH FLOW FORECASTS UNDER THE DISCOUNTED CASH FLOW METHOD

Forecasts are used to estimate the cash flows in the discounted cash flow method. Therefore, we will start by reviewing forecasts, then estimating the present value discount, and finally showing how to estimate the terminal year calculations.

The first step, review and analysis of the forecast itself, is often skipped by valuators. And no wonder, this is where the most common sense and professional judgment are required. With smaller businesses, often the forecasts do not make sense. With larger businesses, the forecasts can become so complex that even when the analyst has a strong opinion as to the reliability or likelihood of reaching the projected result, the issue becomes (due to complexity) how can an analyst make the changes?[26]

Fortunately with smaller companies, if there are forecasts, it is easier to apply some common sense to check reasonableness. Remember, the forecast is unlikely to be correct with the addition of hindsight. Valuators can only work with the information in hand as of the valuation date, if it is reasonable, to ensure accuracy and supportability based on assumptions and data.

In most cases, do not build the forecast yourself. That can be criticized as valuing your own work. Have management prepare the forecast. Yet there are circumstances where a simplified and clearly explained forecast generated by the valuator may be the best that can be provided.

Review of Forecasts

Below is a checklist that should be used to review projections and forecasts. Clearly the more complex the company and the forecast, the more time and attention that will need to be applied.

- Look at historic data: three to five years.
  - Understand revenue, expense, and profit trends.
  - Understand management structure and product or services.
  - Look for bottlenecks and weaknesses in the soft side of business that could improve or worsen financial results.
  - Has something changed significantly with management, products, production, etc. (for instance, a transportation company went from using their own trucks to subcontracted trucks) during the historic period or going into the projection period?
- If the business is a start-up or if major changes are projected from the past, review all assumptions and the facts or basis for those assumptions.
  - What is the support for the changes?
- Carefully review the future forecasts.
  - Who prepared the forecast?
  - Why was the forecast created?
  - What date was it created?
  - Where did the key facts and assumptions come from?
  - If based on contracts or other existing back-up, can you review the back-up?
  - Is there a history of forecasts?
  - If so, compare forecasts vs. results. Are they reasonably consistent or is the variance consistent?
- Overall forecast review
  - Does it reasonably transition from historic data to forecast?
  - If there is a "hockey stick" effect, do the assumptions and facts and other support make sense? Unfortunately there often is an unsupportable jump or a jump that happens far faster than is likely to do so in real implementation. (Due to the time value of money moving up cash flows a year in the early years can *greatly* swing value.)

- Harder to evaluate is a growth rate which is reasonable in one year but not over many years.
  - High growth over five or ten years is difficult for most companies even if the rate is reasonable for one or two years.
- Detailed forecast review. Look at cost of goods sold (COGS) and gross margins, expenses, and profits.
  - If gross margins and profits are increasing, is the increase supportable?
  - If gross margins and profits are falling, where does growth become unprofitable or unsupportable by cash flow or borrowing ability?
  - Where are breakpoints for the fixed costs, such as rent?
  - Are there other major capital investments required?
  - If so, what are the volume or dollar break points?
  - Are those being adequately addressed?
- Again, with long-term growth, can the soft side expenses such as the management team appropriately expand?
  - A $10 million revenue company may get by with a controller-level person but a $20 million revenue company might need both a controller and a true CFO. Is this addressed?
- Many small businesses are primarily labor or skilled labor providers (including many "service" businesses) or perform light assembly with similar types of people. Management is critical particularly if work is performed in multiple, possibly changing, locations.
  - What is the timing of and what is a realistic rate for adding quality managers and skilled employees?
    - This is often the true limiting factor and too often overlooked.
  - What systems, training, and checks are in place to manage the managers as necessary?
    - Many fast-growing service companies in cyclical businesses lose control of work quality and profitability in spurts of growth. Often this shows up in lower margins

and warranty costs a year or two later. An example, a demolition contractor tore out two office bathrooms in an office building so they could be remodeled. Only they were on the wrong floor. A very expensive mistake due to quick recent growth and inexperienced middle management. This is not as unusual as you may think.

- While a generality, for smaller companies, less professional-looking forecasts prepared by the owner or key manager often are more likely to be supportable than fancy forecasts prepared by financial consultants who better understand how to "make the numbers look right" and sometimes use industry standard numbers that poorly tie into past financials.
  - Often valuation-adjusting entries will need to be made to the forecast. Document your work.
- Write down all questions and concerns.
  - If possible, have a conversation with the person who produced the forecast to make sure you fully understand assumptions, calculations, and the like.
  - Review with the owner or appropriate manager (or both) all your questions.
  - "Why" is a powerful question. Ask "why" and "how" often. Ask "why" three times in a row. You will be amazed at what you learn.
  - If you cannot have a direct conversation, get questions answered via email.
- Take notes and think about what was said. Write down key thoughts on why it works and/or why it does not work. Review Chapter 13, Assisting the Small Business Buyer or Seller, the section on How to Ask Questions Effectively.
- If the forecast is simple and needs adjustment in some circumstances, the analyst might make the adjustments. Be sure to document the assumptions and adjustments. You likely will want to show the original and the adjusted version in the report.

- If the forecast is complex, adjust either the discount rate (if using very long holding periods) or a likelihood adjustment prior to calculating a discount.
- At some point, the forecast may not be meaningful enough to use at all. This is quite common with small and very small businesses.

Once the forecast is understood, then adjustments need to be made to develop the cash flow that is going to be used in the discounted cash flow calculation.

Often EBITDA or after-tax cash flow is used to show cash flow for small businesses. Because, in theory, this is return to investors (in practice with small businesses, it tends to be potential return to investors), some decisions need to be made to determine what investors could receive. These areas include necessary increases or decreases in working capital, necessary capital investments, and obtaining additional credit and/or paying credit.

If the forecast is well built, it will include these factors. Yet, with small businesses, balance sheets are usually not provided (maybe never provided) and matters related to balance sheets are not considered. Therefore, the valuator may need to add them or, at a minimum, check if it is reasonable that the business could expand at the projected rate with the internal cash flow for working capital and capital investment.

Forecasts and Balance Sheet Accounts

Because balance sheets and other financial checks are often missing, important limitations on growth, or restrictions on distributions while growth is occurring, may be missed.

If possible, a balance sheet should be prepared each year as part of the annual forecasts. Since that possibility is unlikely with small and very small companies, the analyst should perform some level of analysis and, if necessary, make adjustments to the forecast or the discount or cap. rate when necessary. These should be factored into the forecasts each year in the discounted cash flow method.

Working Capital

In many industries where the small company is providing materials or labor to large companies, the subject company will be expected to extend short-term credit in the form of accounts receivable to their client base. The credit collection time term is often 45–60 days with some extending to 90 days. Many engineering firms, industrial manufacturers, construction subcontractors and the like can fall into this category.

Therefore, the first concern is, can the company generate enough cash to support growth? If not, what is a realistic growth rate or can the company borrow the cash, perhaps on a line secured by receivables? Just remember, receivables financing at reasonable rates tends to vanish in many industries during recessions.

A fairly detailed analysis on estimating working capital is shown in the "Working Capital" section of Chapter 11, Accounting Issues with Small and Very Small Businesses. If possible, adjust the forecast (even if a simplified model for your work papers) to understand the growth limits based on working capital needs.

Do finally note, excess assets, including excess working capital, on the balance sheet as of the valuation date should be added to the value found under this method.

Capital Expenditures

Certain industries require heavy capital equipment spending, e.g., excavation and some other construction trades, equipment rental companies, certain manufacturers, even distributors or retailers experiencing rapid growth. Rapid or high investment reduces otherwise distributable cash. With high levels of accelerated depreciation for small companies, a review of tax implications should also be performed if using an after-tax cash flow.

So carefully review the necessary level of capital investment to grow at the rates projected in the forecast. Is a proper cash flow set aside for these purposes? If not, adjust.

Increase or Decrease in Debt

Increasing debt provides cash to use for investment in working capital and capital goods. While somewhat rare with small and very small businesses, increasing debt can also provide cash for distributions.

Small company debt is likely to include personal guarantees, so the credit worthiness of the owner and potential collateral outside the business also may be factors that need to be reviewed, if valuing a high growth company. But, if increasing debt is a viable solution, make sure interest and, where applicable, principal payments are factored into the ongoing cash flows.

One issue with discounted cash flow models that is more pronounced with very short forecasting periods is the effect of working capital, capital investment, and debt that may not have properly stabilized when the forecast ends and the terminal value is calculated.

Example

A five-year debt was taken out for major capital investments that will last twenty years. Shortly after, the company management provides a three-year forecast. This requires a fourth year terminal value. If unadjusted, that terminal value would still include the full leverage. Depending on the situation, it may make sense to make the adjustment and it may just provide more complexity with little improvement in the estimate.

Generally, debt is not subtracted from the value found when using the discounted cash flow. With small businesses where debt tends to be called and required to be paid at conveyance (again, what is the purpose of the valuation?), there may be times when subtracting the debt from the value found is appropriate.

All valuators can do is use or adjust to reasonable forecasts. It will be very rare when they actually look like the future. But, they can be a reasonable model of a likely outcome.

CALCULATING A DISCOUNT RATE OR CAP. RATE

A discount rate will be estimated first. Additional steps necessary to estimate the capitalization rate will then be shown. All the steps and factors discussed when estimating a discount rate apply to the capitalization rate. In most cases the capitalization rate formula and the terminal value rate formula (before discounting to present value step) used in the discounted cash flow are similar.

The discount rate is the pricing method to determine how much an investor will pay for the cash flow of a business (or anything else such as a public share of stock, investment real estate, a debt, or perhaps a government bond) with the same level of risk as the subject company. Therefore, the valuation analyst must keep the following in mind:

- Investors are looking across all investment classes and types. It is the risk of this investment as compared to all other investment alternatives to as viewed by the market of investors. This is driven by the investment market. This is what creates value for investors, not the value to the current owners. (Most businesses do not sell or are not on the market because the value to the current owners is significantly higher than the value to investors or other potential owner-operators.)
- Risk of not making the projected cash flows is a primary determinant of the discount rate. As risk goes up, it drives down the value. Investment risk as defined for investors is the degree of uncertainty that future payments or earnings will be obtained.[27] Note that this risk is the *apparent* risk, hence the need for judgment as there is no certainty.

Once the history, forecast, and subject company's strengths and weaknesses are understood, then a discount rate needs to be calculated. As in many other areas of business valuation, there used to be one, then two methods to calculate a discount rate, but now there are many.

Sources of Data for Discount and Capitalization Rates

The income method appears simple and when there only was the Ibbotson data available, it was. One needed to simply pull data from one page in a book and maybe look up the industry adjustment in another table that was maybe six pages long. It was simple to apply. Of course, very few people ever read the thick book where the one page was located.

The income method is often used by valuation professionals in litigation because of this apparent simplicity. This simplifies the understanding by a judge and jury and reduces the risk of cross-examination. In addition, since it is the most commonly used method, it clearly meets the judicial test of being a proven method.

The income method was never simple. Read the *Valuation Handbook: Guide to Cost of Capital* book by Duff & Phelps to begin to understand the complexities and assumptions made in the method. (This book can be downloaded, by chapter, from the Cost of Capital Navigator website at www.dpcostofcapital .com.) Another really curious issue that is rarely raised is the lack of clarity or connection between the history back to 1926 for the Center for Research in Security Prices (CRSP) data used in the Ibbotson calculations by Duff & Phelps and what that really tells us about tomorrow. Duff & Phelps' own methodology is calculated from 1963 onwards.

That being said, commonly used or referenced sources at the time of publication include:

- Duff & Phelps/Ibbotson (Duff & Phelps continue to publish the Ibbotson methodology)
- Duff & Phelps

- BV Data
- Aswath Damodaran
- Pepperdine Cost of Capital

Sources appear to be multiplying, so more likely do exist.

Duff & Phelps Products. Under Duff & Phelps model, a calculated risk-free rate is used to smooth out fluctuations that are thought to come from quantitative easing and other sources. Yet as time passes, low risk-free rates are looking more and more the norm.[28] How does this really affect small and very small businesses? Certainly small and very small business interest rates have not dropped commensurate with large company rates. (The typical SBA rate at the date of writing in August, 2019 is prime at 5.25% plus 2.5% or 7.75% while Grade A Corporate bonds are at 3.21%.)[29]

Duff & Phelps calculate both the forward-looking and the backward-looking cost of capital figures. Again, valuation theory is forward-looking. Historic data is backward-looking, supply side is forward-looking. Forward looking requires more assumptions. Assumptions about the future vs. using the past (which is not the future, yet we rely on the past for trend analysis). We are looking to predict the near-term future. This is a constant tension in business valuation.

Duff & Phelps also calculate the buildup data using the same formulas as the Ibbotson data. This may be the most commonly used set of indicators as it has the advantage of long-term use and familiarity. This data includes the breakdown of Decile 10 which is very important for valuing small and very small businesses.

The Cost of Capital Navigator is a complex product. There are complaints of it being a "black box"; however, Duff & Phelps have now included supplementary data that clarifies how the results are estimated. Yet the buildup method was always this complex. At least now we can look at different components individually and intelligently select the components that most affect the subject company, and, using professional judgment, select the correct discount rate. This judgment will improve as valuators work with the product.

Duff & Phelps products (https://www.duffandphelps.com/learn/cost-of-capital) are still the most widely accepted and used for most cost of capital purposes.

Aswath Damodaran. He calculates forward-looking cost of capital data that is based on current financial market results.[30] Dr. Damodaran tends to work with very large capitalization companies and therefore the data may not be as useful for small and very small companies. He also calculates and publishes industry beta information and debt to equity relationships. Very useful for the Cap-M buildup method and the weighted average cost of capital iteration. Every business valuator should visit his website, which has a humble appearance, but is filled with information (http://pages.stern.nyu.edu/~adamodar/).

BV Resources. BV Resources' product, "Cost of Capital Pro" (https://www.bvresources.com/products/cost-of-capital-professional) allows valuators to select the start year for data instead of assuming 1926. It uses the CRSP data just as Duff & Phelps does. It does not break down Decile 10. This is unfortunate when valuing small and very small businesses as Decile 10 businesses (even the small end of them) are still huge compared to small and very small businesses. The product is claimed to be simpler and transparent but it is based on the CRSP data, which is quite complex when fully researched.

Different start dates produce radically different results. This leads to a host of questions that did not exist when valuators presumed one start date for all data. At this point there does not appear to be an answer to the questions of which year do we choose as a start date and why?

The BV data originally referred the valuator to the Damodaran Beta charts. They now have the charts as part of their tool. Again, these products are changing rapidly as adaptation from books to databases is opening up more options and ways to compare data. Overall, this is a very good product and has gained market share quite rapidly since its release.

Pepperdine Private Capital Markets Report. This is an unscientific survey of what investors and banks are requesting, which can be quite different from what they receive. (As many investors told me when I was raising capital, "We want 25–35% internal rate of return (IRR)[31] on the forecast but if you really get us 12–15% over three to five years, we will invest again." I will also note that statement was given at a time (1995) when there were much higher treasury bill rates.) The study is based on asking participants, such as owners, private equity groups, bankers, business brokers, investment bankers, and other groups questions about the cost of capital and the state of the sales and finance market.

The 2018 Pepperdine Survey also revealed that 48% of small and very small business owners think that their cost of equity is less than 10%. That is a very questionable assumption to assert, at least for third party money. For years, these reports were free, but now are available for purchase on Amazon. The Pepperdine Survey is a wonderful reasonableness/sanity test but use with caution.[32]

Partnership Profiles. Partnership Profiles' model[33] is used to calculate a cost of capital for holding companies and family limited partnerships, particularly non-marketable minority interests. With the higher estate tax limits, valuations of these interests (particularly small and very small holdings) have become less common and will not be discussed in this book.[34]

There are other sources of discount rates for various valuations in specialized circumstances. These will rarely be encountered or necessary when valuing small and very small businesses.

COST OF CAPITAL BUILDUP METHOD (BUM): CALCULATING A DISCOUNT RATE

The basic premise is that *data primarily from the public markets* will be taken and used to estimate required investment returns at various levels of risk.

It has become common for valuators to take multiple sources of cost of capital data and compare the results from multiple data sources. Yet, most of the data is coming from the same underlying financial data. Therefore, it seems (but I certainly do not have proof) that using more than one source of discount rate data for a buildup just muddies the water. (We all know there are going to be variances but we have no knowledgeable basis for making a selection beyond "the best available data.") Select the best data source and use it. Particularly with small and very small businesses, the cash flow issues and business risk far outweigh the improvement (if there is one) to weighting multiple sources in the selection of a rate.

Part of Duff & Phelps' Cost of Capital Navigator is the off-shoot of the Ibbotson Cost of Capital series of books, *Stocks, Bonds, Bills, and Inflation*, used for years for cost of capital calculations. Duff & Phelps published the data for approximately five years. No other source breaks down Decile 10 data which comes closest to representing small and very small companies. For these reasons, examples in this book will work with data from Duff & Phelps.

One of the aims of this book is to simplify business valuation by focusing on what really matters to obtain as accurate a valuation as possible. With this in mind, I had the opportunity to ask Roger Grabowski how a valuator working with a small company should use the Navigator. His comment was: "Use the CRSP buildup data, namely, the Risk Premium Report Study with the Regression Equation Method button on. This would estimate the cost of capital for small and very small businesses."[35]

Cost of Equity(%)	
Risk-free Rate of Return	3.0
Common Stock Equity Risk Premium	6.0
Small Stock Risk Premium	5.4
Industry Risk Premium	3.7
Company Specific Premium	0.0
Total Cost of Equity	18.1

FIGURE 8.8   Cost of Capital According to Ibbotson's Buildup

It should be noted that caution should be applied when using extrapolations beyond the data. There is no way to be sure the extrapolation is correct but it is the best that can be done. This estimate then needs to be screened to see if the figure provided by the system makes sense independently. Again, this is a problem with the income model, not Cost of Capital Navigator data. Review the data and use where it affirmatively answers the question, "Does this make sense?"

Figure 8.8 shows a typical Duff & Phelps Ibbotson's process for estimating a buildup. It is further explained below.

Below is a high level summary of a common set of buildup classifications.[36]

- The first tier of the buildup method is the risk-free rate. This is usually derived from the current day or beginning of the month or year rate of 20-year treasury bonds.[37] Sometimes 10-year term or 30-year term T-Bond rates are used. Duff & Phelps have a "calculated rate" that can be used with their version of cost of capital.
- The second tier is the equity risk premium, which is the additional risk premium that needs to be paid to invest in large company stocks over long-term government bonds. The selected rate needs to correlate with the risk-free rate selected.
- The third tier is a size premium or small stock risk premium which is an additional risk premium assessed for smaller businesses. This data is generated by breaking down equities

by total market value of an equity into deciles and then further breaking down the 10th or smallest decile. Again, this needs to be correlated (same start date and data set) with the first and second tier selections made.

- The fourth tier is an industry risk premium which calculates an adjustment for industry based on the industry beta. Beta is the ratio of the particular stocks correlation of movement with the market. The market is 1. If the stock swings more than the market over time, the beta is above 1. If less than the market as a whole, it is below 1.
- The fifth tier is then the company-specific risk premium, which is an adjustment based on the subject company's soft data and financial results, as interpreted by the valuator's judgment. It should be emphasized this is company cash flow risk going forward, not the owner's or any shareholders' cash flow risk which can be quite different.

Not all methodologies have multiple tiers. Each of the tiers have variations in how they are calculated under the different buildup methods.[38] Extensive information is provided by most data sources on their website or in their publications.

The first two tiers are quite established and need no further comment at this time. Most valuators appear to respect Duff & Phelps' work on the calculated risk free rate but use 20-year t-bonds for the rate. The large cap equity risk premium is firmly established.

The third tier, size premium has recently had questions asked about its existence. Apparently in the decade of the 1980s, small capital stocks actually had lower returns than large company stocks. This may be due to popular investment strategies that were heavily promoted at the time. Long-term data and data since the 1990s show a size premium.[39] For middle market companies, the jury may still be out at least with certain data start dates, but most valuators agree there is a size risk premium for small and very small businesses.

The fourth tier, industry risk premium is used by many valuators. Again, the question should be, does the industry risk premium make the comparable data more or less like the subject company? Remember this data is pulled from very large chains and companies. For instance, the restaurant industry risk premium is -2.00. If the subject company is a McDonald's or perhaps even a Subway (the oversupply of Subways may have changed this performance in recent years), perhaps the business does have a below normal volatility. But small local independent restaurants do not. For an independent restaurant, the SIC Code 58 Eating and Drinking Places Industry Risk premium may not be reflective of their risk.

When in doubt, you can look up the companies compiled into the industry data and the number of companies the data is based on. In addition, sometimes surprising companies are in the classifications. In a recent look-up for general contractors (by SEC Code as required), the companies in the category were primarily large homebuilders. Not general contractors.

The fifth tier is the specific company risk premium. Pratt, Hitchner, and Fishman indicate that the typical inside range of values for the specific company premium is 1–6% with an outside range of 0–10%.[40] They further indicate that a negative, specific company risk premium does rarely occur.

A few courts have ruled against the use of the specific company premium. This is understandable, for while it is common practice, there is no real data supporting most of the adjustments other than "this is how it is done," but that logic is a bit circular.

Specific company premium is where valuators adjust for the differences in risk to the large public companies and the risk to the small company being valued. These are unsystematic risks beyond the risk captured in the larger public stocks and industry adjustments.

This tier is where all the subjective company-specific factors (depending on the standard of value, this may be from the buyer's and/or seller's points of view) are taken into account.

These may include adjustments for concentrations, management depth, tax matters, threats to the industry the company cannot adjust to, and so on. A longer list of factors that may apply is given below.

- Growth rate
  - Risk of not meeting the growth rate
  - Strategic risk
  - Changing business model
  - Historic growth success/failure
- Financial risk
  - Risk of leverage
  - Risk of contingent liabilities or lawsuits
  - Profitability/cash flow
  - One-time expenses
  - Casualty loss
  - Control systems
  - Treasury/loss of assets
  - Credit risk
  - Ability to obtain credit, loss of credit, loss of lines
  - Gross margin coverage
- Operational risk
  - Uncertainties from daily activities, human risk
  - Owner concentration/goodwill
  - Management limitations/leaving
  - Lack of insurance
  - Labor issues
  - Ineffective systems, growing beyond systems
  - Recruiting, training, human resources
  - Product/service development
  - Equipment maintenance
  - Purchasing
  - Inventory management
  - Compliance risk

- Intellectual property risk
- Non-competes, non-solicits
- Industry risk[41]
  - Regulation
  - Commodity/supply issues
  - Changing technology
  - Supply chain
  - Owner status/certification-dependent
  - Economic risk
  - Recession
  - Tariffs
- Concentrations
  - Customer concentration
  - Supplier concentration
  - Referrer concentration
  - Regional limited location risk
  - Key word/search dependent
  - Depending on Amazon for sales

Remember, this list of factors equals the total unsystematic risk that cannot be derived from the larger investment market analysis.

Specific company premium is often weighted or calculated using the same techniques discussed in Chapter 6, Market Approaches, the section "How to Present Soft Factor Analysis." This includes the percentage or direct weighting method, the major factors method, and the list method.

At this point the discount rate has been fully estimated. Discount rates are used when the growth is reflected in the forecast projected cash flows. If you wish to continue with the discounted cash flow method, skip down to "Estimating Value Using the Discounted Cash Flow Method." Otherwise the discount rate developed is now going to be further adjusted to become a capitalization rate.

CALCULATION OF A CAPITALIZATION RATE

The capitalization rate is the discount rate less the growth rate. Next steps in selecting the growth rate will be covered.

Estimating the Growth Rate

The capitalization of earnings method uses past data to estimate a cash flow. In this regard, the cash flow is adjusted and weighted and an estimate selected in a process similar to the market method, plus a few additional steps.

Note there is the real growth rate, that is growth before inflation, and the nominal growth rate is that underlying real growth plus inflation. Valuators should be using the nominal growth rate. Over time, broad economic measures have grown by about 5–6%. Most valuators view this nominal growth rate as the maximum growth rate to use in most situations. Economic and industry growth data along with the specific company data should be reviewed when selecting a growth rate. Again, if possible, check whether the industry growth data is real or nominal growth.

The historic growth rate should be assessed. Of course, with many small and very small businesses, this is going to be erratic. Also it may not be indicative of future growth. A typical small business growth chart is shown in Figure 8.9.

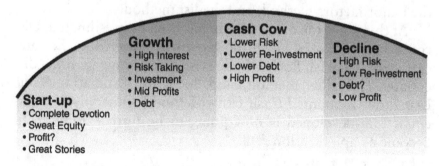

FIGURE 8.9   Business Lifecycle

For many companies, this cycle extends 20–25 years. Sometimes new management or ownership restarts the cycle.

Part of the assessment of the growth rate is determining where the business is in its lifecycle.[42] A business in early growth stages will have a very different growth rate than one that is mature or even in decline. Also consider if there is a reason the business will be reinvigorated and, in effect, move down the business lifecycle by things like new ownership or new management. In those cases (depending on the standard and purpose), those circumstances should be factored into growth.

While in theory the growth rate is in perpetuity due to the nature of present value discounting for small and very small businesses, a 5% or 6% growth rate will NOT produce a company that is larger than GE. As was shown in Figure 8.6, after about 40 years, at most growth rates that would be selected by analysts, the present valuing effect will offset any potential growth.[43]

Certainly, valuators should be judicious with the selected growth rate but when forecasts are not possible, and a company clearly has 5 or 10 years of rapid growth, a higher growth rate may be the best solution. The growth rate is only the growth rate of the earnings or distributable cash flow being used in the valuation. Other measures of growth are not part of this estimate.

Finally, high levels of growth require checking that the working capital, capital investment, and debt adjustments in the cash flow formula are consistent with the growth rate. Growth is often expensive.

Adjusting for Next Period Cash Flow

The capitalization rate is applied to the next year's estimated cash flow. So either the cash flow is grossed up by the growth rate to equal the next year's rate, or the capitalization rate is adjusted by next year's growth rate. The formula to adjust the capitalization rate to this year's cash flow is:

Capitalization Rate/1 + Growth Rate

For example: 16%/(1.04) = 15.4% rounded.

16% is the capitalization rate
4% is the estimated growth rate

ESTIMATING VALUE USING THE CAPITALIZATION OF EARNINGS METHOD

The final step is to divide the selected cash flow by the capitalization rate. Figure 8.3 showed a complete calculation of the capitalization rate using the buildup method. Each step has been completed.

If excess assets exist, they should be added to the value found. This would include excess working capital.

Finally, some method of reasonableness test or sanity check should be applied to the value found. Again, the question, "Does this make sense?" is essential.

Mid-Year Capitalization Rate

The assumption in the capitalization of earnings method is that the company's cash flows are valued at year end. For many businesses, an assumption that the cash flows are received evenly over the course of the year may justify using a mid-year convention capitalization rate. This is a matter for professional judgment.

This often applied to professional service businesses. Outside of seasonal businesses due to weather and perhaps Christmas, it would seem many businesses receive their cash flow evenly over the course of the year. For small and very small businesses, the adjustment will result in an increase of value but materially may be small. The formula for the mid-year convention capitalization rate formula is shown in Figure 8.10.

$$PV = \frac{NCF_1(1+k)^{0.5}}{k-g}$$

PV = Present value
NCF$_1$ = Expected economic income of the full period immediately
        following the effective valuation date
  k = Present value discount rate (build-up cost of capital)
  g = Expected long-term growth rate to perpetuity

FIGURE 8.10 Mid-year Convention Capitalization Rate Formula

WEIGHTED AVERAGE COST OF CAPITAL

The weighted average cost of capital method estimates the cost of capital, including the debt component of the capital structure. If a business is going to have long-term debt on a continuing basis, this can be an effective way to measure value and results. It can also be an effective way to measure value when the buyer is going to have very different financing mechanisms and rates than the current operators do.

Issues with Weighted Average Cost of Capital

Many small and very small businesses are started with some family money (maybe) and a lot of sweat equity. They often have comparably little long-term debt. However, due to the success of the SBA loan programs, when small businesses sell, they often are very highly leveraged and have high debt. But, operating debt is theoretically what is being measured, not purchase price debt. The ability to separate the two types of long-term debt is not common as they are not identifiable in small business data.

Because debt coverage can vary so much, average debt data is likely almost meaningless. (The average of $100,000.00 and $0.00 is $50,000.00 but it is not useful for predicting anything about the two data points.) Another issue is that credit for most small and very small businesses is extended based on personal guarantees in addition to the business credit. Namely, for most financing, the owner's assets are being relied on in addition to the businesses. This restricts the buyer pool and often restricts the ability of the company to expand using debt.

As mentioned, the weighted average cost of capital recalculates the cost of capital based on the full capital structure not just equity. But as debt increases, so does the risk of default. This increases investors' required rates of return. This risk adjustment is very hard to measure and estimate with small companies.

Another issue is how to handle the principal payments during the payment period since investors are in theory interested in what they can receive, and they cannot receive what is due to the note-holder. Further, at some point typically in five to ten years, the long-term debt will be paid, the capital structure will be all equity. Again, most small and very small businesses carry little debt "forever." The model has no way to replicate this.

For smaller companies debt has tax advantages, as interest expense is deductible.

If valuation theory is correct, an equity discount rate buildup and a weighted average cost of capital buildup would produce nearly the same value. In practice, except with the most experienced valuators, the weighted average cost of capital tends to product a lower discount rate and higher valuation.

In most cases for smaller businesses, the weighted average cost of capital is likely a level of detail that will not produce more effective results because there are too many assumptions for which there is not effective data. But, there are always exceptions, so a limited presentation will be made. Figure 8.11 shows a typical weighted average cost of capital calculation.

Weighted Average Cost of Capital (WACC) Calculation

In the weighted average cost of capital calculation the valuator estimates the portion of the capital structure that will be represented by long-term debt. The estimate can be based on specific company and fact pattern factors, industry data,

Line No.	Determination of After-Tax Cash Flow		Historic Year 3	Historic Year 2	Historic Year 1
1	Historic Adjusted Pretax Cash Flow		$609,900	$609,900	$609,900
2	Weighting		1	1	1
3	Weighted Average Cash Flow		$609,900		
4	Deduct Average Depreciation/Amortization		$40,000		
5	Taxable Income		$569,900		
6	State Corporate Tax Rate		8%		
7	Estimated Tax		$45,592		
8	Subtotal		$524,308		
9	Estimated Federal Tax Rate		21%		
10	Estimated Federal Tax		$110,105		
11	Subtotal		$414,203		
12	Plus Depreciation/Amortization		$40,000		
13	Decrease (Increase) Working Capital		$0		
14	Decrease (Increase) Capital Expenditures		$0		
15	Decrease (Increase) Long-Term Debt		$0		
16	Selected After-Tax Cash Flow		$454,203		
17	Next Period Cash Flow (Sustainable Growth 3%)			$467,829	
18					
19	**Calculation of the Cost of Debt**				
20					
21	Weight of Debt	25.00%			
22	Cost of Debt				
23	Interest Rate	7.00%			
24	Tax Rate	35.00%			
25	One minus Tax Rate	65.00%			
26	Total Cost of Debt	4.55%		1.14%	
27					
28	**Calculation of the Capitalization Rate**				
29					
30	Weight of Equity	75.00%			
31	Cost of Equity				
32	Risk-free Rate of Return		3.0%		
33	Common Stock Equity Risk Premium		6.0%		
34	Small Stock Risk Premium		5.4%		
35	Industry Risk Premium		3.7%		
36	Company-Specific Premium		0.0%		
37	Total Cost of Equity		18.1%		
38	Less Sustainable Growth		3.0%		
39	Next Year Capitalization Rate		15.1%	11.33%	
40	Selected WACC Capitalization Rate (27+40)			12.46%	
41	Indicated Value Total Investment Value with Debt			$3,753,897	
42	Less Long-Term & Interest Bearing Debt			$938,474	
43	Selected Value Equity, WACC			$2,815,423	

FIGURE 8.11   Weighted Average Cost of Capital Calculation

This Chart will be broken down and explained in detail.

Line No.

1	Historic Adjusted Pretax Cash flow is adjusted pretax profits plus depreciation and amortization.
	Normalization adjustments will be made similar to those shown for the market method.
	Interest is always added back when calculating WACC.
5	Average depreciation/amortization is subtracted from the cash flow before taxes are adjusted.
1-16	Cash Flow is calculated as previously shown for cost of capital calculations plus interest as mentioned above.
17	Beginning of next year cash flow is estimated. (1+sustainable growth)*current period cash flow.
21	Weight of the debt is estimated.
23	Interest rate is estimated. Make sure you look at rates for small and very small businesses.
24	Estimated tax rate. Interest is still tax deductible for small business.
25	After tax debt expense formula is (1-Tax Rate)* interest rate.
26	Estimated after tax cost of debt. This is multiplied by the weight of debt to calculate the contribution to cost of capital.
30	Weight of equity is shown.
32-39	Buildup cost of capital is same as shown for estimating capitalization rate.
39	Next year capitalization rate is multiplied by weighting (33*42).
40	Total WACC capitalization rate (26+39).
41	Indicated value with debt.
42	Less debt, in this case debt is calculated as (30*41).
43	Selected Value of Equity Interests.

NOTE:

Current Year Capitalization Rate - The analyst can either increase the cash flow to reflect next year's after growth earnings as done here (Current Year earnings times 1+long term growth) or adjust the capitalization rate for the same amount. Namely take next year's capitalization rate and divide it by (1 + long term growth). Per the Gordon Growth model theory the immediate next periods cash flow is applied against the capitalization rate.

FIGURE 8.11 *Continued*

or a combination. In some cases, the subject company's current structure can be used. As mentioned above, while questionable in theory, the figure used is often an "average" estimated debt from recognized comparable data sources. This data is often obtained from RMA, or Integra or other data services.

The cost of the debt is then estimated. This can often be found by checking with banks. For small and very small businesses, it is often in the prime plus 2 to 3% range. Sometimes the bank rate includes a floor rate such as 7%. At times of very low interest rates, the valuator must check the floor value or run the risk of understating interest.

Interest payments on debt are tax deductible (that is still the case for small and very small businesses) so the estimated tax benefit is calculated by deducting the tax benefit on the interest payments. Then the portion of the capital structure represented by debt, perhaps 30%, is added to the portion of the capital structure represented by equity, in this case, 70%. The two figures are added and the cost of capital is calculated.

When estimating the equity value of the company being valued using WACC, remember that the interest-bearing debt (usually both short- and long-term) must be subtracted from the value found when estimating equity interests.

Again, common sense dictates that as the amount of debt rises, investors' cost of equity will increase due to the increased risk that they will not be paid their required return on investment. In fact, because debt is paid before equity, equity holders run a greater risk that they will lose their investment.

Rule of Thumb: Finance Method

The finance method is called a rule of thumb. Basically it is the reverse of the weighted average cost of capital. In the finance method, the valuator takes the cost of financing across the entire capital structure and divides it into the cash flow to come up with a value. This is a practical and easy rule of thumb to use as a check for any value found with small businesses, particularly where small business sales markets are driven by SBA loans or other debt that is easy to price. An example of the calculation is shown in Figure 8.12.

Example

XYZ Company has a seller's discretionary cash flow of $400,000. The prospective buyer estimates that he needs $125,000 for his salary initially and another $75,000 for contingencies, capital investment, and some taxes on principal payments. This leaves $200,000 for annual payments. Using a present value of periodic deposits calculator in Excel with an expected interest rate over the life of a 10 year loan at 8%, the approximate value estimate is $1,374,000. If a "typical" SDE multiplier is 3, this is close to the range of values (3 x $400,000 = $1,200,000) and as a rule of thumb would support the valuation.

Discretionary Cash Flow	$400,000
Uses of Cash Flow	
Owner Salary	$125,000
Capital Investment	$25,000
Contingency	$50,000
Total Uses of Cash	$200,000
Cash Available for Financing	$200,000
Rule of Thumb Finance Method Value	$1,373,685.94

Principal Loan Amount Calculations

Interest Rate	8.00%	
Number of Payments	120	Monthly Payments
Available for Payment	($16,667)	Monthly Payment Amount (Cash Available for financing / 12 months)
Compounding Periods Per Year	12	

NOTE: This chart is "live" and will work if formulas are left intact.

The "Interest Rate" can be an estimated cost of capital or a true interest rate.
Either way this is an efficient sanity test.

FIGURE 8.12   The Basic Finance Method Rule of Thumb

The finance method can be further enhanced to take equity investment into account also. That would generally raise the overall rate.

Example

If we assume 20% down and an internal rate of return of 35% to equity holders, our new "rate" is 13.4%. ((.2 x 35)+(.8 x 8)) = 13.4. (You could go on and tax affect it, for instance, using 6% for the adjusted interest rate.) Assuming 10 periods with a $200,000 payment at 13.4% generates a present value of $1,098,800. Again, in the ballpark for a sanity test.

These estimated rates are drawn from reasonable approximations available by talking to local bankers and estimates from the Pepperdine Survey. They are estimates. While 35%

was used, an analyst may be able to justify a 50% internal rate of return on a 20% equity investment with 80% leverage because of the increased risk of loss.

While this is viewed as a rule of thumb type sanity test, if thought is put into the inputs, the model will produce useful results.

ESTIMATING VALUE USING THE DISCOUNTED CASH FLOW METHOD

In theory, the most accurate method of business valuation is the discounted cash flow method. In the discounted cash flow method the valuation analyst takes a forecast of future cash flows and discounts it back to a present value. The major problem with this theory is that the management of most small businesses cannot prepare forecasts or projections. Small business owners tend to have an attitude that they do not have that much control over their businesses. Seeing as they often serve small geographic market areas with limited product or service lines, this may be true. If the people who know the business best cannot put together a reliable forecast, what is the valuation analyst to do?

Yet there are situations such as turn-arounds and start-ups where the discounted cash flow may be the only method available. Also, for larger companies, or companies that do have a history of financial projections and/or forecasts and perhaps even analysis of downstream results against the forecast, this is the best method in both theory and fact. Finally, there are situations such as when there are going to be major short-term changes, then a stabilizing of growth where a forecast created by an analyst (if management cannot develop one) may be the best method available.

The discounted cash flow method forecasts an income stream, often from three to ten years and discounts it to a present value. Because businesses are assumed to last into perpetuity, the terminal year is calculated to represent perpetuity. Two methods are shown below to calculate the terminal year.

The advantage of the discounted cash flow method is that a company with varying cash flows over time can have those factored into the forecast. That is why start-ups and turn-arounds are best measured using this method. The rapid cash flow growth can be captured in the forecast years and then more measured growth can be captured in the terminal year.

Estimating Value Using the Discounted Cash Flow Method

The next step is to estimate the value for the discrete periods shown in the forecast. These will be added together along with the terminal value estimate that will be shown later to determine the full value.

The formula with a three-year forecast looks like this:

$$\text{Period 1 value} + \text{Period 2 value} + \text{Period 3 value}$$

$$+ \text{ terminal value.}$$

$$\begin{array}{l}\text{Present values of net cash flows} \\ \text{during the explicit period}\end{array} + \begin{array}{l}\text{Present value of terminal} \\ \text{period}\end{array}$$

$$NCF_1/(1+k)^1 + NCF_2/(1+k)^2 + NCF_3/(1+k)^3 + \dfrac{\dfrac{NCFn \times (1+g)}{(k-g)}}{(1+k)N}$$

NCF = Net Cash Flow

k = Discount rate

g = Growth

During the discrete periods (each year) the discount rate is geometric series to determine future cash flow. (The first year is the estimated rate, the second year is squared, the third year is cubed, and so on.) This adjusts the discount rate for present value. An example of the calculations to estimate each year's rate are shown in Figure 8.13. It may be easier to actually

Income Approach: Discount Rate Calculated PV Factors

Year:	2016	2017	2018	2019	2020	2021	2022	2023	2024	2025
n Year #	1	2	3	4	5	6	7	8	9	10
k (built up)	24.1%	24.1%	24.1%	24.1%	24.1%	24.1%	24.1%	24.1%	24.1%	24.1%
PV Factor	0.81	0.65	0.52	0.42	0.34	0.27	0.22	0.18	0.14	0.12
PV Factor =	$1/(1+k)^n$									

Remember, for each each discrete year the formula is Net Cash Flow / PV Factor.

k   The buildup method is generally used to develop the discount rate shown as K as shown below.

k =   Buildup Method - Discount Rate Calculation

Risk-free Rate of Return	3.0%
Large Stock Equity Risk Premium	6.0%
Small Stock Risk Premium	5.4%
Industry Risk Premium	3.7%
Company Specific Premium	6.0%
Total Cost of Equity	24.1%

FIGURE 8.13   Calculating the Discount Rate Each Year

understand how this works by downloading the Excel version on the website and looking at the formulas.

We will address the final step, terminal value next.

Terminal Value

In most cases, business valuation relies on the assumption that businesses will exist into perpetuity. This assumption is poorly supported by facts even for very large organizations but any other assumption would likely be even more difficult to model.[44] Discounted cash flow forecasts are for discrete periods usually between three and ten years. With small and very small businesses it is rare that forecasts extend beyond five years and many may only be for two years. Therefore, the value derived from the cash flows for the years after the forecast period need to be calculated and added to find the full value.

One of the concerns of the discounted cash flow is that the terminal value often makes up far more than 50% of the total value found.[45] With very short forecast periods, this will be even more common. Still, it is likely to be more accurate than using the capitalization of earnings method, particularly where investment or cash flow change is forecast in the near term.

Two methods are used to determine terminal value. The most common used by valuators is a version of the capitalization of earnings model. This calculation assumes that growth will be a constant rate into perpetuity. An estimated growth rate into perpetuity must be selected. These are often between 2% and 6%. With inflation running between 2–3%, anything below that figure is actually losing value after inflation. Negative growth can be selected if the company is expected to contract but this is fairly rare in practice. Most valuators use between 2–4% most of the time, depending on real growth prospects.[46] Roger Grabowski and Ashok Abbott recently performed a detailed study and came up with "real" growth rates (above inflation) for most established (called "Long Term") publicly traded companies in the 2% range counting acquisitions.[47]

Calculating the Terminal Value

For simplification as in the capitalization of earnings method, a variation of the Gordon Growth model is used to account for the value of free cash flows that continue growing at an assumed constant rate in perpetuity.

The projected free cash flow in the first year beyond the forecast horizon (N+1) is used. This value is divided by the discount rate minus the assumed perpetuity growth rate:

$$T_0 = D_0/k - g$$

T_0 = Value of future cash flows (price).

D_0 = Cash flows at a future point in time which is immediately prior to N+1, or at the end of period N, which is the final year in the forecast period.

k = discount rate.

g = growth rate.

- The cash flow (CF) for the first year past the forecast period is assumed to grow at the estimated long-term growth rate.
- The discount rate then has the long-term growth rate subtracted from it to estimate the capitalization rate.
- CF is then divided by the capitalization rate which is then multiplied by the present value factor of the last period in the projection to find the terminal value.

The terminal value is then added to the value found for the discounted years to find the total value. See Figure 8.15 on p. 213 for an example of a complete discounted cash flow calculation.

This is the end of the 4th year of the projection	
	2023
Projected Cash Flow to Equity	$1,113,900
Cash Flow Multiplier	5.5
	$6,126,450
Present Value Discount	0.47
Terminal Value	$2,879,432
Discounted Cash Flow:	
Present value of Periods, 4 years	$2,389,150
Present value of Terminal Year	$2,879,432
Indicated Value of Equity	$5,268,582

Check the cash flow multiplier source to determine if it is pre- or post-tax.
The cash flow multiplier may need to be adjusted to reflect taxation.
Present value discount is from prior tables shown.

FIGURE 8.14   Calculating the Terminal Value Using the Exit Multiple Approach

Exit Multiple Approach

The other method used to determine the terminal value is the exit multiple approach. Yes, it is a version of the market method. This method tends to be used by investment bankers and not valuation professionals but, remember, multipliers and capitalization rates are really just two ways to say the same thing.

In the exit multiple approach the analyst estimates the multiplier for the cash flow being used which is usually based on EBITDA. The multiple as selected is applied to the last year in the forecast's cash flow. This is applied against a present value factor and added to the discrete period's total. Again, this method is often used by investment bankers and does not have strong endorsement by the valuation community if for no other reason than it is combining two methods. See an example of this calculation in Figure 8.14.

		2020	2021	2022	2023
Forecast Net Operating Income Plus Dep & Amort		$ 1,000,000	$ 1,300,000	$ 1,400,000	$ 1,500,000
Projected Corp. income tax (VA)	6.00%	60,000	78,000	84,000	90,000
Projected Corp. income tax (Fed)	21.00%	197,400	256,620	276,360	296,100
		257,400	334,620	360,360	386,100
Effective Tax Rate		-25.7%	-25.7%	-25.7%	-25.7%
Projected Net Cash Flow to Equity		$ 742,600	$ 965,380	$ 1,039,640	$ 1,113,900
Portion of Year Remaining		1	1	1	1
Cash Flow to Equity Remaining		$ 742,600	$ 965,380	$ 1,039,640	$ 1,113,900
Apply: Present Value Factor		0.83	0.69	0.57	0.47
Present Value of Cash Flows - Periods		$ 614,735	$ 661,553	$ 589,769	$ 523,092

				2024
Terminal/Perpetuity Value:				
Net Cash Flow to Equity 2023				$ 1,113,900
Assumed Growth Rate into Perpetuity				3.00%
Assumed Stable Cash Flows				$ 1,147,317
		Discount Rate	Growth	
Apply: Capitalization Rate (Discount Rate - Growth)		20.80%	3.00%	17.80%
Capitalized Terminal Value (Stable Cash Flows / Capitalization Rate)				$ 6,445,601
Present Value of Terminal Value (Last Projection Year Present Value)		PV Factor	0.47	$ 3,026,883

Discounted Cash Flow:	
Present Value of Periods 4 years	$ 2,389,150
Present Value of Terminal Value	$ 3,026,883
Indicated Value of Equity (DCF)	$ 5,416,033

FIGURE 8.15 Discounted Cash Flow Income Approach: Forecast Projected Net Cash Flow to Equity Holders

Estimating the Value Using the Discounted Cash Flow Method

The final step is to add the discrete year calculations to the terminal year calculations to come up with the final enterprise value. Cheryl Hyder sent me the original version of this format and I have found it very useful over the years. See Figure 8.15 for the complete calculation. Note that the Excel file on the website also includes tabs for estimating the discount rate and estimating the present value factors.

This completes a basic discounted cash flow calculation. Please note this is a basic model suitable for small companies. Models can be adjusted to include debt and for partial years or for a mid-year discount rates. For very small businesses the effort is unlikely to materially change the results. But if necessary for your project, see Hitchner's *Financial Valuation*.[48]

NOTES

1. I will not address the little used (for small business) excess cash flow method.
2. James R. Hitchner, *Financial Valuation*, 3rd Edition (Hoboken, NJ: Wiley, 2011), p. 181.
3. Aswath Damodaran, "Basics of Discounted Cash Flow Valuation," p. 9; "Never mix and match cash flows and discount rates," undated presentation.
4. This is shown as an example. It is assumed that the rate includes all growth and period adjustments.
5. Again, this is a simplification—not all adjustments have been made.
6. SSVS 100 .23 and .31–.42.
7. Note that the commentary in this section is limited to what is typically required for small and very small businesses. It is not intended to cover all situations in all valuations—even in the case of very small businesses.
8. As will be covered later, this is a gross simplification to make a point. As will be seen below, the capitalization rate is applied to the next year's estimated cash flow. So either the cash flow is grossed up by the growth rate or the capitalization rate is adjusted by next year's growth rate (i.e., Cap. rate/1 + growth rate or 16%/ (1.04) = 15.4% rounded).
9. Tax affecting is currently a contentious area in business valuation. Ask 100 valuators and you will receive 100 different answers and variations in methods.
10. It appears business valuation experts believe they have a much clearer understanding of the effects of TCJA than tax experts as to what the law really means and how to properly apply the

law. Tax experts report the current tax law becoming close to unmanageable.

11. The cases include: Gross T.C. Memo 1999-254, aff'd. 272 F.3d 333 (6th Circuit) 2001, cert denied 537 US 827 (2002) (Corp); Wall TC Memo 2001-75 (Corp); Heck T.C. Memo 2002-34 (Corp); Adams T.C. Memo 2002-80 (Corp); Dallas T.C. Memo 2006-212 (Corp); Guistina TC Memo 2011-141 (Limited Partnership); Gallagher TC Memo 2011-148 (LLC).

12. *Estate of Aaron Jones*, TCM 2019-101. Beginning on page 24 of the opinion, there is a summary of prior case law on tax affecting for estate purposes. The gist is that, in the past, tax affecting was not done properly but would be considered if done properly. The court continued, in this case, a rough estimate was provided that is fair and sensible and therefore it is being accepted by the court. Pardon my paraphrasing.

13. *Kress v. United States*, 372 F.Supp.3d 731 (2019) while a lower district federal court case, the IRS expert tax affected.

14. *Estate of Aaron Jones*, TCM 2019-101.

15. Often in those cases the discount rate or capitalization rate may be adjusted to reflect all or part of the tax adjustment.

16. Again, this goes back to our basic standard of value question—who is our buyer?

17. Wyoming is proposing a limited corporate tax of 7%. Read https://taxfoundation.org/wyoming-proposed-corporate-tax/ for an interesting analysis that has implications on profitability, hence value.

18. Nancy Fannon, "Incorporating Research Relating to Tax Effects Into Your Income Approach Analysis," May 15, 2017.

19. American Society of Appraisers, "Valuing C Corps and Pass-Through Entities Under the New Tax Law," *Business Valuation Review* vol. 37, no. 1 (2018).

20. Eric Barr and Peter L. Lohrey, "Inside Pratt's Stats: Impact of Entity Form on Selling Price (Part2)," Business Valuation Update, BVR, January (2018). www.bvresources.com/articles/business-valuation-update/inside-pratts-stats.

21. Many valuators are currently tax adjusting to the personal taxpayer rate as opposed to corporate rate for pass-through entities. I disagree for many reasons but one is that it is unlikely that the public stock was being valued by individuals, as most

public stocks are owned by institutions supported by the fact that 78% market capitalization of the Russel 3000 index stocks are owned by institutions which may have different tax outcomes. Support for the 80% statement: https://www .pionline.com/article/20170425/INTERACTIVE/170429926/ 80-of-equity-market-cap-held-by-institutions

22. Other resources include https://www.irs.gov/statistics/soi-tax-stats-corporation-data-by-sector-or-industry#_bm2

23. Other resources include https://www.irs.gov/statistics/soi-tax-stats-corporation-data-by-sector-or-industry#_bm2

24. This gets very complex and can result in double taxation. See https://taxfoundation.org/very-short-primer-tax-nexus-apportio nment-and-throwback-rule/

25. Fannon, "Incorporating Research."

26. Perhaps in these cases instead of raising the discount rate, a separate discount should be applied to clearly adjust for the projection overstatement or understatement of earnings.

27. *International Glossary of Business Valuation Terms*, June 8, 2001. www.nacva.com/content.asp?contentid=166

28. For a discussion of how Duff & Phelps generates its Normalized Risk Free Rate, see https://www.duffandphelps.com/insights/ publications/valuation/us-normalized-risk-free-effective-september-30-2019

29. 5.25% prime plus 2.5% or approximately 7.75%) Corp Spot Rates FRED 10 year high quality market (HQM), *Wall Street Journal* August 16, 2019. Prime has been dropping during the writing of the book but small business financing is significantly more expensive when available than large company financing.

30. *See* http://pages.stern.nyu.edu/~adamodar/New_Home_Page/ datacurrent.html

31. Internal Rate of Return is the financial return on an investment. It is a discounted cash flow without factoring for additional financial and inflation risks. It can be calculated in Excel.

32. *See* https://digitalcommons.pepperdine.edu/gsbm_pcm_pcmr/

33. *See* https://www.partnershipprofiles.com/

34. *See* https://www.partnershipprofiles.com/

35. Immediately prior to interview with Roger Grabowski, NACVA Conference, "Around the Valuation World," June 6-8, 2019. See

also comments on Video Around the Valuation World SLC2019 https://www.youtube.com/watch?v=Ap4ZPUyq5Eo

36. Jim Hitchner, "Best Practices" presentation, November 28, 2018, NACVA, New Jersey, Slide 18 recommends BUM (Buildup method) for very small companies where betas are not relevant.

37. Technically 20-year T-bonds do not exist. This is the rate of 30-year T-bonds with 20 years left.

38. The CAPM and MCAPM models, which use the beta coefficient to adjust for risk are not being reviewed here. As stated above, these are more appropriate when valuing larger businesses.

39. James P. Harrington, "Size Effect Analysis," NACVA, New Jersey, State Chapter Presentation, November 28, 2018.

40. J. Hitchner, S. Pratt, and J. Fishman, *A Consensus View: Q&A Guide to Financial Valuation* (Portland, OR: BVR, 2016); Valuation Products and Services, LLC, Question 73.

41. As previously mentioned, some valuators omit the industry risk premium if it does not reflect the risk of the subject company. Some show the industry risk premium anyway and then show a contra adjustment.

42. Roger Grabowski and Ashok Abbott recently performed a detailed study of observed long-term growth and concluded that "real" growth rates (inflation removed) of earnings (before taxes) (titled "Long Term" organic growth; that is, removing effect of growth by acquisition) for most publicly traded companies are less than 2%.

43. As discount rates drop and growth rates increase, the effects of present valuing cash flows reduce the value of early cash flows and increase the value of later cash flows. Still under most selected capitalization rates, the early cash flows will have more influence on the value found than later ones.

44. While somewhat anecdotal, see "Fortune 500 firms 1955 v. 2017: Only 60 remain, thanks to the creative destruction that fuels economic prosperity," October 20, 2017. https://www.aei.org/carpe-diem/fortune-500-firms-1955-v-2017-only-12-remain-thanks-to-the-creative-destruction-that-fuels-economic-prosperity/

45. Of course, this same methodology is used for 100% of the value in the capitalization of earnings method. Again, no. model is perfect.

46. Grabowski, "Real Growth Rates."

47. Ashok Abbott and Roger Grabowski, "Estimating Long-Term Growth Rates," paper presented at 2019 NACVA Conference, pp. 34–40.
48. James R. Hitchner, *Financial Valuation: Applications and Models*, 4th Edition (Hoboken, NJ: Wiley, 2016).

CHAPTER 9

Valuing Partial Interests
in a Business

Up to this point the focus has been on 100% control owner-ship of the business, i.e., estimating the value of the entity, the enterprise value, and once debt is removed, the 100% equity value. Yet business valuations are often for partial interests in the business. Adding partners, removing partners, divorce when an owner has partners, gifting interests, estates, and more are all situations where partial interests are valued. When valuing a partial interest, the interest must be investigated and under-stood above and beyond the business itself. In many ways this is equivalent to performing a second valuation.

When a business has multiple owners, the different owners often have very different rights and responsibilities and in that case each owns a different interest. At the highest level, rights may be broadly broken up along the lines of:

- cash flow
- control
- tax benefits.

In addition to owners, lenders through loan covenants, including security agreements on assets or stock, can exert control over a company. Lenders or others may have option agreements entitling them to buy stock or equity in the future. These other interests may also be valued by the analyst, such as options and debt.[1] Finally, the interplay between the rights of an interested party can affect the rights and value of the others.

The rights and risks of any interest are determined by statutes, court cases, and agreements between the parties. The relationship between governing rules, the interpretation of the rules, and private agreements that often, but not always, modify the rules must also be studied and understood to properly value an interest.

Classifications of levels of value of equity interests are based on control, availability of a market, and in some cases synergies or cash flows. In the simplest form these levels are called control, marketable minority, and nonmarketable minority. These and additional levels are covered in the next section. These levels of value are useful shortcuts to guide in selecting proper methods for review and estimating the discounts or premium to adjust the underlying entity value. But, each interest must be investigated, thoroughly analyzed and valued on its individual merits.

The rights of shareholders' or members' equity-type interests in a company will directly impact the risk of the cash flow to the interest and therefore the value of the interest. This chapter describes the process of properly determining the true rights of the interest and then placing a proper value on the interest based on those rights or restrictions.

Example

A 20% owner, who was fired as an employee, receives no severance, no distributions of profit, and a tax bill on $100,000, which is his share of the pass-through earnings. He has a very different situation (and value) than a 20% owner, who is being paid $100,000 a year, who feels he is fairly compensated plus receiving $50,000 a year profit distribution (out of his $100,000 share) to cover taxes and maybe a little bonus. In addition, the second owner has a fair buy-out agreement in place.

> *These are both a 20% interest in companies with the same earn-ings power but the interest values are very different. That part is simple. Determining a more precise interest value is not simple.*

LEVELS OF VALUE IN BUSINESS VALUATION

Levels of value are shorthand ways of calling out where inter-est holders are in the spectrum of shareholder value. Figure 9.1 shows Traditional Values and an updated Unified Theory of Value in business valuation. This chart was first formulated by Chris Mercer.[2]

The different levels of value are determined by the level of control over the business by the interest holder, the possibilities of profit growth, and the marketability of the interest. Levels of value serve as a shorthand description of these key characteris-tics of the interest being valued.

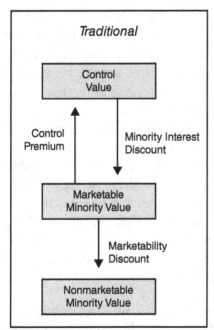
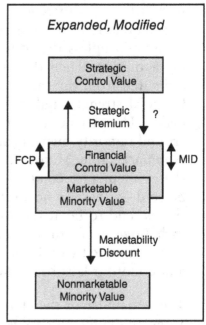

FIGURE 9.1 Unified Theory Value Chart

- **Control Value.** Control value is the highest value under the traditional chart. Control owners have final say over most matters with the business. Because they have control, their interests are usually marketable even with private companies. Under the expanded value chart, control value is further broken down into strategic control and financial control. Strategic control combines strategic cash flow savings or gains (profits) with control. For small businesses, cash flow is usually adjusted to determine the strategic premium. Financial control is closer to the traditional control value often determined by direct comparison with private market data and income method buildup calculations for small businesses.
- **Marketable Minority.** This is the usual value for shares of public stocks listed on the exchanges. These shares do not represent control but they are fully marketable. It should be noted that public financial control shares usually have very little price difference from marketable minority shares. Marketable minority shares are very rare in small private companies unless the company or another owner is making a market. Then the minority value would be usually estimated from the cash flows, repurchase agreement, and financial strength and other characteristics of the market maker. The variance in cash flows between the control owners and minority owners constitutes a minority discount.
- **Nonmarketable Minority.** These are minority ownership shares in private companies. Usually these shares cannot be sold as there is no market for them. Owners of these shares tend to be at the whim of control owners, making cash flows from these interests very risky. This value is often estimated with both a minority interest discount and a discount for lack of marketability.

The remainder of the chapter is about understanding and adjusting the enterprise value found for these equity interest levels of value and the underlying risks and benefits.

UNDERSTANDING PARTIAL INTEREST FACTORS

This section of the chapter provides an overview of corporate documents and other agreements between co-owners and perhaps key people and lenders. These documents are reviewed to understand the ability of an interest holder to influence or control a company or other shareholder action (control). Also, in some cases the documents may create an obligation to buy or sell stock and create a limited market (marketability).

The sections on partial interests and discounts are about accounting for the increased or reduced risk that a partial interest holder has above the company risk as a whole. The simplest way to look at it is with the driving analogy.

Example

Think of a car ride. Is it a pleasant Sunday afternoon ride where we enjoy the scenery and have an enjoyable conversation with a good driver, or is it the ride of your life with a breakneck driver and you're not sure if you will get there alive? Or is it somewhere in between?

While this is a simplified view, these are two extreme situations where the pleasant drive might be viewed as a "fair" control owner and the breakneck driver an "unfair" owner in the business world creating different value equations for the non-control owners.

In addition, there is the risk that the control owner may treat the non-control owner differently or could change attitudes on being "fair" with the current non-control owner. Finally, there is the risk of a new or different control owner taking over. These matters are all different risks that need to be accounted for in valuations of partial interests. These risks are usually assessed after finding the value of the company as a whole.

When reviewing documents, remember that you are trying to determine the following for the interest being valued:

- What actions does this interest holder have control over?
- What actions does the interest holder not have control over?
  - Who has control over those actions?
  - What could they do?
  - Are there any protections under state statutes, case law or elsewhere?
- How do these situations/risks compare to the comparable set being used?
- How do we show these relationships clearly?
- How are the numbers impacted?

Examples of actions that may impact future cash flows to an interest holder are:

- Major corporate actions:
  - Adding or removing partners
  - Mergers, liquidations or going public
  - New debt
  - Board appointments, particularly the ability to control the board
  - Ability to change the rules (a real wildcard).
- Normal operations:
  - Products, services and pricing
  - Employment and salaries
  - Select contractors and vendors
  - Distributions
  - Reinvestment
- Individual freedoms:
  - Ability to explicitly compete or have related investments
  - Non-competes and non-solicits
  - Employment contracts
- Cash flow preferences:
  - Above or below market salaries
  - Benefits, particularly uneven benefits
  - If pass-through, distribution for taxes policy

- Buy-sell and dispute matters:
  - Arbitration or waiver of jury
  - Restrictions on sale
  - Restrictions on value (e.g., book value, declared nominal value)
  - Required sale at end of employment
  - Put options (agreements to buy the stock)
  - Valuation process and payment terms
  - "Swing" vote with two other owners having equal shares

For more on this, see Pratt, Reilly, and Schweihs, *Valuing a Business*,[3] where a list of prerogatives of control includes twenty items.

These rights are specified in the various organizational documents, meeting minutes, buy-sell agreements, employment agreements, and other related documents. In addition, where the documents are silent, or in some cases regardless of what the documents say, state statute and case law provide more guidance. Finally, in different situations and in different jurisdictions the courts may enforce these agreements differently.

Our job as valuators is to distill the factors that create or mitigate risk to the perceived future cash flows and adjust the values accordingly. In different situations, different factors will be more important than others. As usual, we will look at the past to give indications of the future. But, the past is not the future, particularly with small businesses where a control owner can become arbitrary with relative impunity. Definitive documents, court cases, and work by thought leaders have produced agreed methods for presenting the analysis of these matters. Not all of those will be shown here. But, consistent with the theme of the book, appropriate methods for most situations involving small and very small businesses will be presented.

Clearly valuing partial interests is an area full of professional judgment and subjective review. Now let's begin to examine how we better assess the level of control or lack of control and make appropriate adjustments to value. This starts by reviewing the legal framework that establishes these rights and restrictions.

Examining the Interest

All business entities are governed by state, federal, and local law. The relationships between the different owners is generally a state law matter. Many of the laws governing the relationships between the different owners and the company are in state statutes. Those statutes and, in some instances, older common law are then interpreted by the courts. Many rules provided in the statutes can be modified by the agreement of the parties involved. Therefore, any time an interest that is less than 100% ownership is being valued, a working level (not the level of an attorney but a reasonable understanding for a valuation professional) of both the state law and the documents agreed to by the parties is necessary.

Of major importance to the valuator when examining an interest is the standard of value (typically either fair value or fair market value but it can be others) to be applied to the interest. Most of the discussion in this chapter concerns valuations under the fair market value standard. See Chapter 2 for a discussion of standards of value. These standards may vary based on the type of organization, the nature of the problem, purpose, or cause of action at hand.

If your client is working with an attorney, it is always advisable to talk to the attorney and obtain standard of values and statutory framework laws from them. Experience dictates that for many smaller legal disputes and cases where many valuation analysts start out, the lawyer may not know what the standard of value or the correct valuation date is or know much about these valuation matters. Frightening but true, as you are likely to be working with a junior attorney also. Yet your valuation depends on a correct starting point. At that point, do your own research and confirm your findings with your client and their counsel. While we do not want to cross the line and be determining law, we must understand exactly what we are valuing.

Valuation professionals are not lawyers, therefore, we cannot properly evaluate interests in companies without understanding the rules that the different parties live by. With the ease of registering new entities over the internet, there are now many small companies who are solely governed by state law. Individuals go to the state website and create an entity simply by filling out the filing document, making the payment, and performing no other tasks. In those cases, state law determines the relationships which influences the relative value of shareholder interests and other interest holders. Unfortunately, the one-size-fits-all approach rarely turns out to be fair to all parties.

Statutory Framework

Organizational documents must be reviewed. If the valuation is of a 100% control interest of one owner or for a sale where an underlying assumption is that the sale is approved by shareholders, then corporate documents and shareholder documents have less significance. If the value of an interest is less than 100% then the organizational documents become critical.

The organizational document, usually Articles of Incorporation for a corporation, or Articles of Organization for a Limited Liability Company (LLC), are the organizational documents of the two most frequently used types of business entities. These are recorded in the state of formation. General partnerships do not have to be recorded but often a trade name certificate is filed for the partnership. State law specifies the requirements. Usually the entity needs a unique name in the state and a person or entity to receive service of process for lawsuits. In most states, the public filing says little else for private companies.

Each entity type will then have other documents that specify rights and control. For corporations it tends to be the by-laws and directors' or shareholders' meeting minutes and consents. For limited liability companies, it tends to be the operating agreement. In all cases, other agreements may also need to be examined.

Corporations have been in existence longer than other entities that limit liability. State laws tend to have a more robust framework for the various relationships in corporations. There is often less flexibility in the structure of the ownership interests due to this framework.

One area of particular importance in entities are minority or non-control owner rights. Most corporate statutes require approval of more than 50% ownership to perform major actions, such as taking on substantial debt, liquidation, mergers, etc., 76% is a typical percentage, according to many state statutes. Therefore, while a 51% owner can control many things, there are still a few major actions where the minority owner may have some say.

Some states (approximately sixteen) have "Close Corporation" statutes or the equivalent where unanimous consent is required for all major and some less major corporate actions. Registering under the Close Corporation or equivalent statute creates more of a common law partnership. These statutes also require unanimous consent for owners to buy or sell stock.[4] While the statutes protect against unwanted partners or sales, they can be cumbersome in dispute situations and must be understood by the analyst. Often, they are not fully understood by the owners when agreed to until a problem arises and attorneys enter the fray to sort out what it all means.

Outside of the Close Corporation statutes, many states have statutory protections for minority owners. For instance, in Maryland, an owner with under 20% ownership can petition the court to force a majority owner or a new owner to buy their stock if the majority owner is selling only his stock.[5] This is referred to as an Oppressed Owner statute. Other states may have different protections, including broader or more limited protections for minority shareholders.

Limited liability companies are a much newer entity type. Limited liability companies have much more flexibility in how they can be set up and what the rights and responsibilities of various interest holders in the entity are. The standard of value under most state laws loosely parallels state corporate provisions but not always. There also may be less protection for minority interests in limited liability companies under state law. Again, carefully check state law. Do not make assumptions based on similar but different situations.

Corporate Documents

The article of incorporation is the filing document. Again, usually very little information of value to valuators is contained in that document but it will have been filed and should be reviewed. An exception to this is if the document says it is a Close Corporation. In many states those few words can completely change the statutory framework of the rules that apply. If it says that the company is a Close Corporation, research what that means in your state carefully, review further agreements of the parties through that lens, and using professional judgment apply those rules when evaluating the interest.

Corporate By-Laws. By-laws are the document that defines rights and responsibilities of the different interest holders in the corporation. By-laws are usually approved at the first meeting of the shareholders and directors or they can be approved by a signed unanimous consent. This document is the first place to look to see the rights that majority and minority shareholders have. It explains what shareholder voting percentages are required for different corporate actions. It will specify if the shares are issued subject to sale restrictions. It is fairly common that small private companies issue stock that is not transferable without the approval of all shareholders or of the majority shareholders.

One item to note is if the voting rights described in the agreement or under state law for the board of directors is cumulative voting or straight voting. Straight voting allows a 51% owner to appoint every director, as each director is voted on as a separate election and each shareholder has votes equal to ownership percentage.

Cumulative voting treats the vote for all directors as one election. (For instance, there are three director positions and two shareholders one with 40% and the other with 60% ownership. The three director positions are counted as one vote. So the majority shareholder "wins" two directors seats with 30% and 30% but the minority shareholder can at least win one director seat using the 40% all on one director.) Cumulative voting is thought to protect minority shareholders by better ensuring some representation on the board of directors. The value of this right will then depend on the number of shareholders and size of the share blocks, the number of board members and the requirements for board approvals (i.e., one board member on a board of three where two board votes is an approval may not matter).

Some shares, where there are multiple classes of shares, do not have rights to vote for board members. This is a further restriction. This is fairly rare with small and very small businesses and will not be further addressed here.

Stock Certificates. Stock certificates, if they exist, should be collected. Usually they will specify that they were not registered with the Securities and Exchange Commission (SEC) and that they are not transferable subject to shareholder agreements or corporate documents. Often they are missing or were never officially issued.

Meeting Minutes. Few small and very small companies keep meeting minutes or even unanimous consent documents but major decisions should be approved using these methods at shareholder or director-level meetings. If your clients do not have an annual meeting or a record of unanimous consents for major decisions, you may want to suggest they start documenting those processes as a value added to your clients. In the event of a dispute, proper documentation is very helpful.

Buy-Sell Agreement. A buy-sell agreement is between the shareholders and the corporation and generally specifies terms and conditions for a sale of stock between owners and the company. Often they are quite restrictive. Typically, a buy-sell agreement will specify different terms for the purchase of a shareholder's stock if the shareholder is selling because of choice, death, disability or, termination for the convenience of the company. They also may have non-compete or non-solicit clauses. Sometimes they contain rights of first refusals. In some cases, these documents may provide a price and payment schedule if a shareholder wishes to exit. Sometimes a valuation clause exists in buy-sell agreements. These are often written poorly and can be the source of litigation in itself.[6]

One of the most common clauses requires a value to be agreed to by the shareholders at the beginning of every year. I have yet to see the ownership of small companies reset this value regularly as required in the agreement. But this is a pervasive clause.

Limited Liability Company Operating Agreements

Well-drafted LLC operating agreements act as both by-laws and a shareholder agreement. It is comparably easy to set up different types of interests with different levels of control, cash flow, and tax benefits for each owner, compared to corporate forms. Equity interests can have preferred payouts for investment. Payment ratios can change if goals are not met to better ensure minimum returns (clawback provisions). Equity interests can be non-control so long as goals are met, then become control if goals are not met. Because of this flexibility, limited liability companies are how most small businesses are formed.

Example

A key minority interest owner of 25% is provided with a 60% distribution of the earnings. The earnings share of the cash flow for the "control" owner is 40% in this instance. The minority owner's cash flow has to be taken into account in order to determine the interest value of the two particular ownerships. Terms such as this are quite easy to structure in LLCs and can be quite common.

Employment Agreements, Non-Solicits, and Non-Competes

Sometimes owner-operator partners have further restrictions in their employment agreements that may impact their ability to freely sell their interests. This can include non-solicits, non-competes, and forced sale of stock for various reasons. These may need to be considered when evaluating value as it impacts how freely the stock can be transferred.

Enforceability of the Agreements

Another state law consideration is, are the agreements between the parties enforceable? For instance, in California, non-competes for employees tend to be unenforceable. In many states, while non-competes are enforceable, courts will often go to extremes to find no violation of non-competes for employees or possibly 1% owners with no more rights than employees. In general, most private agreements between interest holders will be enforceable but not always.

A related issue is to ask the question, "Will the company enforce the agreement?" This is particularly an issue in divorce and sometimes in business disputes. Restrictive sale price provisions between partners in small partnerships are often given little weight by courts in divorce. They can also be overridden in some co-owner disputes. If the restrictions and reduction in market price are severe and there is no history of enforcement or uniform enforcement by the company, the court may choose not to apply the restriction and/or specified price. If doing this analysis as part of a lawsuit, be sure to explore these implications with the attorney associated with the case.

Example

> *Start with a dispute between two 50/50 owners of a tech company over a buy-out. The shareholder agreement provided for a "shotgun" type buy-out provision where one partner was to present an offer to buy out the other partner. The other partner then had 90 days to beat or accept the offer. In the specific case the first partner obtained an appraisal and made an offer supported by a bank commitment. The other partner sued in court. The court threw out the offer and ordered each side to obtain an appraisal and begin the state dissolution process. Coincidentally the negotiated settlement was essentially the original offer 12 months later. However, the court refused to enforce what would appear to be a legitimate agreement. In this case it was even reasonably applied (as opposed to a situation with a highly discounted initial offer).[7]*

Therefore, case law is important. Please note not all case law is the same. Typically, the case law from the highest court in the state or the local federal court jurisdiction has the most weight. Then lower court published opinions. Often unpublished opinions (very useful when available for your judge) may offer insights into local jurisdictions.

In some cases, certain courts tend to be influential in certain areas, as they are recognized as dealing with valuation or other issues frequently. The Delaware Court of Chancery, a 100% business court, is looked upon by many courts as an authority on shareholder disputes. The Federal Tax Court for tax matters is another. In the end, as valuators, all we can do is make an informed professional judgment and convert the best available facts and reasonable assumptions into a discount rate or other adjustment. Document your reasoning and ask, "Is this reasonable?"

DISCOUNTS AND PREMIUMS

Discounts and premiums are adjustments in risk and cash flows to account for the interest holder variations that are different from the entity risk and cash flows, and in some cases from the comparable set of companies' risk and cash flows. Comparable set as used here could be either market method comparables or the comparables developed from the buildup method.

> *Fact: Discounts occur in arm's length transactions as a result of an investor's requirement for an increased return.*[8]

Note, the point of discounts is to arrive at an overall rate of return that would be acceptable to an investor or owner based on the interest being valued. Discounts also depend on modeling and are usually comparisons of the subject company with a known sample set. The main discounts affecting smaller businesses will be discussed.

Minority or Lack of Control Discount

This is an adjustment used to estimate the difference in the value of the enterprise which is a control value and the value of an interest holder who does not have "control ownership." Minority ownership due to the lack of control in small and very small businesses tends to be unmarketable and non-liquid. It is very difficult to sell these interests as there is no market.

Example

Father is the 70% majority owner and son is the minority 30% owner. They have worked together for 15 years when the son says he wants to do something else. Dad is angry and refuses to negotiate. Does anyone believe there is a market for the son's 30% interest?

Minority discounts are an issue when the standard of value is fair market value as shown above. Fair market value is the value of the interest to market participants. In the fair value standard, usually enterprise value is divided by the percentages of ownership without regard to control issues. This is usually imposed by statute in an attempt to protect and indemnify minority shareholders from actions taken by the majority that they do not agree with. For instance, the son's 30% interest could have a value at least in litigation with a fair value standard.

It has been suggested by Shannon Pratt that the minority discount can be fully estimated by using an unadjusted cash flow to estimate value.[9] In effect, if the majority owner rarely took excessive salary or benefits and distributed "fairly" to the minority holders, then there was little discount. On the other hand, if a majority owner took a high salary and personal benefits and restricted cash flows to minority holders, then there is a strong case for a large discount. Essentially the same multiplier is applied to the two cash flows to estimate the discount. See an example of calculating the control versus lack of control cash flows in Figure 9.2.

	Estimated Cash Flow	Totals	Selected Multiplier	Estimate of Value	Estimated Discount
Pre-tax Net Profit	$400,000				
Add depreciation & Amortization	$20,000				
Distributable Cash Flow to Minority Shareholder	$420,000	$420,000	2.8	$1,176,000	
Majority Owner Discretionary Add-backs					
Excess Salary	$50,000				
Child at college on payroll	$20,000				
Travel / Conference	$10,000				
	$80,000	$80,000			
Distributable Cash Flow to Majority Shareholder		$500,000	2.8	$1,400,000	16.00%

Notes
Estimated Discount calculated as 1-($1,176,000 / $1,400,000)
Market Multiplier is estimated

FIGURE 9.2 Sample Cash Flow Differences to Estimate Minority Discount

Example

A small strip club was being valued for estate tax purposes. There was no real estate involved. A former stripper inherited a 25% interest from a deceased owner (you can't make this stuff up). The remaining 75% owner was not happy about his new partner. The tax returns showed nominal revenues and a small profit, yet the club was remarkably well maintained. Clearly a cash business. (If there was any doubt, the sign behind the stage said there was a 35% service charge plus 15% tip for all credit card charges.) The majority owner made it clear that the minority partner was NEVER going to see a dime from the ownership interest. There were no buy-sells or other documents in place. Clearly the likely distributable cash flow indicated little value for the minority owner.

This is a reasonable starting point. For larger companies with many shareholders, this may even be a reasonable stopping point. But for small and very small companies it fails to recognize that past treatment of minority shareholders may not be the same as future treatment. This concern about change may be the case where shareholders might remain the same (everyone knows partners who got along for years and suddenly did not) and certainly is within reason where the shareholders may change. Therefore, this analysis should be performed, but it is a first step.

The risks due to the imbalance in the relationships between interest holders as determined still must be reviewed and, where appropriate, further adjusted. If the minority shareholder is getting absolutely nothing under a current cash flow, this review might involve an increase in value (eventually they might sell). But, in many cases it might decrease value beyond the adjustment due to cash flow.

Minority Discounts: Estimating the Discount Beyond Current Cash Flow Risk

The last step is to analyze the restrictions and benefits in order to come up with a reduction in value due to the risk that the cash flow will change in the future. A write up or chart must relate the following points:

- restrictions and benefits from the documents and agreements
  - as impacted by statutes and court cases
  - as impacted by historic actions or inaction (have they uniformly enforced provisions, etc.?)
  - as impacted by possible future change.

The risk to the minority owners as taken into account by the unadjusted cash flow is most pronounced with an "unfair" current owner. (How much worse can it get?) In general, these will require little additional adjustment for minority interest issues. The risk of change in policy with a "fair" current owner needs to be further assessed.

In most cases with private companies, where there is a minority discount, there will also be a marketability discount. The line between minority and marketability discounts can be fuzzy. For this reason, the additional risk to the minority owner beyond that expressed in the cash flow often is addressed in the marketability discount.

DISCOUNT FOR LACK OF MARKETABILITY

The fair market value definition includes the stipulation that payment will be cash or cash equivalences. This is usually interpreted to be cash in three days or less. Clearly it takes time to achieve a full value market sale with small and very small businesses. In good economies it may take six months to a year. In bad economies it may take one or two years. Some cyclical businesses are virtually unsaleable in poor economies.

This gives rise to two main discounts. The liquidity discount, which is the reduction in value due to the time to obtain use of the money and the marketability discount, which is due to the risk from the time involved to find a buyer and to close.

Note, the point of discounts is to arrive at an overall rate of return that would be acceptable to an investor or owner based on the interest being valued. In all cases, the risk of "doubling up" on a risk factor exists. This doubling up could come from factoring the risk both in the discount or capitalization rate and in the further specific discount or by factoring it in both the marketability and minority discount when both apply.

It is essential, once the final value is found, to examine that value in terms of overall rate of return vs. overall risk. If this does not make sense, then the components need to be examined again. Valuation is about finding an acceptable overall rate of return for the investor or other party. Not about how complex our calculations can become.

Liquidity Discount

> The consensus conclusion that we draw is that illiquid investments trade at lower prices than liquid investments and generate higher returns ...[10]

The American Society of Appraisers (ASA) Standards define Discount for Lack of Liquidity as "An amount or percentage deducted from the value of an ownership interest to reflect the relative inability to quickly convert property to cash."

As money moves quicker and quicker, this is becoming less of an issue independent from the marketability discount below. As a practical matter, a three-day clear is defined as being a cash equivalent.[11] Prior to wire transfers being common, it often took a week or more for a check to clear. This was even the case with bank checks and certified funds. Certainly, if the fact pattern does not include wired funds or does include a delay in receiving cash, then a liquidity discount may be in order. These are usually very small, in the 1–3% range, as usually they are based more on time value of money rather than risk-based. If there is a risk of collection, then a larger discount should be used although it probably should be categorized as a collection risk discount or a marketability discount.

Marketability Discount

The adjustment for marketability is based on both the time value of money and the risk that the value will decrease or even disappear. The Business Valuation Glossary definition of marketability is "The ability to quickly convert property to cash at minimal cost." The computation for the discount for lack of marketability (DLOM) is very simple, as shown in Figure 9.3. Justifying the selected discount is much more work.

Note that generally a discount for lack of marketability is applied to a minority interest. (Also note, when both discounts are present, the minority interest discount is taken first. In addition, the discounts are multiplicative, not additive so they would never be added together.) While controversial and sometimes not provided for in state law, it can be applied to controlling interest.[12] As stated in the IRS Job Aid, "The controlling interest holder may not be able to sell the interest quickly or with certainty as to the ultimate sales price."[13]

In many ways this discount for marketability is magnified with small and very small businesses. Small and very small businesses tend to have limited product offerings in limited geographic markets. This means situations beyond their control can very quickly cause a large loss of value. Examples of situations that can quickly cause a loss of value are loss of major clients, owner illness, the calling of a line of credit, supplier or vender loss, dispute, or disruption, loss of franchise or license agreement and the like. While all of these items are foreseeable in the aggregate, they usually are not foreseeable during day-to-day operations. This is an issue for a valuation as of a specific date.

Indicated Value	$1,000,000
DLOM Percentage	30.00%
DLOM	$300,000
Value Found	$700,000

FIGURE 8.3 Calculation of Discount for Lack of Marketability

What may happen over a reasonable amount of time after the valuation date? No one has a crystal ball.

One of the hardest issues is that sometimes the risks are all-or-nothing situations. A company with essentially one contract (and few easy replacements) that can be terminated at will, probably would justify a large discount for value. Yet it may have a high cash flow that continues for a long time (or ends tomorrow).

Example

An example is a business valuation for divorce where the business owner spouse has had a contract with a local school system for over five years that brings in $2,000,000 of annual revenues. SDE is $500,000. Yet the contract is at the will of the school administration. Just to add to the complexity, it was in a jurisdiction where the school administration tended to change every two or three years. (This could be factored into the discount or capitalization rate, or a separate concentration discount or a marketability discount for the entity.)[14]

Fact patterns such as in the Example above require additional background, experience, and professional judgment. Be careful not to double-count the risk in both the discount or capitalization rate and the discount for lack of marketability. For clarity, put the defined risk (for instance, concentration risk) all in one place and clearly specify how you are treating the adjustment. If you must break the risk up and put it in a few places, clearly explain why and how you are not double counting.

Remember, valuation is comparing a subject company or interest to a comparison set. If there is a risk to the cash flow of the subject company beyond the comparison set, then an adjustment should be made.

The review here is going to be specifically for small and very small business. If larger businesses are being valued for estate or gift tax, for example, a more detailed analysis and review should be applied.

Currently the primary methods used to estimate the discount for marketability are:

- **Quantitative Approaches.** These use databases and data to attempt to quantify the discount for lack of marketability (DLOM). Quantitative means measuring by quantity or amount.[15] Typically, when valuing larger businesses, business ratios and data can be used as a comparison to the database dataset. Quantitative approaches provide a framework to compare the subject company to the databases.[16]
- **Option Pricing Models.** For example, Longstaff, Finnerty, and Chaffe. These each attempt to "model" the discount based on statistics and available option pricing formulas.[17]
- **Qualitative Methods.** Most small businesses are not going to have meaningful detailed quantitative data for comparison. Qualitative means relating to, or involving quality or kind.[18] Therefore, the situation along with relevant numbers is reviewed. Qualitative methods are further covered next as the primary means for estimating a discount for lack of marketability appropriate for small and very small businesses.

Qualitative Methods

Most small and very small businesses are not going to have the quantitative data internally to properly compare to larger company data. The theories are the same but the data cannot be proven to apply based on ratio analysis and other financial measures. For this reason, for most valuations of smaller businesses, qualitative approaches are likely to be sufficient.

Qualitative methods include:

- benchmark restricted stock discount studies
- pre-IPO Discount Studies

- Mandelbaum factors
- the acquisition method
- IRS DLOM Job Aid factors.

The most supported methods for determining the discount for lack of marketability as of the time of publication for small and very small businesses will be further reviewed below.

Restricted Stock Studies

Restricted stock studies adjusted by Mandelbaum-type[19] factor analysis are probably the most frequently used methods and are suitable for small and very small business valuations. We will briefly review those along with the adjustment factors suggested in the IRS Job Aid here.[20]

Restricted stock studies are studies of publicly traded shares that are restricted from public resale. This is due to Rule 144 which provides a safe harbor rule from public company registration requirements for restricted stock. The restricted stock has a minimum holding period before it can be sold on public markets. Those minimum holding periods have been getting shorter. From 1972 to 1997, the holding period was two years. From 1997 to 2008, the holding period was one year. Currently the holding period is at least six months for reporting public companies and at least one year for companies not subject to reporting requirements of the SEC Act of 1934.[21]

Many studies have been performed since the original study by the SEC in the 1970s. Many of the most important ones are shown in Figure 9.4. One of the concerns about using restricted stock studies is that the discounts reflect more than just the discount for marketability. These other factors may include monitoring costs of the investment, assessment of true value of stock vs. a discount at all, and other factors. These and other factors may or may not apply to the company being valued. Note the range of discounts found in the various studies are far more varied than the mean and medians might indicate.

In Figure 9.4, the median discounts in the Studies range from 9 percent to 45 percent. Looking at the FMV Opinions (769 transaction) data the Mean is 19.33% and the Median is 15.05%. Presumably small nonmarketable discounts will be higher. But, these figures can be used as a starting point. The discount would then be increased or decreased based on how risky the interest being valued is compared to typical securities in the studies.

IRS Job Aid Factors

One should incorporate the above starting point into account when using the IRS Job Aid and Mandelbaum-type factors to adjust the data. IRS Job Aid Factors (IRS Discount for Lack of Marketability Job Aid for IRS Valuation Professionals, August 2011) is a job aid, or guide developed for use by IRS engineers to use when preparing or reviewing valuations involving discounts for lack of marketability.

The IRS Job Aid specifies factors the IRS considers as impacting the DLOM. It describes many methods and the pros and cons for each method based on the IRS review. This Job Aid certainly should be read before preparing a discount for IRS use. It is recommended reading before estimating any DLOM.[22]

Subject company factors

- value of company private securities vs. publicly traded securities
- dividend-paying (or distribution) ability and history
- dividend yield
- attractiveness of subject business
- attractiveness of subject industry
- prospect for a sale or public offering of company
- number of identifiable buyers

Study	Period of Study	Transactions	Discount for Lack of Marketability	
			Mean	Median
Securities Exchange Commission	1966 – 1969	398	25.80%	n.a.
Gelman	1968 – 1970	89	33.00%	33.00%
Trout	1968 – 1972	60	33.45%	n.a.
Maher				
All Transactions	1969 – 1973	34	35.40%	33.30%
Adjusted Transactions	1969 – 1973	28	34.70%	33.30%
Moroney	1969 – 1972a	146	35.60%	33.00%
Arneson	Opinionb	n.a.	n.a.	50% or greater
Stryker and Pittock	1978 – 1982	28	n.a.	45.00%
Wruck				
Unregistered	1979 – 1985	37	13.50%	12.20%
Registered	1979 – 1985	36	−4.10%	1.80%
Barclay et al	1979 – 1997	594	18.70%	17.40%
Hall and Polacek (FMV Opinions Study)	1979 – 1992	Over 100	23.00%	n.a.
Hertzel and Smith	1980 – 1987	106	20.14%	13.25%
Management Planning, Inc. (Original)				
All Transactions	1980 – 1996	231	29%	28%
Shares excluding Registration Rights	1980 – 1996	53	27%	25%
Shares with Registration Rights	1980 – 1996	27	12.80%	9.10%
Management Planning, Inc. (Update)	1980 – 2000	259	27.40%	24.80%
FMV Opinions, Inc.	1980 – 1997	243	22.10%	20.10%
Silber	1981 – 1988	69	33.75%	n.a.
Willamette	1981 – 1984	33	n.a.	31.20%
Bajaj, et al.	1990 – 1995	88	22.00%	21.00%
Hall and Polacek (FMV Opinions Study)	1991 – 1992	17	21.00%	n.a.
Johnson Study	1991 – 1995	72	n.a.	20.20%
Columbia Financial Advisors Inc.	1996 – 1997	23	21.00%	14.00%
Columbia Financial Advisors, Inc.	1997 – 1998	15	13.00%	9.00%
Management Planning, Inc. (Update)				
All Transactions	2000 – 2007	1,600	14.60%	n.a.
Registered Shares	2000 – 2007	100	9.50%	n.a.
Unregistered Shares	2000 – 2007	200	18.70%	n.a.
Management Planning, Inc. (Update)				
All Transactions	1980 – 2009	1,863	15.90%	13.30%
Registered Shares	1980 – 2009	203	8.70%	n.a.
Unregistered Shares	1980 – 2009	402	22.10%	19.60%
Other Shares (w/Reg.Rights)	1980 – 2009	1258	15.00%	n.a.
Pluris Valuation Advisors (LiquiStat)	2005 – 2006	61	32.80%	34.60%
SRR	2005 – 2010	98	10.90%	9.30%
Trugman Valuation Associates, Inc.	2007 – 2008	80	18.10%	14.40%
Trugman Valuation Associates, Inc.	2007 – 2010	136	16.60%	14.30%
FMV Opinions, Inc.				
All Transactions	1980 – 2015	769	19.33%	15.05%
Transactions Excluding Premiums	1980 – 2015	727	20.97%	16.11%

Source: J. R. Hitchner, R. J. Alerding, J. B. Angell, and K. E. Morris (2017). *Discount for Lack of Marketability Guide and Toolkit*. Ventnor City, NJ: VPS, pp. 137–139. Reproduced with permission from Valuation Products and Services, LLC, Ventnor City, NJ.

FIGURE 9.4 Summary of Restricted Stock Studies

- attributes of controlling shareholder, if any
- availability of access to information or reliability of that information
- management
- earnings levels
- revenues levels
- book-to-market value ratios
- information requirements
- ownership concentration effects
- financial condition
- percent of shares held by insiders
- percent of shares held by institutions
- percent of independent directors
- listing on a major exchange
- active versus passive investors
- registration costs
- availability of hedging opportunities
- market capitalization rank
- business risk.

Subject interest factors
- restrictive transfer provisions
- length of the restriction period
- length of expected holding period
- offering size as a percentage of total shares outstanding
- registered versus unregistered
- general economic conditions
- prevailing stock market conditions
- volatility of stock.

Any applicable Job Aid Factor can be underwritten and placed in a chart or analysis such as described below in Mandelbaum. Remember, the analysis could be used to analyze both how the interest is different from the overall entity risk and how the assessed risk varies from the comparison set used to estimate an adjustment.

Mandelbaum-Type Factors Analysis

Judge Laro in *Bernard Mandelbaum, et al. v. Commissioner*, TC Memo 1995-255 rejected the IRS and the taxpayer's experts and developed a ten-factor adjustment process to estimate the discount for lack of marketability. The ten factors with excerpts from the IRS DLOM Job Aid, p. 28 are:

1. Private vs. public sales of stock—review of the restricted stock studies can serve as an important reference
2. Financial statement analysis—historical and projected trends, profitability, leverage, distributions, liquidity, volatility, and other measures
3. Company's dividend policy—distributions are preferred as they provide capital recovery
4. Nature of the company—positive results attract investors
5. Company management—intangibles such as systems, management, and how they contribute to financial success
6. Amount of control in transferred shares—control reduces risk
7. Restrictions on transferability of stock—specific clauses that increase discounts include:
   - Rights of first refusal that tend to reduce third party interest and offers
   - Transferee limitations reducing or eliminating potential buyers
8. Holding period for stock—for non-marketable securities, the unpredictable and likely substantial time to liquidate is a substantial negative
9. Company's redemption policy—put rights or an expected monetization event reduce risk
10. Costs associated with making a public offering—even marketable securities can be impacted by severe liquidity discounts during bear markets.

Mandelbaum Factors	Comments	Increase	Neutral	Decrease
History and Outlook Business and Industry,				
Financial Factors, Revenues, Earnings, ratios,				
Management				
Holding Period				
Redemption Policy				
Transfer of Control				
Restrictions on Transfer				
Cash Distribution Policy				
Competitive Position/ Nature of Industry, Risk Growth Rate				
Cost of Public Offering				
Other Tax Court Factors				
No of Potential Buyers				
Size of Business				
Volume of Comparable Private Transactions				
Restrictions on Transfer				
Dividend History and Yield				
Share concentrations, Size of Block of Stock				
Attributes of Controlling Shareholder, Shareholder Relations				

FIGURE 9.5 Sample Mandelbaum Analysis Chart

Figure 9.5 is an example of one type of Mandelbaum analysis chart. Note that each factor is presented with an overall impact (increase, decrease of the discount) and an explanation. It is a useful example and model. Each analyst may choose to expand or contract the chart based on both Mandelbaum and Job Aid factors as they gain experience and confidence in their methodologies. A working Word file of this template is included on the website. Finally, the Sample Conclusion of Value report available at the website demonstrates one way to apply these concepts in a report.

A final way to look at these same factors is to consider the following:

- number of shareholders
- concentration of control owner
- number of potential buyers
- access to capital markets
- size of the business
- desirability of the business
- existence of non-compete agreements
- existence of key employee contracts
- divergence of owners' business philosophy
- yield (high profitability)
- volatility of assets
- liquidity of control owners
- size of subject block
- quality and competence of management
- existence and impact of impending litigation
- investor required holding period
- secondary market liquidity
- multiple classes of stock.

Other Discounts

Remember that the point of discounts is to adjust risk for things related to the interest being valued that are not well represented in the model and comparable cash flow. These adjustments can be taken when calculating the discount or capitalization rate or as a separate discount. In general, if the discount is very small, for example, 5–10% of the overall rate, it probably makes sense to make it part of the specific company adjustment. If the adjustment becomes significant, say, 10–50%, for clarity, it makes sense to show it as a separate discount.

Table 9.1 is a summary of a presentation that Lance Hall developed that shows the breadth of situations that can occur and provide a rationale for a discount in the business valuation estimate.

TABLE 8.1 Lance Hall's Discounts Chart

Key Person Risk
Personal Goodwill
The Mafia Discount
Non-Homogeneous Property Discount
The Corporate Form Discount
The Emotional Discount
The Uncertainty Discount
The Williamson Act Discount
The Lack of Full Control Discount
 The Prior Court Decisions Discount
The Swing Vote Premium
The Influence Premium
The Assignee Discount
The Right of First Refusal Discount
The Tiered Discount

Source: L. S. Hall (2016). "Gift and estate tax valuation: discounts, discounts, discounts." ASA, Jan./Feb.

An example of a situation where other discounts may apply to small and very small businesses is customer concentration, if the companies in the comparable sample did not have this characteristic. Or, dealing with likely fair market value when the sample may have a large number of earn-out transactions like the sale of accounting firms. Or, a professional practice like a dental practice, when there are possible eminent health issues preventing the provision of services and a smooth transfer. These discounts are likely to be completely justified depending on the fact pattern.

Control Premium

There is a good amount of controversy over whether a control premium actually exists above public stock prices and the related buildup methods used for the discount for marketability.[23] For larger companies, it is an area that is currently disputed though synergies and similar situations with undervalued assets can be considered a control premium and those do exist (see Figure 9.1 on p. 221). In some regards, the question is, is that really a control premium or, at least in the case of undervalued assets, just a case of mispricing?

For small and very small businesses, in limited cases where a small block of stock being transferred will create a new control owner there certainly may be a premium paid on a per share basis in that situation. In theory, the analyst can use the likely cash flow benefits to the new control owner and use a multiplier or discount it back to estimate the maximum that could be paid.[24] Usually only a fraction of that is paid.

Final Thoughts on Discounts

The purpose of a discount is to fully factor adjustments between the interest in the subject company and the comparables that are not fully accounted for elsewhere in the valuation model. Discounts are even more justified with small and very small companies due to the high levels of risk because of owner relationships, limited customers, limited suppliers, small geographic market, limited management depth, etc. These concentrations create volatility and risk that do not exist with larger companies and often are not fully accounted for in market data, capitalization rates, and discount rates.

It is important to tie the subject company risk into the best data available. Usually there is no perfect or even good data. At that point, a logical weighting and explanation of the factors are the best that can be done to show the process. Common sense and professional judgment greatly matter in these areas.

Be careful that you do not double-count the risk in two or more places in the valuation. Remember to use a commonsense approach to verify that the ultimate value found produces a reasonable return for the true risk at hand. One final check is to step back and ask, would you or anyone reasonably pay the value found for the interest being valued? The Art of Business Valuation is making sure reasonableness and common sense prevail.

NOTES

1. Because valuing options and debt is quite rare with very small businesses, it is not addressed here.
2. Z. Christopher Mercer and Travis W. Harms, *Business Valuation: An Integrated Theory*, 2nd ed. (Hoboken, NJ: Wiley, 2008).
3. Also *see* S. Pratt, R. F. Reilly, and R. P. Schweihs, *Valuing a Business*, 4th ed.n (New York: McGraw-Hill, 2000), pp. 347–348.
4. Depending on the specific state statute, number of owners, elections of the owners under the statue, and other considerations the control owner has reduced authority and/or there may be no control owner or marketable control owner in those cases. For example, *see* MD-CODE TITLE 4 – CLOSE CORPORATIONS.
5. MD Code Ann. Corporations and Associations article, section 3-202 et. deq. : Section 3-210 Court to appoint 3 appraisers; Section 3-211 Court order based on appraisers' valuation; Section 4-602 Close corporation petition for dissolution; Section 4-603 Right to avoid dissolution and pay fair value.
6. Chris Mercer has written extensively on buy-sell agreements, including how valuation clauses should be written. *See* http://www.buysellagreementsonline.com/
7. This was a case that reached settlement in lower court. There is no cite.
8. S. Pratt, *Valuing a Business: The Analysis and Appraisal of Closely Held Companies*, 5th edition (New York: McGraw-Hill, Inc., 2008), p. 228.
9. Bruce Johnson, Partnership Profiles, NACVA AVW Presentation, May 2019.
10. Aswath Damodaran, New York University, Stern School of Business.
11. J. R. Hitchner, *Discount for Lack of Marketability Guide and Toolkit* (Ventnor, NJ: VPS, 2017), p. 2.
12. S. Pratt, *Business Valuation Discounts and Premiums* (New York: John Wiley & Sons, 2001), p. 167.
13. *See* IRS Job Aid, pp. 8 and 9.
14. As an aside, in this case the valuator got off easy as the contract was lost before the valuation report was to be submitted.

15. "Quantitative" in Merriam Webster dictionary, *see* https://www.merriam-webster.com/dictionary/quantitative

16. The following are some resources for quantitative approaches: Stouts FMV Restricted Stock Study. The Stouts data can be used independently or Stouts has a system to sort the data to create "comparables" based on indicators of the marketability discount. *See* https://www.bvresources.com/products/the-stout-restricted-stock-study; Pluris DLOM Database, *see* http://www.pluris.com/pluris-dlom-database; Valuation Advisors Lack of Marketability Discount Study (pre-IPO), *see* https://www.bvresources.com/products/valuation-advisors-lack-of-marketability-study; J. R. Hitchner, R. J. Alerding, J. B. Angell, and K. E. Morris, "Discount for Lack of Marketability, Guide and Toolkit," May 2017, *see* https://www.bvresources.com/products/discount-for-lack-of-marketability-guide-and-toolkit

17. The following are some resources on Option Pricing Models: https://www.valuationproducts.com/wp-content/uploads/2018/06/FVLE-Issue-32_Duffy.pdf; the following article contains an easy to use table, *see* https://www.withum.com/resources/discount-lack-marketability-finnerty-model/; the IRS Job Aid on DLOMs has citations for Longstaff and Chaffe, *see* https://www.irs.gov/pub/irs-utl/dlom.pdf. These all require an estimate of volatility. An easy-to-use public company volatility calculator is found in https://www.fintools.com/resources/online-calculators/volatilitycalc/

18. "Qualitative," in Merriam Webster dictionary, *see* https://www.merriam-webster.com/dictionary/qualitative

19. *Mandelbaum, et al. v. Commissioner*, TC Memo 1995-255.

20. *See* https://www.irs.gov/pub/irs-utl/dlom.pdf

21. For a history of Rule 144, *see* J. Hitchner, *Discounts for Lack of Marketability* (Portland, OR: BVR, 2017), starting at p. 34.

22. In addition, For working with the IRS *see* "Business Valuations and the IRS" Michael A. Gregory, 2018, Birch Grove Publishing.

23. *See* E. W. Nath, "Control Premiums and Minority Interest Discounts in Private Companies," *BV Review*, June 1990, for a very good summary of the lack of control premiums in public company guideline data.

24. Pratt, *Valuing a Business*, 5th ed,, p. 228.

CHAPTER 10

Goodwill and the Small Business

In small and very small business valuation, goodwill is often used as the general classification for all intangible assets. Calculating goodwill is fairly straightforward. Goodwill is the residual when subtracting all physical assets value from the total business value. Goodwill in its broadest sense is the value attributed to all business assets and activities other than the physical assets.

There are many potential classifications of intangible assets. These include licenses, intellectual property, such as patents, copyrights, trademarks, trade secrets, and the like. There are intangible assets associated with the customer list and relationships with suppliers, contractors, and the like. These can all be broken down and estimated. The Generally Accepted Accounting Principles (GAAP) require this for larger companies but these estimates are rarely if ever done for small and very small businesses. With small and very small businesses, intangible assets are not further broken down except when there are reasons to determine personal goodwill and company goodwill.

In many jurisdictions for divorce, and in some federal tax matters including when C corporations are sold in asset sales, and for estate and gift tax, personal goodwill can be very important to determine.

In many states, in divorce, personal goodwill is a personal asset and not part of the marital estate. For federal tax purposes, if a C corporation is being sold in an asset sale, double taxation can provide an onerous burden and leaves little after-tax profit for the shareholder owner.[1] But, if personal goodwill exists, the owner can sell his or her personal goodwill directly to the buyer and that portion of the transaction will avoid double taxation.[2] There are also interesting planning situations that can arise in estate planning but that rarely comes up with small and very small businesses and will not be covered here.[3]

Many state courts have very different definitions of personal goodwill from those of other states and the IRS or Tax Court. In some cases, there is no consistent definition within a jurisdiction. Always make an attempt to understand the definition being used by your user and if it is applied consistently.

Small and very small businesses tend to have owner operators running the business. Therefore, there often is goodwill associated with the business and additional goodwill associated with the owner. Because the owner and the business are somewhat indistinguishable to customers, suppliers and the like, some of the value of personal goodwill can show up in the business value.

A few situations where business goodwill value and owner personal goodwill value may be lumped together as goodwill are:

- If the owner operator is well known by the suppliers and customers and people work with the company because of the owner.
- Sometimes the owner operator's name is part of the business name.
- In professional situations, such as medical centers, perhaps people only want "that" surgeon not the associates.
- Artists and high creatives may be desired like the surgeon, for their personal talents that do not pass to others well.

These are all situations that indicate personal goodwill may be present.

There are three categories of personal goodwill:[4]

1. **"Pure" Personal Goodwill.** This is goodwill completely owned by the owner. This cannot be conveyed under any conditions. In a properly prepared business valuation, it will not be shown other than perhaps with a value to the holder standard as it cannot be conveyed. If it cannot be conveyed and turned into future cash flow by a buyer, then under most standards it does not exist as business value. Because the past is usually looked at to estimate the future, the cash flows may not be properly adjusted to remove the "personal component" of the cash flow.[5] So, there can be disputes about this value existing in a business valuation that must be countered but, in reality, if it is shown, it is an error as it does not exist as business value.

2. **Transferable or Conveyable Personal Goodwill.** Most personal goodwill qualifies under this category. It can be conveyed with proper non-compete clauses and perhaps a transition plan. Of course, the asset value is likely to be lost by the business if the owner chooses to compete or walks off and does not properly transition the business. For many businesses these transitions can be as short as a few weeks and in some personal service businesses, it can take two or three years. To restate this concept, people like buying from me but will happily buy from you if you can meet my price, terms and service level. A second version is the owner has a "special process" that needs to be (and can be for a reasonable cost) taught. This personal goodwill really exists but will often be shown as company goodwill. It really comes down to who owns the goodwill (do they think they are calling the owner or the business?) as opposed to how hard this is to convey.

3. **Entity Goodwill.** Entity goodwill is true business goodwill. No one really cares who the owner of a local McDonald's is (except perhaps the owner). Suppliers and customers are relying on the corporate franchise and the local managers and employees to take care of them. This is entity or corporate goodwill. If the business changes hands (and in this case keeps the franchise rights), there will be no impact because of the name, personality, or relationships or the like of the owner. The owner of a McDonald's franchise does not have personal goodwill.

A few "real-world" facts about personal goodwill. Most people, including clients, suppliers, employees and the like, are creatures of habit and a little lazy. They tend to go back if nothing was wrong. Therefore, some professional services that are required every day or year, such as bookkeeping, audit, and tax accounting, have high personal goodwill but it is transitional goodwill. Many traditional small businesses also have transitional goodwill. Remember the lead case "Martin Ice Cream" (cited below) was an ice cream distribution company.

Artistic-type businesses, such as architects, interior designers, advertising, that are subject to trend and style, still often have strong personal goodwill. This is particularly the case with smaller companies that only have one principal or maybe two, each of whom have their own following. There are often very few comparables for these types of firms in market data, again demonstrating that they are difficult to sell.

In medicine, small office general practitioners have little or no transferable personal goodwill anymore. Some people find primary care doctors through insurance lists, others through clinics and may change affiliations based on insurance. A few really highly ranked specialists have personal goodwill but this is true personal goodwill with little market value. Even where this does exist, the hospital system referral networks along with insurance have removed a lot of personal goodwill in the space.

CALCULATING GOODWILL

There are many tests for personal goodwill. Most valuators look at a range of indicators and use a chart format to create a weighting mechanism and then apply judgment to determine the ratio of company goodwill to personal goodwill. Similar to discounts for lack of marketability, the calculations are simple. Justifying the selected discount takes work and professional judgment. A typical calculation is shown in Figure 10.1. Typical indicators are discussed next.

Business Size and Systemization

- **Personal.** Small entrepreneurial business are highly dependent on employee-owner's personal skills and relationships. All decisions get attributed to the owner, employees do not have authority (or will) to make decisions. There may be quite a few employees but most are ministerial.
- **Institutional.** Larger business which have formalized their organizational structures and institutionalized systems and controls. Indicators are many employees with clearly defined tasks. Employee handbooks, job descriptions, defined, somewhat stable teams. Reporting systems and standards. Forecasts, budgets, along with accountability review. Decisions and customer contacts are pushed lower in the organization.

Total Indicated Value	$424,200
Tangible Asset Value, going concern	$132,400
Goodwill - Intangible Asset Value	$291,800
Personal Goodwill Percentage	60.00
Personal Goodwill	$175,080
Personal Goodwill (Rounded)	$175,100

FIGURE 10.1 Personal Goodwill Calculation

Non-Compete and Other Agreements

- **Personal.** There are no pre-existing non-compete and/or employment agreement between the company and the employee-owner.
- **Institutional.** The owner-employee has pre-existing non-compete and/or employment agreement with the company.

For IRS purposes, this has been held by the courts to be a complete bar to personal goodwill. "You cannot sell what you do not own. If you conveyed it, you do not own it."[6] Rulings are more likely to vary with state courts of equity such as divorce or even partnership and shareholder type disputes. The state case law is likely to be very fact dependent. Check your state law precedent.

Personal Service

- **Personal.** Personal service is an important selling feature in the company's product or services. The fact that the owner will be overseeing or managing or performing the service is viewed as comforting and helpful. Artists, designers, architects, Certified Public Accountants with known specialties, lawyers, medical doctors, particularly specialists, and so forth. Personal services denote personal goodwill.
- **Institutional.** The business is not heavily dependent on anyone's or any group's personal services.

Capital Investment

- **Personal.** There is no significant capital investment in either tangible or identifiable intangible assets.
- **Institutional.** The business has significant capital investments in either tangible or identifiable intangible assets. High capital investment indicates that financial resources and deployed capital in the form of plant, equipment, vehicles, and the like are necessary and create value more than any one person.

Ownership

- **Personal.** Only employee-owners own the company. Often owner-operators have their own practices, customer bases, or specialties.
- **Institutional.** The company has more than one owner, some of whom are not employees. Again, this is an attribute of larger organized companies.

Sales Relationships

- **Personal.** Sales largely depend on the employee-owner's personal relationships with customers. A high percentage of customers or the larger customers are still "sold" by or loyal to the owner, not the business.
- **Institutional.** Company sales result from name recognition, sales force, sales contracts, and other company-owned intangibles. This is similar to an auto dealership where the owner usually has no direct customer involvement.

Company Knowledge

- **Personal.** Product and/or services knowhow, and supplier relationships rest primarily with the employee owner.
- **Institutional.** The company has supplier contracts and formalized production methods, patents, copyrights, business systems, and so forth. While the owner may have intimate knowledge of this, the knowledge is well dispersed through the proper departments and parts of the company.

Based on the judgment of *Martin Ice Cream vs. Commissioner, 110 T.C. 189 (1998)*, the finding of personal goodwill does not require an even application of the above tests or any other test. It is generally viewed that if the attribute is strong enough, such as the ability to take the customer base, that will prevail, even if other factors indicate an institutional goodwill

Personal Goodwill	Comments	Personal	Neutral	Institutional
Business Size				
Entrepreneurial				
Owners' Involvement				
Other management				
Decision-making is delegated				
Written systems				
Non-compete and other agreements				
Employment Agreements				
Non-compete				
Non-solicit				
Personal Service				
Is this a high trust or high creative type service?				
Capital Investment				
Volume of comparable private transactions				
Restrictions on transfer				
Dividend history and yield				
Share concentrations, Size of block of stock				
Attributes of controlling shareholder, shareholder relations				

FIGURE 10.2 Potential Goodwill Factors

situation. This should apply in any case where an owner has relationships with suppliers or customers or other group that could cause serious damage to the existing company.

Figure 10.2 provides a chart that is a useful format for presenting personal goodwill considerations and weightings.

MUM METHOD FOR GOODWILL

Another commonly used method is the MUM or multi-attribute utility model.[7] This is a methodology that attempts (the factors and analysis *remain subjective*) to add some standardization and quantification to the process. It is extremely detailed. In fact, some analysts are reported to be using a simplified model due to the "illusion of precision" when using MUM.

Again, the valuator must still choose the ranking for each item. The rankings are still based on professional judgment. The other problem with the method is a few attributes may carry significantly more weight than other attributes. This is hard to account for in a pre-determined matrix as there is no completely satisfactory quantifiable way to estimate entity vs. personal goodwill.

Brainteaser

Multiple partners. An interesting aside is how to deal with the personal goodwill of multiple partners? Certainly if your spouse cannot own your goodwill, how can you own your partners' goodwill? When does a high goodwill firm such as an architecture firm or law firm have anything beyond personal goodwill?

This may be most difficult in law firms. In law firms, lawyers and/or the firms they work for, cannot have non-compete clauses as it is against professional ethics. In addition, there are many conflicts of interest problems which can limit work as firms grow. This does present some very interesting problems.

NOTES

1. While this problem has been moderated for Federal taxes with the TCJA, state taxes can still present a major issue, particularly in high state tax jurisdictions.
2. *Martin Ice Cream Co. v Commissioner*, 110 T.C. 189 (1998); *see also H & M Inc. v. Commissioner, T.C. Memo. 2012-290.*

3. *Estate of Adell v. Commissioner*, T.C. Memo 2014-155 and *Bross Trucking v. Commissioner*, T.C. Memo 2014 – 107.
4. For more information, *see* "How to Determine, Support, and Testify on Personal Goodwill in Divorce" webinar presented by Jim Alerding, CPA/ABA, ASA, CVA and Harold G. Martin, Jr., CPA/ABV/CFF, ASA, CFE in the VPS Straight Talk Series, January 31, 2012, p. 29 of presentation materials.
5. The adjustment can also be in the multiplier. Presumably if similar sale transactions can be identified, they would have a reduced multiplier to adjust for likely reductions in future cash flow.
6. Howard No. 10-35768 (9th Cir. 8/29/11)
7. *See* https://www.valusource.com/wp-content/uploads/2016/11/MUM_Sample.pdf

Accounting Issues with Small and Very Small Businesses

One of the major differences between larger business and smaller businesses is the quality of the financial information available to management and valuators. Small businesses, as a rule, have poor quality financial and management information. Many small business owners and managers manage by walking around. They are in the middle of every decision. Therefore, they are relying on direct observation instead of reports that summarized other people's observations. Of course, when it is time to value a business, the valuator does not have the ability to directly observe matters on a continuing basis. This is why many small businesses can be run well yet have few proper reports. This lack of reporting creates many difficulties for valuators. Some of the difficulties and starting points for solutions are discussed below.

CASH, ACCRUAL, AND TAX BASIS STATEMENTS

Accounting statements and records are kept in many formats or methods. Each method has its advantages and disadvantages.

One of the most important principles of accounting is consistency. The theory is that if accounting is not performed consistently, the data will not be valid and useful. Consistency starts

with the basis of accounting used. Consistency is very important in the application of cut-offs between accounting periods.
Consistency applies to coding the same expense to the same category every year. (Yes, one client did code rent over a two-year
period as: mortgage payment, lease, rent, and building—figure
that one out.)

Cash basis and accrual basis are the major bases of accounting. Another hybrid method, tax basis, is also used frequently as
tax returns are often used for small business valuation. Finally,
GAAP or Generally Accepted Accounting Principles is a very
formalized accrual basis that is used by medium-sized and larger
companies in the United States.

Each basis has advantages and disadvantages for valuation
work. Below each basis is discussed.

Cash Basis

Cash statements are tied directly to the checkbook. If cash is
received or spent, it is recorded. Revenues are recognized when
goods sold are paid for by customers. Expenses are recorded
when they are paid by the business. Receivables and payables
are ignored and in its most pure form not even shown on the
balance sheet. Again, in extreme cases, inventory is an expense
when paid.[1] Typically equipment is recorded as capital assets
and depreciated. Loans are placed on the books as liabilities.
For small businesses with poorly trained bookkeepers, do check
if the loan principal is being expensed as part of the loan payment. This is an error even for cash basis accounting.

Some analysts believe the cash basis or at least the ability
to generate cash is the proper way to measure value. After all,
cash available or distributed to investors and shareholders is
viewed as the truest measure of earnings power and investor
return. Yet, accounting periods are artificial. They involve
cut-offs. Those cut-offs are necessary for reporting but do
not really exist in time. Because we are working with defined
periods and fairly short terms for small businesses, getting

cut-off procedures correct is important for comparability. The lack of good cut-offs between periods is the major problem with cash basis accounting.

Cash basis is very simple. But simple is not always useful. For small restaurants and consumer service businesses that tend to be paid when service is provided and that do not have extensive inventory, cash basis can work quite well and provide credible measurement. For businesses with inventory or large receivables, cash basis can become quite misleading and difficult to compare results over time.

For instance, a company with a large inventory that has been expensed when purchased (therefor no inventory is shown on the balance sheet but it sits in the warehouse) may show no profit in the year that it buys large amounts of inventory. Yet it now owns a valuable asset in the inventory. Assuming the inventory is sold and NO new inventory is purchased, the company should be highly profitable the next year. Unfortunately, neither year's results are particularly useful. The first one's profits is understated and second one's profit is overstated.

The same thing happens with receivables. Many companies that provide goods or services to large companies do not get paid for 60 days or so. As the company is growing, these receivables consume all extra cash and on a cash basis reduce profit. If the company stabilizes or contracts and the receivables are paid, the company will show a high profit for a while.

Therefore, many cash basis companies can actually appear more profitable on their financial records even as they contract. This is not what is actually happening but because of the accounting method combined with short cut-offs, that is what the statements will indicate. The cash is being generated by assets being depleted – not from new earnings.

Example

During the severe recession beginning around 2008, many small construction subcontractors using a cash basis had several good years, according to their books and records. They were collecting old receivables which was shown as new revenues and profits under the cash basis. (The work had been paid for when performed years ago in some cases.) But, when they actually started growing again in 2013 they did not have cash remaining to re-invest in their client receivables and went out of business.

There are several ways to work with cash basis companies that have these issues. The first is by obtaining five years' data. Often the problems with cash basis will average out over time. Cut-offs are often the main issue. A one-year period is an accounting concept and cash basis does not address cut-offs. At the end of the year or other period, if checks are held to lower revenues and taxes, this will tend to average out over time. Namely, if $100,000 of checks are held at year end, the first year revenues are $100,000 lower. If the same amount is withheld, the second year revenues would be correct. If the company had a "bad" third year and did not withhold the $100,000 of checks at year end, then the company now overstated revenues by $100,000. While two of the three years could be materially inaccurate for valuation purposes, the average of the three or better yet five is likely to be reasonable.

Figure 11.1 is an example of averaging out cash basis financial information over a period of time. The information is further used to develop an estimate of current, year-end earnings. A common size income statement is used to better view the situation over time. In the case below, the averages look reflective of the future but that may not always be the case.

Another way to review cash basis statements when looking to adjust somewhat consistent intentional timing matters is to obtain the twelve months data for the year by month with a total column. This is an easy download in QuickBooks. It makes it easy to see the types of games cash basis taxpayers often play such as reducing income and increasing expenses at year-end. (Compare all months and particularly December and January for revenues and expenses.) Figure 11.2 is condensed, showing

	Cash Basis: Estimate Based on Averages					Est Year End	2013 – 2017	YTD
	2013	2014	2015	2016	2017	2018	Average	Aug–18
Rev	$6,340,800	$6,125,800	$6,867,900	$5,854,600	$7,095,300	$6,000,000	$6,456,880	$4,037,900
GP	$976,200	$1,134,500	$1,092,300	$851,600	$1,239,000	$800,000	$1,058,720	$451,300
Profit	$327,300	$267,600	$72,900	($65,500)	$295,800	($100,000)	$179,620	($174,000)
Approximate Add Backs	$325,000	$325,000	$325,000	$325,000	$325,000	$325,000	$325,000	
Discretionary	$652,300	$592,600	$397,900	$259,500	$620,800	$225,000	$504,620	

Percentages Based on Straight Line Projection Above

	2013	2014	2015	2016	2017	2018	Average	
Rev	100.00%	100.00%	100.00%	100.00%	100.00%	100.00%	100.00%	
GP	15.40%	18.52%	15.90%	14.55%	17.46%	13.33%	16.40%	
Profit	5.16%	4.37%	1.06%	-1.12%	4.17%	-1.67%	2.78%	
Approximate Add Backs	5.13%	5.31%	4.73%	5.55%	4.58%	5.42%	5.03%	
Discretionary	10.29%	9.67%	5.79%	4.43%	8.75%	3.75%	7.82%	
					4 Year Average SDE		7.16%	

Notes:

Using a long period of time cut-off issues from cash basis taxpayers will often average out.

The data reflects that revenues are up and down in a reasonable range.

Further common size ratios were reviewed and show a reasonable range.

This analysis can be used in a calculation to estimate values, future cash flows, and the like.

In this case an eEstimated Year End 2018e was projected from year to date data and reviewing prior year data. With the advantage of hindsight GP and Profit came in higher and closer to historic averages.

FIGURE 11.1 Cash Basis Averaging Financial Analysis

Yacht Maintenance	13 January	13 December	14 January	14 December	15 January	15 December
Revenues	$96,600	$37,800	$85,000	$60,200	$138,700	$38,900
COGS	$18,800	$69,200	$18,200	$81,100	$21,600	$73,800
Expenses	$28,800	$8,100	$11,300	$23,400	$34,000	$44,200
Profit	$49,000	($39,500)	$55,500	($44,300)	$83,100	($79,100)

FIGURE 11.2 Year End Cash Management Example

December and January entries for each year. This is a seasonal yacht maintenance business in North America so the reported monthly entries are unlikely to reflect actual collections.

If the company is growing or contracting through all periods reviewed, then the averaging process is less likely to be accurate. This solution is still likely to understate or overstate the amount of growth or contraction. Yet, it is still likely to be more accurate than any one period.

Another method is to attempt to convert the records to accrual basis. If accounts payable and accounts receivable records can be obtained for each period beginning and end, then simple math can be used to estimate the revenue understatement or overstatement. Simply subtract the beginning receivables from the ending receivables. If the number is positive, add it to revenues. Do the same with payables. If payables have increased, add the difference to the cost of goods sold or other expense. An example of this is shown in Figure 11.3.

The problem with this method is that many small companies have no idea what their receivables and payables are at any given date. Many small businesses do not enter the data until the payment is made or the check is cut, meaning they do not know their payables and receivables. (Worse yet, they think they do but they don't.)

If a supplier or contractor working for them bills late or if there is a dispute with the supplier or contractor, the payable may not have been entered at all sometimes for months. The same applies for receivables. There also is the issue of

		Year 1	Year 2
Accounts Receivable	Beginning Balance	$200,000	$250,000
	Ending Balance	$250,000	$300,000
	Change in Receivables	$50,000	$50,000
Accounts Payable	Beginning Balance	$100,000	$100,000
	Ending Balance	$100,000	$125,000
	Change in Payables	$0	$25,000
Income Statement	Revenues	$900,000	$925,000
	Accrual Adjustment	$50,000	$50,000
	Adjusted Revenues	$950,000	$975,000
	Expenses	$800,000	$800,000
	Accrual Adjustment	$0	$25,000
	Adjusted Expenses	$800,000	$825,000
	Adjusted Pretax Income	$150,000	$150,000

Note: Often with cash basis taxpayers, the entire accounts payable and accounts receivable will need to be added to the balance sheet.

FIGURE 11.3   Method for Estimating Accruals

bad debts that needs to be investigated. Cash basis does not require recognition of bad debt. In some industries a certain level of negotiation and adjustment is expected. This can be very difficult to estimate if there is no history of the write downs. Professional judgment (again, this includes how does this compare to the treatment of what we are comparing it to?) is required to estimate those amounts particularly in the absence of data. See Figure 11.4 for an example of this type of adjustment.

One way to work with this issue with companies that track gross margins is to review the gross margin data over many years. This is most effective when the cost of goods sold mainly contains subcontractors and materials because these tend to be the long pay period items. If company's salaries are included in the cost of goods sold, the analyst may want to perform the

Adjust Revenues for Increase In Revenues and Expenses In Records

	Cash		Accrual Estimate	
Revenues	$4,000,000		$4,800,000	
COGS	$2,800,000		$2,900,000	
GP	$1,200,000	30%	$1,900,000	40%
Sales & Admin	$1,000,000		$1,000,000	
Profit	$200,000	5%	$900,000	19%

Note that the gross profit appears unsupportably high.

Further Adjusted COGS based on Historic Percentages

	Cash		Accrual Estimate	
Revenues	$4,000,000		$4,800,000	
COGS	$2,800,000		$3,360,000	
GP	$1,200,000	30%	$1,440,000	30%
Sales & Admin	$1,000,000		$1,000,000	
Profit	$200,000	5%	$440,000	9%

Notes:
COGS is materials and subcontractors.
If labor is included in COGS, you need to break that out.
At a minimum a multi-year analysis should be used to estimate GP margin.
Need to book payables liability for increase in COGS.
Other factors could still indicate that future results are better or worse.

FIGURE 11.4 Estimating Revenues and Profits / Cash to Accrual Estimate

same analysis, but removing salaries. Salaries tend to be paid quickly (compared to suppliers and subcontractors) and therefore are less of an accrual issue when a cash basis is used.[2] This will both serve as a check on whether "current" estimated accruals are likely to be correct and will provide back-up for any projections or adjustments necessary.

Note, as with all of these analyses, the level of valuation and the purpose are very important in determining if and how to use the data developed. An example of estimating the gross profit for the last seven years of a 12-year analysis is shown in Figure 11.5.

Specialty New Construction Contractor: Gross Profit 2007–2018

Year	2012	2013	2014	2015	2016	2017	2018	12 Y AVERAGE
Revenues	$1,617,800	$2,124,800	$2,383,800	$2,850,600	$3,225,800	$3,412,700	$4,069,200	$2,156,308.33
COGS	$871,000	$1,393,400	$1,444,500	$1,815,100	$2,222,800	$2,489,600	$2,640,600	$1,381,346.58
Gross Profit	$746,800	$731,400	$939,300	$1,035,500	$1,003,000	$923,100	$1,428,600	$774,961.75
GP % Rev	46.16	34.42	39.40	36.33	31.09	27.05	35.11	37.23
								5 Y Average
GP % Rev			39.40	36.33	31.09	27.05	35.11	33.80
								3 Y Average
GP % Rev					31.09	27.05	35.11	31.08
				Selected				32.00

Notes:
As projects become larger, gross profit tends to go down. That is reasonable.
Only 7 of the 12 years are shown due to space considerations.

FIGURE 11.5 Cash Basis Gross Profit Analysis

OTHER CASH BASIS ACCRUAL TYPE ADJUSTMENTS

Construction contractors and large project-based manufacturers that bill on a percentage of completion basis for projects that extend many months often have an additional issue in order to generate reasonably accurate accrual financial statements. This is the matter of, have they invoiced before they actually did the work or not? This is common in construction even though very few owners or companies admit it.

A partial work in process schedule for calculating over- and under-billing is shown in Figure 11.6. Over-billing should result in an accrual reducing revenues and increasing liability for completion. Under-billing should increase revenues and produce an asset of unbilled receivables. Work in process schedules are important job summaries for contractors. Many important things are tracked such as remaining work in the pipeline, remaining contribution margin, profitability of jobs and more. Of course, most smaller companies do not use them. If a company has two or three jobs, the owner can track this in his head but as companies grow, they should update the WIP schedule every month. Few do.

Software as a service and some other technology companies bill in advance and have the same revenue recognition issue but it is generally acknowledged in the industry. Similar analysis needs to be done.

WIP Schedule				Estimated			
Contract Price	COGS	GP	GP %	% Complete	$ Complete	Invoiced	(Over)/ Under
$3,000,000	$2,500,000	$500,000	16.67%	75.00%	$2,250,000	$2,300,000	($50,000)
$1,000,000	$800,000	$200,000	20.00%	50.00%	$500,000	$400,000	$100,000
$5,000,000	$4,500,000	$500,000	10.00%	30.00%	$1,500,000	$1,800,000	($300,000)

FIGURE 11.6   Work in Process Schedule for Over Under Billings

QuickBooks Issues

The QuickBooks system has become ubiquitous with small and very small business accounting. QuickBooks is a godsend compared to no bookkeeping but because it is so easy to start bookkeeping, many of the complexities of proper bookkeeping are not adjusted for.

All of the various problems in small business accounting mentioned above exist in QuickBooks. In addition, beware of the following:

- The tax accountant made adjustments shown on the tax returns but not in the QuickBooks file. Namely, make sure you pull data from the same source. Add-backs may be larger on QuickBooks. Make sure they tie through to the tax return.
- You have a QuickBooks file that says it is Accrual. Many, if not most, small businesses do not enter the data to have proper accrual records. If the data has not been entered, no matter what the title at the top of the report says, it is still not Accrual. This is pervasive. "Oh, you want accrual, I will just run you the accrual books from QuickBooks." Beware and ask about accounting procedures that would be required to have real accrual records. If payables are entered as checks are cut and/or receivables are not tracked (or as often seen, tracked in another system), it is probably not accrual. In many industries, there are many revenue and expense recognition timing issues that need adjustment and entry in addition to pushing the accrual button, such as Work In Process adjustments, as discussed above.

Cut-Offs

For most small businesses getting the cut-offs correct is THE biggest issue with their financial statements. Check for all sources of cut-off error and make corrections or adjustments as necessary. A few errors to check for are presented below.

- Intentional cut-off error in order to reduce tax liability. Many accountants just shut their eyes or claim to not know. Ignorance seems to be bliss in these cases so don't just ask the accountant.
- Inconsistent data entry processes. Sometimes it is just general sloppiness or not realizing that it matters. Many small companies do not see the difference in entering payables or, when on the cash basis, sending checks between the 28th and the 3rd. Clearly that can impact period results.
- Financials run through today. Again, many "helpful" bookkeepers and owners want to run the financials through today. Often but not always these will show all revenues as sales are booked immediately by the company but expenses such as payroll and suppliers or contractors are only booked when paid or when the invoice is received. Therefore, the results are often too high. This is also why some owners are always surprised by their actual results. They always have a few weeks to a month more of revenues than salaries and most expenses. In short, the data through today is incomplete data which is often biased with every sale and not every expense. In general, work with internal data that is 30–45 days old so at least most data has been entered.

Beware of cut-off issues and adjust accordingly.

Accrual Basis

Accrual statements attempt to tie the timing of income to the timing of the related expenses. The advantage of this method is that, if performed accurately, it shows the earned profit the most accurately at every point in time. The biggest disadvantage is that management can be making a high level of profit and run out of cash. An accrual basis company (or any other basis) that does not pay attention to cash collections could go bankrupt even though they are profitable. View cash as blood.

An otherwise healthy person can bleed to death. It is also why many small businesses use the cash basis. An otherwise healthy business can run out of cash.

Both cash flow in the short term and profitability in the long term are required for a business to survive and have value.

The disadvantage of the accrual method is, if required allocations are inaccurate, it is easy to distort earnings for a few periods in the short run. This distortion of earnings can be intended or unintended. Because of the complexities in making adjustments (generally known as accruals), inexperienced bookkeepers can have a difficult time producing accrual statements accurately.

As a general principle, revenue is recognized when earned. In general, it is "Earned" when everything expected for its receipt has been performed.[3] Therefore in most cases when the invoice for payment goes out, so does the recognition of the revenue. In some industries, it could be 90 days before the cash is paid on the invoice.

Prepayments and deposits also occur. This is common in information technology businesses. Sometimes up to a year (or even three years with value-priced cloud-based businesses) of future service may be prepaid. Some industries receive large deposits. In proper accrual accounting, this will be booked as a receipt of cash and a liability for future work. As time goes by and the work is performed, the liability is then reduced and revenue is recognized. When working with financial statements of these types of companies, ask how these calculations are made. There will be adjustments in many cases.

In a similar vein, expenses are to be recorded as the work is performed or goods are sold. This is fairly straightforward with items such as payroll and rent that tend to be paid monthly or more frequently. But there are many other expenses that are not incurred necessarily when paid. The simplest is industries with 45–60-day payable cycles. 60 days is 16% of the annual cycle. That is a large material variance if the timing of the "booking" of the payables varies from year to year.

Capital asset purchases are generally understood not to be expenses by even untrained bookkeepers. A truck that will last five years is not fully expensed on a properly applied accrual basis when purchased. The purchase price will be placed on the balance sheet as an asset and the truck will be expensed over time on the income statement through depreciation. The depreciation will also reduce the value of the asset.

Some other common accounting issue are shown in the next few sections.

Loans. In many cases, capital assets will be purchased using loans. The loan provides cash to pay for the equipment. Loans often have three components: points paid when the loan is incurred, principal or the amount of the loan given, and interest also paid for use of the money. Points and interest are the price of the money and are to be allocated over the time the loan is in place. Except for major purchases, in many cases it is not worth allocating points based on materiality (this is not tax advice or bookkeeping advice, it is only advice on how to reasonably clean up these situations for performing a valuation). The interest is expensed as incurred. Most loans require monthly or quarterly payments. Beware of back-end balloon interest payments. While infrequent, this needs to be noted and it may materially impact the valuation both for current earnings and the ability to make the balloon payment and therefore perhaps even the going concern assumption of the valuation. This lump sum interest should be accrued as incurred even though it is not paid.

One thing that is often missed by bookkeepers and small business people is that loan principal is NOT an expense. In general, they understand that the cash received when getting the loan is not income. Yet, they often want to expense the principal payment. But it is a repayment. The loan principal is repaid with after-tax dollars from profits. This is something that needs to be looked at both to see the real cash flow to the business and to investors.

Insurance and Other Prepayments. Many companies pay business insurance on an annual basis. If the company is a retailer, general insurance and even workmen's compensation may not be that big a number. Construction and manufacturing companies can have very large liability and workmen's compensation insurance rates. These are often paid lump-sum annually. Under proper accrual accounting, this expense then needs to be allocated monthly. At the time of the pre-payment, the excess premium is an asset. Each month the amount used should be expensed and deducted from the remaining asset. Finally, if the company has this type of insurance payments and revenue is growing or falling sharply, check for the rate and base that the rate is applied to. These policies contain audit provisions that can increase the total cost significantly as revenues go up, particularly for subcontractors and other labor-providing companies in dangerous industries. This can be a very material adjustment to overall profits and value when applicable.

Software as a service and other expenses can have pre-payments or be pre-paid. Again, they need to be allocated in the same way as that explained for insurance above.

New or Lease Renewals with "Free Rent Periods". The free rent period should be allocated over the term of the lease. For example, if the landlord gave six months' free rent and then the rent is $5,000 per month for five more years, the free period should be calculated ($30,000 = 6 x $5,000). The $30,000 should reduce rent by $455 (rounded) per month over the period ($30,000/66 months). This is a particularly material issue when the "Free" period is improperly booked in one of the periods under review. For example, rent shown for the year is booked at $30,000 (6 x $5,000) instead of $54,540 calculated as (($5,000 - $455)*12) because the company had six months' free rent in that period.

Retailers of Wholesalers Purchase Inventory for Sale. Inventory is an asset of the company on the balance sheet. Even when it has been paid for, it is not supposed to be expensed until sold or otherwise disposed of.

Inventory should be physically taken at least annually. Physical counts provide the best inventory method as they accurately adjust for shrinkage or theft. Many small companies never take inventory. If the business is small and simple, that may be manageable for day-to-day operations but it creates problems to really understand the cost of goods sold (COGS) and profitability of the company.

Inventory Methods

Most small businesses currently use a form of specific ID. Namely they track the actual item sold. Otherwise they tend to use first in first out (FIFO).

Few still use last in first out (LIFO). Unless the company has large excess inventory or stale inventory, this is unlikely to affect small business results. There is just not enough spread. Of course, on a liquidation basis, LIFO inventory may be understated and could be worth a higher percentage when liquidated than inventory under other methods. If LIFO is used, which is rare to see with small businesses, the inventory on the balance sheet, and beginning and ending inventories on the income statement would require adjustment to properly mark to market.

There are other inventory items to look for. Many small companies never write off stale, excess, or unsaleable inventory. If there is a significant adjustment in inventory, it needs to be reflected on the income statement as additional expense. If unsaleable inventory accumulated over many years exists, then perhaps the write-off should be deducted over multiple years for comparability.

In industries such as manufacturers or contractors that are making things, work in process or WIP, namely, the product being made is a form of inventory. In general, on smaller projects the work in process will be expensed as the completed units are sold. On larger projects like large construction projects taking months or years, the company may use percentage of completion method where the project revenues and expenses are recognized or written off as the work is performed.

Smaller inventory than actually exists—many companies overstate COGS in order to understate income and reduce taxes paid.

Example

Often a somewhat small amount on a yearly basis is overstated, for instance, $30,000 for a company with $400,000 of inventory. Of course, after ten years, net inventory shown on the balance sheet is $100,000 while there is actually $400,000 inventory.

This requires some form of adjustment in the valuation or at least recognition of the issue. It does create an issue at sale because in a stock sale, the buyer is assuming the risk of tax audit and, in an asset sale, the seller or the buyer is going to receive a "bad" tax outcome as the inventory write-up will be ordinary income (as is the case in all deferral of income strategies).

A related issue with the same likely outcome is when companies always use the same beginning and ending inventory. In effect, they are either over-stating or under-stating the cost of goods sold. A similar issue is always using the same percentage of cost of goods sold. Usually this is justified as being based on some sort of historical experience or overall mark-up. But it does not reflect likely changes in pricing due to premiums or more likely discounts to sell through inventory. In both cases it is very difficult to really understand the profitability of the business. If possible, a physical inventory should be taken. While it is only an ending inventory, at least a real number exists to use for adjustments.

Tax Basis Accounting

Tax basis accounting is a combination of cash and accrual accounting that complies with IRS guidelines for preparing taxes. Tax basis accounting will vary across industries. In some cases, it is similar to cash basis accounting though inventories are tracked and adjusted on an accrual basis. In some cases and above a certain size (currently $10 million), it will be accrual accounting. Even in that case, some adjustments to the financial statements such as depreciation rates will vary from the GAAP accrual accounting. Because most small business valuations are prepared based primarily on tax returns, the tax basis of accounting is frequently relied on.

Obvious other differences between normal accrual and tax basis accrual are that depreciation under tax accounting is much quicker than under most financial accounting including GAAP. In equipment-heavy industries the amount being written off under Section 179[4] needs to be reviewed. Because the write-off does not appear on the business tax return income statement, it is not added back but it is also not deducted. It is often ignored.

When the owner is buying a small amount of equipment compared to the revenues and value of the business, ignoring the write-off is often immaterial. In equipment-intensive industries, Section 179 write-offs and depreciation need to be reviewed and may require adjustments for capital investment in the cash flow.

Adjustments will also vary with the valuation method being used. Market data from comparable companies was likely to be maintained on a basis similar to what you are seeing (assuming you are using small-revenue private businesses as comparables). Data from the income method, if material in amount, should be converted from tax depreciation to GAAP rates. (Fortunately, with small and very small businesses, it is rarely material.) In industries with large capital investment; the investments, depreciation, and the age of equipment must be carefully reviewed. Heavy reinvestment requirements will lower multiples, or be an adjustment to the cash flow, or may be a direct reduction in value, particularly if the fleet or equipment is very old.

GAAP

Generally Accepted Accounting Principles (GAAP) are the authoritative guide to accrual accounting in the United States. Very few small businesses comply with GAAP. GAAP is very technical and cumbersome for small and very small businesses to implement. If a small business has substantial outstanding bonds or loans, the bonding company or bank may require "Reviewed" or "Audited" financial statements conforming to GAAP.

Another new issue with GAAP statements is there are a number of clarifications and corrections in the form of new rules, including items like revenue receipt, showing equipment leases and real estate leases on balance sheets that may make it difficult to compare results over time.[5] The jury is out on how this will affect financial analysis, including business valuation.

CPA Statement Levels

Certified Public Accountants (CPAs) are allowed to issue four types of statements. A new category, "Basic Financial Statement Preparation" has recently been introduced. Basic Financial Statement Preparation means the CPA took the client's data and formatted it. This is basically the same thing as working with client-provided data. A notice on each page must state that "no assurance is provided." There is no report.

The next level is a "Compilation." A compilation is when the CPA has compiled the records. Usually they will provide a very low level of checks to make sure things like loans are all properly reflected. While this is a low level, at least it is some minor level of third party check.

The next level is Reviewed. Reviewed statements are just that. The CPA has performed some very basic reviews to see that the data is sensible and correct. They have NOT performed audit procedures and are not attesting to the financial statements. Yet, at this level the statements do have some implied reliability. They often include notes to the financial statements. Be cautious of reviewed statements. Experience indicates that reviewed statements often imply a higher level of evaluation than occurred.

The highest level is Audited. Audited financials have had extensive checks made for completeness, accuracy, and correctness. But they are unlikely to disclose intentional fraud. For business valuations, these are the highest quality statements. Usually they comply with GAAP and they are well organized and complete. Unfortunately, they are very rare in the small business world. They are quite expensive and require many disclosures and extensive notes that many small business owners view as unnecessary.

Analyzing CPA-Provided Statements

When you receive financial statements from a CPA, the process to analyze them is straightforward.

- Start with the cover letter. Check on the level of work that is being performed. The cover letter will state if it is a compilation, a review or an audit. Read on what basis the statements are compiled: cash, income tax, accrual. Does it comply with GAAP? What are the variances?
- The cover letter will state if there are going concern issues and if the company is out of compliance from GAAP or other standard used. These notices can be big red flags. Investigate carefully.
- If the statements have notes, go there next. Read the notes. When complete, notes provide a wealth of information on real estate leases, debts, contingent liabilities, industry information, and so on. Notes are often the most useful part of

reviewed or audited statements. Notes often contain details the company would like to keep hidden.
- Study the financials. Flip back to the notes to make sure you fully understand details.
- If Supplementary Schedules are attached, assess them. Often details on overhead accounts, cost of goods sold, break-downs and other useful information are presented in supplementary schedules.
- Even with CPA-prepared financials such as compilations and reviews, investigate one-time add-backs and contingencies beyond the statements and notes. Some companies "manage" earnings which is sensible from their perspective but may not reflect true earnings power in the correct period. An example is a company that has substantial earnings from prior periods that it is not recognizing due to potential "contingencies" that did not appear to exist.

Unfortunately, very few small and very small companies have reviewed or audited financials. When available, they make business valuation much simpler because financial statements are clear, consistent, and notes provide a level of detail that can take many questions to uncover.

WORKING FROM COST ACCOUNTING OR UNIT DATA

Sometimes a unit of a multi-unit operator needs to be valued. Often in these cases all that exists is unit performance data. In most cases it is reasonable to use the unit data. Of course, certain checks and likely adjustments need to be made.

- How does the unit data compare to the "average" unit data or other reasonable measure?
- Again, when comparing "average," remember to check same size data for key measures across units, such as COGS, labor, and so on.

- Is the unit data complete? Often overhead items such as accounting, H/R, insurance, and other necessary operations are not included. Make sure you fully understand what costs and expenses are paid in unseen parts of the financials. Take the time to understand all costs of operating independently and make sure reasonable adjustments are made.
- Often these individual units when sold are going to be franchise units. Make sure franchise fees and continuing charges are estimated according to the franchise agreement the new owner will operate under.
- If the unit is a franchise or co-op, are there additional fees and charges that have to be paid as part of the transfer? Small $5,000 or $7,000 franchise transfer fees probably do not affect value but large ones in the $35,000 range and up certainly may impact the value of smaller operations.
- Does the franchisor require updating and improvements as part of the transfer or to remain in the system? These costs can be significant. Often updating a location can cost $100,000 or more. (For Burger King, it can be $250,000–$300,000 every 10 years.) For many small businesses, this can be much of the total value.
- Occasionally hardware, farm, and grocery stores belong to a co-op for group purchasing. Make sure you have investigated what the cost to join the co-op is and how it is being paid for by the business. In rare cases these may have a market value, in many, the cost will be repaid assuming the store sells again in the future. But, for valuation purposes, in most cases, it is a capital-type cost of doing business.

BALANCE SHEETS

Balance sheets are important to fully understand the operations of many businesses, yet often small businesses do not maintain proper balance sheets. Balance sheets show what the name implies. They show the balances of accounts, what is owned and what is owed, as of a given date. It is a view of the business, like an X-ray is a view of a body. Also like an X-ray, it may only be valid at the minute it is taken.

From no balance sheets, to balance sheets that are not properly adjusted as loans are paid and assets are purchased, every level of maintenance of balance sheets is seen.

Another frequent issue is that the balance sheet is stripped of cash regularly. Basically, the owner and the company move cash back and forth as needed. Many small business owners view the business as another personal checking account.

Often for small and very small businesses these situations mean that ratio analysis and common size balance sheet comparisons cannot be performed. For many small businesses, it really does not matter. The data sources for the small business data presumably are aggregating the same businesses valuators are looking at which causes the comparable data to be somewhat questionable too.

All of these problems make balance sheet review and ratio analysis hard to perform for small and very small businesses. For many purposes with small companies, the balance sheet is not necessary. Estimating the sales price of a small retailer where the analyst can assume inventory is above the value found at closing and liabilities will be paid by the seller is an example where a complete balance sheet may not be necessary. But, when determining an equity interest value, or minority interest or for some purposes and some standards of value, the full balance sheet needs to be determined.

Yes, estimates of future cash flows are the greatest indicator of future earnings and value but a company that has a very strong balance sheet should have a different "value" than one with a weak balance sheet. The data for these adjustments comes from the balance sheet.

Many small and very small businesses operate from their income statement and pay little attention to the balance sheet. Here we are going to review how balance sheet accounts impact valuation of small and very small businesses.

Assets

Assets are what the business owns, including the obligations owed to it.

Cash. Cash is generally retained by the seller in a very small business sale and is not part of the delivered assets. Cash is a component of working capital which will be discussed below.

Accounts Receivable. Accounts receivable are money owed the business for services that typically have already been provided. Small business owners will be quick to tell you that that this is their money because they already earned it. They sold and delivered the product or service. As discussed in Chapter 7, accounts receivable should be reviewed and in some cases adjusted for collectability.[6]

Of course, for many businesses, accounts receivable is a very necessary component of the business, just like the delivery truck. In some industries, particularly those with large clients the ability to wait for payment is very important to obtaining premium pricing on their work and to growth.

Example

In construction, subcontractors who cannot finance their payroll will take 20% or more discounts and are only be able to obtain work from smaller owners and general contractors who have the ability to be flexible in order to get paid in time to make payroll every Friday.

The market method databases generally specify that for asset sales the cash and accounts receivable will be retained by the seller and are not part of the purchase price in a sale transaction. Often the databases with stock sales assume a balanced working capital. Beware, in practice, as discussed elsewhere, neither of these assumptions is always or perhaps even generally correct. Accounts receivable are also a key component of working capital and will be reviewed below.

Inventory. The value of inventory is often added to the price for small businesses when using the market method. According to some transaction databases and most rules of thumb, the value of good and usable inventory is not included in the price. For small businesses this is often the case. See the section, Inventory, in Chapter 6, Market Approaches, for more ideas on how to adjust inventory for different size and types of businesses.

Other Current Assets. This is a catch-all account for payments due to the company in under one year. Often it will contain real estate deposits and the like. Technically a real estate deposit is not current (except during the last year of the lease) as it cannot be received back until the end of the lease. Technically it should be moved to Other Assets. Usually the amount is immaterial.

Fixed Assets. Fixed assets generally are equipment and vehicles. Tenant improvements also fall into this category. These should be marked to market. (If the real estate lease is unlikely to be continued, the tenant improvements mentioned above likely have a market value of $0.0.) Except in liquidations and for a few asset-heavy businesses the fixed assets of most small businesses have little impact on value. If fixed assets are a major contributor to value, it may make sense to bring in a real estate appraiser if it is real estate-based, or an equipment valuation expert, if it is equipment-based.

Liabilities

Liabilities are what the business owes to others.

Accounts Payable. Accounts payable are the short-term debts the company owes to its vendors. The significance of these is that they are a low-cost loan to the subject company. Yet many small businesses must pay much quicker than they are paid. In general, for small business sales, the market database assumption and real-world situation are that accounts payable are paid by the seller through the closing date.

Other Current Liabilities. This is often where taxes and pay-roll due reside. Unpaid retirement and other benefits also are shown here. In general, with smaller companies and asset sales, this is paid off. This can also contain lines of credit. Lines of credit are often secured by receivables and inventory.

Long-Term Debt. Long-term debt for small businesses are often truck, vehicle and equipment loans. They can be lines of credit depending on the terms and SBA loans also. Long-term debt is almost always personally guaranteed by the business owners. (Often accounts payable and the real estate lease may be personally guaranteed also.) Typically for small business sales as reflected in the market method data, long-term debt is typically paid off at the time of a sale and therefore needs to be deducted from the value found.

Contingent Liabilities. Contingent liabilities are liabilities that may or may not happen based on a contingency. Common contingent liabilities are loan guarantees on other people's or companies' loans (due on default by the other), uninsured claims in lawsuits with a likely chance of loss (due on loss of suit), and union pension obligations (usually due on sale of the business). If not revealed by the owner or management, these can be hard to find. Once found, it can be hard to determine proper adjustments.

In the case of loan guarantees, understanding the loan terms and the financial strength of the primary borrower is a starting point. For lawsuits, often the attorney handling the case will give an opinion letter assessing the likely outcomes. Finally, demand letters to the pension managers will produce estimates of the union pension liability. In many cases, these estimates, or a portion of them, would be adjusted from the value found.

Owners' Equity

Owners' equity is the sum of all the assets of the business less all the liabilities of the business. It should also total the equity investments in the business by the owners plus cumulative earnings of the business less cumulative distributions of the business. Therefore, as the name implies, owners' equity shows the owners' investment in the business. Owners' equity shows the worth of the business on a book basis.

Owners' equity indicates if the company has resources and resilience to survive downturns and change. Further regular distributions to the owners should be reviewed, particularly when valuing minority and lack of control interests.

Finally, the ability of the company to make money over time is the ultimate determinant of value. Regular distributions or increasing retained earnings in owners' equity is the surest sign of long-term growth.

OTHER ADJUSTMENTS AND CALCULATIONS BASED ON THE BALANCE SHEET

Below are common adjustments necessary to develop a more accurate balance sheet and calculations that arise as part of the valuation process to develop the final estimate of value of the interest being reviewed.

Lack of Adjustments

Many accounting systems automatically make balance sheet entries. Many small business owners never make the other half of the entry, therefore the account over time becomes misleading.

Example

A distributor had software that automatically put variances between the purchase order amount and the invoice amount into a purchase price liability, noting there was likely to be a future payment that was not already in the system. This account needed to be cleared when the invoice variance was resolved. Yet it was not. Over time, this became a very large liability that did not exist.

Other areas are loan balances that are not reduced as payments are made. Depreciation adjustments that never get posted at year end. You may also find an account that is an 'unidentified' summary account or that accounts receivable have a credit balance instead of a 'normal' debit balance, and/or accounts payable have a debit balance instead of a 'normal' credit balance. For many of these types of adjustments, if the amounts are material to the value of the business, then the valuator must do the clean-up or have the business accountant or bookkeeper make adjusting entries.

WORKING CAPITAL

Working capital is the net current assets over current liabilities. Often the interpretation for small and very small businesses is net current assets over all liabilities.

For small and very small businesses, the assumption using the market method is that all current assets (except inventory which might be paid for above the price) will be retained by the seller and all liabilities will be paid off by the seller. This is the assumption used for asset sales by several comparable databases. Much like inventory in practice (and therefore what is likely reported to the database services), it does not always work that way when negotiating a price in actual sales. Part of this bias may be that main street business brokerage started primarily with retail businesses like gas stations, convenience stores, restaurants, and liquor stores that do not have significant accounts receivable.

All but the most naïve buyers recognize that any money they have to put into a business in the first 60–90 days is an additional part of the purchase price, namely, it is part of the original investment that must be paid back and earn a return.

In sale transactions under a $1,000,000 of business value, the standard rule of thumb that the seller will retain the net working capital usually applies even to B-to-B companies that may have significant receivables compared to their size and earnings. But at some point, the discussion of working capital and leaving behind accounts receivable as part of the base stock business price (or a conveyed asset in the case of an asset sale) becomes part of the negotiations.

Some valuators argue that current assets are "automatically" included in a stock sale. This has not been my or other brokers' experience with small businesses. It is very easy to distribute assets and pay liabilities immediately before the sale. With small and very small businesses using both asset and stock methods, the specific assets and liabilities can be and often are managed. In addition, reported asset values for market transactions are often swayed by tax considerations as there can be a large variance in market value of used assets.

To make matters more complex, when the economy becomes strong, banks are far more likely to lend working capital. Particularly in low interest rate environments, this reduces pressure on buyers to obtain working capital from the sellers and may change the willingness to borrow working capital vs. receive it from the seller.

Example

A concrete subcontractor works for large general contractors. The company has $5,000,000 of revenues per year. Between retention (a hold back to ensure completion of work) and accounts receivable, the company has over $1,000,000 of receivables. (In our local markets they get paid in 45–60 days less a 10% retention paid eventually at the end of the job.) Let's further assume that the company has typical earnings and sells for 30% of revenues. So now we have a value of $1,500,000. But is the value really $1,500,000 purchase price or, assuming the seller can retain the accounts receivable, the $2,500,000 that will be invested in the company in the first 90 days? Or perhaps something negotiated in-between?

In sales/price situations this is a negotiated factor. For small and very small businesses one logical way, based on the author's experience, to handle working capital is to provide an estimate of working capital and adjust the valuation findings based on professional judgment.

Estimate of Working Capital

Many small businesses are essentially labor suppliers or material suppliers, or both labor and material providers to much larger businesses. In this role they often have to pay labor weekly or bi-weekly and pay suppliers on 30 to no more than 45 days terms. Yet they get paid somewhere between 45–90 days by their large clients. This financing is not poor cash management, it is an expectation in their industries.

This means, as revenues grow, so does required working capital. Namely, net current assets over current liabilities will grow and require more and more cash. For most small business valuations, it is important to estimate if the company will be able to generate the cash to invest. If not, the company will not grow at the projected pace or will go bankrupt due to cash shortages. This increase in working capital may also need to be adjusted in the cash flow.

The simplest rough estimate that is often sufficient:

- Obtain income statements, balance sheets, accounts payable aging and accounts receivable aging as of the same date. In addition to year-end, request balance sheets and A/R and A/P agings for another typical month in the year.
- If the company has seasonality, you may need to look at A/R and A/P agings several times during the year. Also check if suppliers give special terms in season. For retailers in some specialties, many vendors give payment terms of 90 days for Christmas season purchases.
- Do not just look at year-end data. Year-end data is often manipulated for tax purposes by cash-basis small and very small business owners.

- Review the ratio of salaries and wages to revenues over the three years. If the company has COGS, make sure you add the wages in COGS to the review.
- Usually wages will be fairly consistent with revenues. If not, estimate the cash increase or decrease based on the trend.
- In addition, check if there are large capital investment needs, borrowing needs or perhaps principal payments not showing that would modify the estimated cash flow gap. For most small companies which operate on little long-term debt and have policies of periodic replacement of their small amount of equipment, this is generally not a factor.

Then, for non-seasonal businesses, take the revenues and subtract profits (total costs). Divide by 12. This is the rough monthly cash needs of the business. Multiply this by the time it takes the company to collect receivables. Subtract typical payables. This is the working capital needed. Of course, this will vary month to month but if reasonable months are selected. it should be in the ballpark.

If the business is seasonal, this needs to be done in the busy and slow season. Payables need to be checked to make sure terms are being taken advantage of. In some cases, if available, this is done with monthly data. Often income statement data can be pulled out of QuickBooks. Balance sheet data will depend on the quality of the bookkeeper.

Example

A company has $6,000,000 of revenues and $300,000 of profit. Working capital required is approximately $475,000 per month calculated as (($6,000,000 - $300,000)/12). If the payment period is 60 days or two months and the typical balance on A/R is $200,000, then the working capital needed is $750,000 calculated as follows:

$475,000 x 2 = $950,000 – $200,000 = $750,000.

This is a reasonable estimate of the required working capital. (If all billings have to be made at the end of the month, it is possible that

> *the company needs another month billings. If that is more realistic,*
> *then using the same formula, the working capital is $1,225,000.)*
> *Remember this is a NEGOTIATED part in underlying transactions*
> *so we can only estimate and assume.*

Construction contractors commonly have a withholding called retention. The purpose of retention is so the contractor comes back and completes the job 100%. It is often 5–10% of the revenues for the work. This can further exacerbate cash flow issues and the need for working capital. Some contractors keep retention in general receivables and many have a special category. If retention is in a special category, make sure to account for it in the working capital calculations. The easiest way to do that is to add average retention to the accounts receivable balance when doing the calculations above.

This can be done at several time points if necessary, to check consistency and develop an estimate. If this process is done several times over the period reviewed, a working capital ratio to revenues can be established.

Applying Working Capital in Forecasts

The working capital estimate can then be used to determine increases in working capital based on revenue growth. For instance, in the example above, when revenues are $6,000,000, working capital is $750,000. This means the working capital is 12.5% of revenues. So, if revenues are projected to become $8,000,000, the next year working capital is now $1,000,000. This could result in an adjustment of $250,000 in increased working capital. If company profitability does not support that level of re-investment of earnings, either growth is likely to be slower or third party lines of credit need to be investigated.

A more thorough estimate of working capital could be performed by examining historic working capital over the prior growth period and confirming if more or less is needed as revenues grow.

Of course, long-term growth for most small and very small businesses is very modest compared to the above example.

Applying estimated working capital requirements as calculated above directly to estimates of value for the capitalization of earnings and the market methods are addressed in Chapters 5, 6, and 8 of this book.

Estimating Capital Investment

It is hard from a purely "financial" perspective to estimate capital investments for many businesses. Many manufacturing businesses can run multiple shifts if necessary. New technologies can make perfectly operable equipment obsolete on an operating cost basis. Furthermore, in most businesses, capital investment is not an even steady state thing. Often large capital investments occur in chunks from time to time. Not in even drips or drops. This makes estimating a steady state capital investment adjustment very difficult.

To estimate capital investment, examine the prior capital investment. Often depreciation schedules will be the best source of this information. Note the age of equipment. If equipment is getting old, you may be able to obtain wear and tear indicators such as mileage on vehicles. You can also see how the current owner handles replacement. Some sell vehicles at 100,000 miles and some run them for 20 years and replace the engine at least once.

When estimating equipment needs for a manufacturer, try to get an indication of current volume and when the owner believes replacement or additional equipment will be required. This is something that often needs to be handled as part of the owner/management interview.

Take the information obtained from all sources and see how it ties into growth forecasts. If growth is not forecast, check on replacement costs. Make sure these are reasonably included in forecasts or in estimating the cash flow for the capitalization of earnings method.

In some industries, replacement cost may be factored into the market method multiplier. For instance, printers may require a lot of capital equipment investment. Printers always had a lower multiple (even before the internet) than some other businesses because of the high level of capital investment. In other industries, it may not. Use your judgment in trying to align the size and type of companies in the market data as compared to the subject company.

Owner Debt

Some small business owners are well advised. These owners will often fund much of the capital for their business with debt they provide as opposed to equity. In certain liability and creditor situations, if done properly, this can be advantageous for the owner.

In addition, as part of tax planning, sometimes the owner will lend money from the company to themselves in lieu of a distribution. In those cases, they are required to have a note and pay or accrue at least the legally required interest for IRS purposes. Of course, it raises this issue for business valuations – is a debt to or from the owner really a debt?

Clearly for legal purposes, in most states, if the debt has been properly set up, properly documented, and interest paid, the debt exists. There are court rulings in some states indicating that where no one would give a market loan to the company, the debt is really equity.

Excess Assets

Excess assets are assets that are not required by the company to generate the revenues and resulting cash flows that generate value for the company. Examples include vacation homes owned by the company (often for "entertainment"), personal vehicles, old or obsolescent equipment no longer used in production (of course, does this have a value at all?), gold coins, excess working capital and/or retained cash.

Conservative owners often keep excess cash on the balance sheet, just in case. I suspect it helps them sleep at night. Excess cash beyond reasonable operating needs should be treated as an excess asset.

Excess assets should be recast as non-operating assets on the balance sheet,[7] it will not change the adjusted equity amount. The non-operating asset amount is required to be added to the value of the enterprise in the income and market approach analyses.

BIG Taxes

Excess assets held by C corporations may have a BIG tax on them. BIG taxes are built in gains. C corporations are separate tax-paying entities. Their tax effects do not pass through to the shareholders. Therefore, two sets of taxes are applied to money earned by C corporations. The tax at the corporate level and then the tax at the shareholder level. Pass-through entities, namely, partnerships, limited liability companies, and S corporations are only at taxed at the partner, member, or shareholder level.[8]

Common sense says that the estimated BIG tax should be deducted from the excess assets when adding the asset value to the estimated value using any valuation approach. BIG taxes are addressed in Chapter 7, Asset Approaches. If significant, excess assets might be subject to BIG taxes, it is dependent on the purpose and professional judgment of the valuator if they should be deducted from the value found in determining the estimated value of the excess assets. For instance, if excess assets are likely to be distributed as part of a settlement, then they likely should be at pre-tax values. If the valuation was for purchase or sale of a minority interest, then likely the excess assets would be shown at a post-tax value.

CONCLUDING THOUGHTS: THE BALANCE SHEET AND VALUE

The balance sheet is an important contributor to value that is often forgotten about when valuing small and very small businesses. If a company is unprofitable, then the balance sheet can be used to determine the net asset value in an organized sale or liquidation. In other cases, the balance sheet is used to adjust the value found under cash flow-oriented valuation methods. This adjustment will vary with the valuation method and purpose of the valuation. Most of the material adjustments for small business focus on working capital accounts (cash, accounts receivable, accounts payable), inventory as its own component independent of working capital, and excess assets.

NOTES

1. Cash basis is not supposed to be used with inventory but occasionally it is.
2. Salaries paid monthly may behave more like suppliers and contractors. I suggest using cut-off dates for current financials of about 60–90 days prior to the current date to allow most of these costs to be included in the statements.
3. Accounting Standards Codification (ASC) 606.
4. Section 179 allows an immediate deduction for qualifying equipment purchases. On pass-through entities it is an item that directly passes through to the owners, therefore, it is not show on the return. It is shown on the related K-1s.
5. ASC 606 for revenue recognition, ASC 842 for lease accounting.
6. If adjusted, then the Income Statement is likely to need adjustment also.
7. If preparing a valuation for a price, it might be removed from the "conveyable" balance sheet.
8. Limited liability companies do not exist as a tax classification. Owners of LLCs choose C corporation, S corporation, partnership, or if an individual single member owner, schedule C.

CHAPTER 12

Details for Business Valuators

This chapter discusses topics of particular relevance to business valuators. They include final selection and weighting of the valuation method, standards relating to calculations and conclusions of value, meeting clients' wishes for multiple purposes, engagement agreements, and more on professional judgment.

SELECTION OR WEIGHTING OF METHODS

Often multiple methods will be used to calculate indications of value. As part of a conclusion of value, one method needs to be selected or several methods need to be weighted in order to select a final value.

If the purpose is for estate and/or gift tax, or if you agree with its philosophy, Revenue Ruling 59-60 specifies selecting the best method.[1] The ruling argues that multiple methods muddy the water.

Many analysts support, and standards allow a weighting to select a final value. After all, this is an opinion and multiple methods may contribute to the logic and value found. Therefore, for many purposes, valuators perform a weighting of two or more credible methods. Some purposes allow the selection

Method	Indication of Value	Weight	Weighted Value
Asset Method	$120,000	0.00%	$0
Market Method – Revenues	$900,000	25.00%	$225,000
Market Method – Cash Flow	$860,000	75.00%	$645,000
Income Method – Cap. of Earnings	$960,000	0.00%	$0
Estimate of Value		100.00%	$870,000

Notes: Example of basic weighting of estimates of value to calculate final value. The calculation is simple.
Clarity in the explanation for why the weighting was selected is essential.
When a range of values makes sense, some valuators will select two values as a high and low for the
range. An example might be to select the high value as $960,000 and the low value as $860,000.
Again, the logic and judgment for the selection are key.
Revenue Ruling 59-60 mentions selecting one method but it also mentions that the valuator
should apply common sense specific to the facts when determining value.

FIGURE 12.1   Selection and Weighting of Valuation Methods

of a range of values. Again, it is important to explain how and why the range was selected.

An example of a weighting of methods is shown in Figure 12.1.

Along with the fairly simple presentation comes the explanation of the process and reasoning for the weighting. Typically, valuators will provide a final summary of the logic of the method and the logic of the weighting. This is a final check on the sensibleness of the value found. Some factors to consider are listed below.

- Are there strong reasons to choose the selected or weighted methods compared with other methods?
- If there are large variations between the methods, is the choice made reasonable?
- Why is there a large variation, should it be explained?
- What would the effect have been if one method was selected over the other?
- Is the other method or is the less weighted method likely to be materially more correct?

In most cases if there is a large variation, one method should be selected. It is one thing to weight a reasonable range and another to pick a mid-point that is highly unlikely to be correct.

Finally, is the selected method weighting reasonable?

Weighting four or seven methods or more indicates a lack of thought and selection. At a minimum it looks like averaging of rules of thumb. Blind averaging is not supportable.

CALCULATIONS AND CONCLUSIONS (OPINIONS) OF VALUE

Formal business valuations are classified by two different standard levels: a calculation of value and a conclusion of value. Conclusion of values are commonly thought of as opinions of value but the American Institute of Certified Public Accountants reserves the word "opinion" for audits exclusively. Conclusions must meet all valuation standards. Calculations of value cover a large range of work product agreed to by the valuator and the client.

In addition to the work produced to estimate a conclusion or calculation, a report is also produced. Generally, reports are written to standards. The Standards are somewhat but not completely interchangeable. The National Association of Certified Valuators and Analysts (NACVA) publishes a guide showing the relationships of the differing Standards.[2] The NACVA Standards are based on principles. Principles-based systems state the principles that are to be met and leave more of the details to the valuator. The AICPA SSVS (Statements on Standards for Valuation Services) standards are much more rules-based. Uniform Standards of Professional Appraisal Practice (USPAP), developed by The Appraisal Foundation, of which the American Society of Appraisers is a member, are a mixture of both.

While principles-based standards may work best with the fluid and varying nature of valuation work, rules-based systems tend to have more detail and in this case work better as an outline. For that reason, the AICPA SSVS No. 1 standard will be used for convenience. Because rules are rigid, if you are a certified public accountant, make sure you follow SSVS. In all likelihood the other standards will be met.

Valuations prepared for litigation are exempt from the reporting standards but not from the developmental standards. There is also a reporting exception if a governmental body has specified a different work product. Conclusion reports are submitted as a summary and in detailed format. They may be oral or written. In general, calculation reports can vary greatly, based upon the agreed-upon procedures with the client.

According to SSVS 1:

.02 the term engagement to estimate value refers to an engagement or any part of an engagement (for example, a tax, litigation, or acquisition-related engagement) that involves estimating the value of a subject interest. An engagement to estimate value culminates in the expression of either a conclusion of value or a calculated value.

This is further refined in .04

.04 In the process of estimating value as part of an engagement, the valuation analyst applies valuation approaches and valuation methods, as described in this statement, and uses professional judgment. *The use of professional judgment is an essential component of estimating value.* [emphasis added]

The SSVS has many examples of when professional judgment is used and not used, but it is a fine line. If valuations are being prepared and you have a certification, it is probably prudent to assume that even a back of the napkin estimate is using your professional judgement. (Presumably, at some point, even choosing a rule of thumb is a judgment.)

CALCULATIONS OF VALUE

A calculation is produced when:

> a. (1) the valuation analyst and the client agree on the valuation approaches and methods the valuation analyst will use and the extent of procedures the valuation analyst will perform in the process of calculating the value of a subject interest ... A calculation engagement does not include all of the procedures required for a valuation engagement. (SSVS #1 .21b)

The difficulty with trying to show what is in a "typical calculation" is that a calculation to a large extent is what is agreed upon to be provided between the valuation analyst and the client. This can and does range from a simple "almost or barely" calculation to a calculation just short of the opinion of value. In fact, some analysts (and they may well be right) will insist that what is shown in the companion documents on the website as an opinion is just a fairly complete calculation.[3]

Calculation Report

AICPA SSVS No. 1 paragraphs .73 through .77 describe the requirements of a calculation report. A sample calculation report is included as part of the materials included with the book on the website. The sample includes information useful for an internal exit planning situation. The report also is annotated to further show applications of the concepts discussed in the book.

VALUATION ENGAGEMENTS

Regarding a valuation engagement, AICPA SSVS No. 1 paragraph .21a. states this occurs

> when (1) the engagement calls for the valuation analyst to estimate the value of a subject interest and (2) the valuation analyst estimates the value ... and is free to apply the valuation approaches and methods he or she deems appropriate in the circumstances. (SSVS #1 .21a)

Valuation engagements result in a conclusion of value. Note that there are no exceptions when performing a conclusion. All work that the valuation analyst feels must be performed along with all work required by the standards must be performed.

Valuation Reports

Valuation reports are broken down into a detailed report and a summary report. Detailed report requirements begin at SSVS .51 and run through .70. Summary reports are covered in .71 and .72. The Standards again provide a high level of clarity about what must appear in a detailed report.

When the valuation is prepared for controversy purposes, then the reporting requirements are exempted. The developmental standards still apply. Remember for litigation your report is all or part of your testimony so make sure the report is credible. Check for the requirements for the jurisdiction you are working in. Some do not require a report be filed, just testimony. Others only allow information in the report to be testified. A big swing in requirements and possible strategy.

If you are subject to the AICPA SSVS or NACVA, USPAP or other standards, do review them carefully to ensure compliance.

A sample Summary Report is included as part of the materials included with the book on the website. The sample was prepared for a bank loan approval purpose. The report is also annotated to show applications of the concepts and methods used in the book.

MEETING CLIENTS' NEEDS

In many small business valuations, the client is the small business owner or his attorney representing him. For many small business owners, cost is a huge factor in business valuation. Most clients do not begin to comprehend the complexity of this specialized work, the theoretical framework or the standards that are to be followed. They believe a rule of thumb is all that is needed and they know their cash flow (or at least believe they do), so what is the big deal?

Most small business owners are practical people who just want an answer. In addition, being human, they usually want the answer they want which may or may not be a supportable value. Clearly, working for clients who are creating fee pressure for you and have strong desires, which may be beyond your opinion, can lead to ethical pressures. Yet that is the reality for most practitioners on most assignments. How do we as professionals resolve this?

In business valuation, valuators represent their "opinion" of value. Valuators represent the work. They should be as persuasive as possible about the opinion of value. (Sometimes that includes being understated.) What should not be done is attempting to sway the opinion or findings to represent what any other party wants. Independence necessitates that the analysts be an advocate only for the opinion. Analysts owe the client, and if different, the users, an accurate calculation or opinion. As specified in the engagement agreement letter, that user has the right to rely on our findings.

A few circumstances for small business valuations and questions to determine "what is important":

- **Internal planning**—usually calculations of value will do. If truly for internal planning purposes only, or early planning purposes, a low level of verification of add-backs and adjustments may be warranted.
  - How is the tool of the business valuation going to be used by the client?

- Are they going to just use "the number" or are they looking for guidance on how to improve the business?
- Are they seeking guidance on what market transaction terms will look like?
- Your ultimate report or notes or oral guidance should be directed to meaningfully assist the client with their uses in addition to finding the correct number.
- **Mediation/negotiation** that may or may not lead to litigation
  - What quality level documents are being worked from?
  - Are clients both parties, a company representative, a third party? (Should that matter?)
  - What is the cost/benefit of whatever level of work we are doing?
  - What are the rules of engagement for the parties and for the valuation analyst?
- **Litigation** (often divorce)
  - What is the standard of value and premise of value?
  - For smaller entities, is this a business?
  - What other tasks might be performed as part of the service (e.g., available funds reports, support tests)?
  - What documents are available?
  - Is there access to the same documents as the opposing side?
  - What is customary or required in the jurisdiction for computations and/or reports or exhibits as it becomes full litigation? For example, is a full report required early or is no report required at all? Will a calculation report suffice?
  - Are forensics likely to be required?
  - Does the valuation date move during the process?
- **Compliance** (SBA Loans, ESOPS, Fair Value Appraisals, Estate, Gift Tax Matters)
  - What is the size of the business?
  - What is the purpose or use of the report?
  - What expectations or requirements has the user provided through publications, court cases, and so on?

Valuation professionals are not reviewers or auditors or even compilers of financial statements for direct use of the statements as such. But, we are providing an assessment of the value and providing an opinion based on the data. When performing work for third parties, we must recognize our third-party obligations and apply professional prudence to our work.

One of the standard ways to adjust for risk of poor financial documents is to reduce the value or increase the marketability discount. Certainly, this is how buyers in market transactions deal with uncertainty.

That may be fair (but is it really correct?) when the "keeper" of the documents, namely, the owner will be negatively impacted by the reduced value. But what if you represent the out-spouse in a divorce? Or if a value is being determined for cashing in stock options? Or if you are retained for a mediation to do work for both parties? While every case is different, it would be unfair to in effect penalize a party for someone else's refusal or inability to clean things up. Easy to say here and yet this requires a high level of professional judgment and experience to solve.

DETERMINING WHAT MATTERS

Again, as stated earlier:

> USPAP STANDARDS Rule 9-5 Comment, The value conclusion is the result of the appraiser's judgment and not necessarily the result of a mathematical process. (2018-2019 USPAP)

How Do We Determine What Matters?

Clearly determining what matters ties in with professional judgment. In accounting parlance, what matters is what is "material" to the work. What matters are those things that lead to a finding that is "approximately right." It is the Art of Business Valuation. It also includes those things that will allow you to sanity-check and reasonableness-test your findings, increasing your likelihood of being reasonably right. Reasonably right is accurate in business valuation applications.

How Do We Really Know What Matters?

> Businesses at their simplest are: People, Processes, Profits.[4]
> Simplicity can be deceptive.

What matters are understanding the major building blocks of measuring cash flows or profits and evaluating the risk of those cash flows that come from people and processes, to estimate value for any given purpose.

Of major importance is the interaction of people and systems to maintain relationships with customers, suppliers, regulators, and others to create resiliency around the numbers or perhaps indicate weakness. Can these systems withstand change and uncertainty? Again, what is the company story and how does it affect the analysis and treatment of the numbers.

The numbers and profits are a score. The financial results over time produce trends that are used to judge the likelihood of the results of the next "game" or financial period. The exact building blocks will vary with each engagement based on the business, industry, economy, actual financial statements and other components of a proper business valuation. Finally, a liberal dose of "Does this make sense?" is needed at every step.

Emphasis is placed on the purpose of the business valuation. The valuator may use very different methodologies and levels of documentation depending on the purpose. For instance, let's look at a small business valuation being developed for litigation versus preparing a valuation to price a business for market sale.

In both cases, the "correct" number or value is important. But in litigation, surviving cross-examination may sway the selection of valuation methods and create a real need for excessive detail in working out some portions of the business valuation. For instance, a site visit to an office of an engineering firm might be performed simply to avoid the cross-examination challenge of "not knowing what the place looks like."

When possible, in litigation, determine who the judge is and find out what the judge's preferences in prior valuation cases were. Some jurisdictions have reporting services for unpublished cases. These can be very helpful.

In market sale estimates of value for small and very small business calculations, it probably just makes sense to use a market multiplier and, for the smallest businesses, maybe even a rule of thumb and apply this against an adjusted cash flow as a proper sales process will determine the real price. Since the valuation for possible mergers and acquisitions work here is for internal planning, there is no third party reliance on backup documentation. (A "fair value opinion" valuation for a buyer or seller with third party users is a very different engagement.) Purpose also ties into the standard of value that is to be used by the valuator and in many cases whether an opinion or calculation is required.

What matters is what will materially affect the estimate of value. That includes its believability and supportability where credibility may be questioned.

How is the valuation work seen, measured, recorded, analyzed, and then explained to the user? Items that materially affect the analysis and the ability to support the analysis are what matters. Business valuators build an argument for their concluded business value. When properly completed, the argument addresses weaknesses and problems with the analysis, as these always exist.

PROFESSIONAL JUDGMENT

Business valuation uses more professional judgment than most accounting functions which tend to look backwards at the past.

The past happened. There are a finite number of choices and outcomes about the past. Business valuation is really about the future with unlimited choices and options. Business valuation is more of a finance function looking at financial stability and growth or contraction in the future than it is about compiling accounting data.

But what is professional judgment? Merriam Webster's dictionary does not treat it as one word or phrase.

Professional is "1 a: of, relating to, or characteristic of a profession. b: engaged in one of the learned professions. (1): characterized by or conforming to the technical or ethical standards of a profession (2): exhibiting a courteous, conscientious, and generally businesslike manner in the workplace."[5]

Judgment is: "1 a: the process of forming an opinion or evaluation by discerning and comparing. b: an opinion or estimate so formed."[6]

Boiling it down, an engaged professional in a learned profession is characterized by his technical or ethical standards. Certainly, those both apply to valuation. Most people who engage in business valuation belong to at least one professional association and follow standards both as to ethics and technical matters.

Judgment is the hard part. What does, "the process of forming an opinion or evaluation by discerning and comparing" really mean? Discerning and comparing what to what? Which also begs the question of what is it that is being discerned and compared? When valuing smaller businesses, we have issues both with the relevance and correctness of what is being compared and the comparable. Namely, both sides of the equation or model are flawed.

In simple terms, professional judgment (yes, this is the art) becomes how we best improve the overall equation to get the best answer possible even if it is not likely and in fact will never be perfect. Over time many practitioners do learn how to do this in a variety of situations.

One of the goals of this book has been to speed up that learning curve and assist practitioners at least in specific areas that are frequently encountered by small and very small businesses. That is why the question of "how does the analyst improve the equation or model?" has repeatedly been brought up. This directly impacts professional judgment.

In addition to the exercise of professional judgment is the question of how the valuator's file should be documented and supported to demonstrate the process of professional judgment.

Simplicity: The Law of Parsimony

Occam's razor and the "Law of Parsimony" form the theorem that the simplest problem-solving method tends to be the correct one. Namely, the most accurate solution tends to be the one with the fewest assumptions. This theory relates to the fact that each assumption tends to bring in a huge number of new alternatives, making it harder to prove a hypothesis wrong. Therefore, simpler theories are more testable and verifiable. Basically, the complex way may be correct but it is almost impossible to prove. With the simpler way it is easier to prove that it is probably not wrong.

The other extreme is the advent of the black box. The black box is where a computer algorithm calculates the answer. Plug in defined variables and get an answer. This appears to involve no judgment by the analyst at all (which begs the questions of how the variables were selected and what biases may be in the algorithm). There is a lot of concern about using black box solutions since they cannot easily be verified. Sometimes a variation of a black box is all there is.

The use of statistics can also fall into this category. If simple statistics, medians and means were all there was to business valuation, valuators would have been replaced by interns with calculators and certainly computers at this point. Statistics does have a place along with the black box in some situations but most businesses are not "average" and even if they were, we still have the problem of comparison, namely, is our comparative data from average companies? In many cases it is not. Finally, statistics can show correlation but not causation.

Conclusions as to Professional Judgment

The problem with professional judgment and business valuation is that a business valuation has so many layers of professional judgment that it is almost impossible to consider them all.[7] Most of these layers are materially important.

The following is a recommended process for working with professional judgment:

1. How important or material is the determination to what we are estimating? This may have to be reviewed several times in the valuation process as importance may increase or decrease as the entire valuation comes together.
2. Assuming 1. above, that the matter is material, do you have experience with the matter at hand? If not, who does and what books and documents do? The more material there is, the more you should research and document.
3. Is there a consensus view? If the consensus view does not apply, clearly document what you have done to verify that and why. The factors listed above are a good outline for that process.
4. Are there other factors or procedures or tests that support or invalidate your view? If they do not support your view, how are you adjusting or justifying your final determination?
5. If a particular user or reviewer is involved (e.g., the Internal Revenue Service (IRS), the Securities and Exchange Commission (SEC), local judge), have they stated a position on this matter? While it may be against ethical standards to vary your opinion for them, certainly it could impact how you present your report and analysis.

6. Document your process to the appropriate level considering the level of the estimate of value (calculation or opinion), the materiality of matter, and your reasoning for variance (if any) from the consensus review. If appropriate, put a summary of the analysis in the report.

Many very important assumptions, such as the economic outlook for cyclical companies, while very material, are usually going to be a consensus view and will require little or no documentation, particularly in a calculation. On the other hand, material adjustments beyond the consensus view (say, a 60% discount for marketability) need to be thoroughly vetted, supported, and backed up in work papers and when appropriate in the report.

For another take on professional judgment, see the "Final Report of the Advisory Committee on Improvements to Financial Reporting to the United States Securities and Exchange Commission," released August 1, 2008.

NOTES

1. While I do not agree with this statement, Revenue Ruling 59-60, Section 7, Average of Factors states that, "Because valuations cannot be made on the basis of a prescribed formula, there is no means whereby the various applicable factors in a particular case can be assigned mathematical weights in deriving the fair market value. For this reason, no useful purpose is served by taking an average of several factors (for example, book value, capitalized earnings and capitalized dividends) and basing the valuation on the result. Such a process excludes active consideration of other pertinent factors and the end result cannot be supported by a realistic application of the significant facts in the case except by mere chance."
2. *See* http://web.nacva.com/TL-Website/PDF/DomesticStandards Chart.pdf
3. Currently, there is some controversy over what work can be performed as a calculation. See AICPA Valuation Services, VS Section, "Statements on Standards for Valuations Services, VS Section 100,

Valuation of a Business, Business Ownership Interest, Security, or Intangible Asset Calculation Engagements, Frequently Asked Questions (FAQs), Non-Authoritative". In summary, calculations can be used for a wide range of purposes.

4. My partner, Eddie Davis's favorite refrain
5. "Professional" in Merriam Webster's dictionary : *see* https://www .merriam-webster.com/dictionary/professional
6. "Judgment" in Merriam Webster's dictionary: *see* https://www .merriam-webster.com/dictionary/judgment
7. Ron Rudich states while teaching business valuation that he constantly is juggling many balls concerning valuation theory in the air (in his mind) before he is able to conclude an opinion.

CHAPTER 13

Assisting the Small Business Buyer or Seller

This is a book about business valuation. Many small business owners or future business owners rely on their accountants, particularly those with valuation certifications, as trusted advisors concerning exit planning and buying or selling a business. This book is only going to touch on these topics. It will not touch on the many variables of deal structures for internal, family, or market sale transactions. It will address creating business value, SBA financing, and some market sale issues.

Suffice to say, planning an exit to family members or management can take five years of planning and another ten years to execute the sale of stock over time or for the payment of notes. All cash, third party sales often take two to three years.

There are a great many misconceptions about the exit planning process and buying or selling businesses. Perhaps the most costly to sellers is the lack of preparation. Next is the concern or belief that growth is more important than profitability. Finally, a reluctance to talk to family members or key management about succession plans. Many owners are shocked to find out that their key employees do not want to buy the business.

Example

Many employees when asked, "Would you like to be an owner?" hear, "Would you like an upside bonus plan?" not personal guarantees and real ownership risk. This requires a clear and detailed conversation – early.

As professionals who want to serve our clients well, the biggest hurdle is getting clients to start thinking about these matters early. Most companies are well run and in reasonable order. Yet, small modifications can make big differences. In addition, many owners would like to sell to key employees. In some cases, the key employees would like to buy the business. But, this too takes time both to plan and execute. Most key employees do not have the capital to obtain a loan and buy the business outright. Therefore, a sale to employees needs to be planned in advance so the employee has capital or equity or buys the business over time.

One area that could use more focus is the emotional side of the business exit and purchase process. Buying or selling a business is a major life change. It is stressful and difficult for most people. Numbers are easy compared to emotion and fear. Therefore, most people, even those who should know better, just avoid the topic. The next topic is asking questions which is the key to having deep effective conversations about buying or selling a business and other sensitive matters.

In the future service/consultant-driven world, being able to deal with sensitive matters and more difficult conversations will be an effective way to differentiate yourself.

HOW TO ASK QUESTIONS EFFECTIVELY

This may seem silly, of course we all know how to ask questions. Yet careful questioning and listening are lost arts. Most of us probably never really learned the art.

The starting point is to be clear about what it is you are trying to determine. If you just need answers to a few technical questions, that is pretty easy to obtain. If you are trying to determine the motivations and resilience of an owner or key leader in a company (this often is the overriding factor in the success of small and very small businesses), that can be more difficult.

To prepare for the interview, do the following:

- Determine your purpose and goals from the conversation—what do you really need to understand?
- What can support that understanding in your work papers and report?
- Write out the questions. If you ask the wrong questions, you will never get the right answer. This sounds basic but is often missed. The perfect answer to the wrong question is useless.
- Write out a second and third question for each important question. Most questions are not that important. A few are. Be prepared in those areas.
- Do not be afraid to interject, why, how, who, what, when, or other clarifiers. In fact, write these down where you may want to use them. Leave white space for follow-up commentary and other questions.
- Before you arrive, if this is not someone you know, research the party on social media. Explore the firm on a search engine. Explore both on LinkedIn, Facebook, Twitter, Instagram, and so on. Network and ask others. Learn all you can about the party and look for a way to connect, based on values and interests. People work better when they are comfortable.
- Recognize that you have a "view." By view, it is meant that you have preconceived notions about the other person, how things are going to go, and so on. This is like wearing sunglasses. After a while you don't even realize you have them on but they change the color of everything. Do your best to let the view go and be open. (Being aware of your own

perspective, along with taking a deep breath three times in a row, is a way to relax and start letting your view go.)
- Recognize that the other side has a view of you. Can you set up the room, the people involved, the snacks, and so forth to improve the situation and create a feeling of ease?

Most interviews in business valuation do not begin from a hostile, unfriendly point. But in litigation, some will. If that is the case, calm the fire. You are there as an expert fact witness to provide unbiased commentary. You need to be perceived as neutral and unbiased. Be respectful and professional regardless of how you are treated. Still outside of formal depositions and the like, follow these rules. (When you can, follow them there too working with counsel.)

- Be cordial. If you are outgoing, ask questions and talk about things you might have in common based on art, awards, books, or any other cues from the room, office, and prior research. If introverted, ask questions or just move into the work. Be who you are and be comfortable in your own skin.
- Start with easy questions. Questions that are not threatening.
- Ask questions about the person and their contributions.
- Be complimentary.
- Work on building a connecting relationship.

You are working to establish trust and confidence in the relationship. As a third party, even in somewhat hostile environments, conflict can often be toned down and trust built up to allow deeper conversations.

- Move into your more difficult questions.
- Listen to the answer carefully. Note not only the words being said, but the tone of the words and the associated body language and facial expressions. (Someone pulling away when

a question is asked may say more than the answer.) It is often helpful to have two people there. One to take notes and the other to ask questions. That way the questioner can be more cognizant of nonverbal cues.[1] Those may suggest other follow-up questions for clarification. Stay focused, yet be professional and engaging.

- Do not be thinking about your next question or what you are having for lunch.
- Ask each question. Ask all three questions on important items. We are asked so many questions that we are trained to deflect them. For many this is an unconscious response. By asking questions three times you will work past the deflection response in most cases. This can be very effective in non-conflict environments but works in conflict ones too. You will be surprised at what comes out if you listen attentively.
- Listening attentively means that besides noting the response, summarize, paraphrase, and ask open-ended questions to draw out answers. If an issue is emotional in nature, empathize. Work with the person. Develop a relationship that will foster greater openness with you.
- One more time: *Listen to the answer carefully. Do not be thinking about your next question.* Your next question will be better if it comes directly out of the answer just given. You can take a moment or two and think between questions. This will be interpreted as you are really listening and absorbing. Everyone likes being listened to.
- Seek the answer behind the answer. What is really driving the results you see? What could change those results positively and negatively?
- Listen for what is not being said. Sometimes what is not said is more important than what is being said.
- Periodically restate in your own words what you believe you heard. Ask for confirmation that you understood. If not, ask for clarification so that you do understand the answer.

Practice this before you meet with the other party a few times, particularly at first. You may want to practice this in front of a mirror to see if you are being as neutral and professional as you think you are. It may seem awkward to ask almost the same question three times. Yet, worked into a conversation, it really is not. This takes practice and is often more about you being comfortable while conversing. In general, if you are comfortable, they will be too.

If this is for negotiation purposes, really try to understand the deep motivating emotions in the parties. A few negotiation tips are provided later in this chapter. Negotiation is very similar to asking questions but with a more focused goal in mind.

This system will greatly improve your insight into the company and the people interviewed about the company. When working with clients and prospects, this will also increase your connection and trust level. Finally, you will be amazed at what people tell you. Just ask and then really listen.

WORKING WITH BUSINESS SELLERS

For most sellers, selling their business is an emotional process. Often this is their last child or at least the child they got along with the best in many ways. Probably the child they spent the most time with. What this really means is that they may not know what they really want. In many cases the most helpful thing you can do as a trusted advisor is listen and ask questions to help them work through determining what they want.

Want to versus Have to

Many owners start from "I should sell" or "it is time to sell" or "my spouse wants me to sell." Yet, they do not really want to sell. This rarely works out well. Listen for the word "should." It usually indicates a lack of commitment. People do what they want and then rationalize how they got there. When you are talking to an owner, if they do not want to sell deep down inside, they should not go to market at this time. That does not mean they should not be preparing to go to market eventually or if the facts make sense, they should not be working with key managers or family members on a long-term buyout plan. Many owners start those processes way too late.

Other owners genuinely reach the decision that it is time to do the next thing or at least move on from the business. They WANT to sell. Which sounds somewhat like SHOULD but is a completely different place mentally. A shorthand is "Want to vs. Have to." "Want to" generally should sell. "Have to" should not. At least not yet.

When talking to your client, listen carefully for if they really want to sell or feel they should and therefore have to. Again, have to clients rarely get to closing, wasting tremendous energy.

Time versus Money

Few businesses outside some narrow tech fields are going to sell for a price that is irresistible. Somehow this is the main focus of most accountants: "but you are making so much money compared to what it will sell for." That is an easy to understand fact even for somewhat befuddled potential sellers.

Your client is probably much more wrapped in the emotion of a possible major life change. Spend time on that.

- What are they going to do next?
- What has changed in the last few years, creating these feelings?
- How do other family members or influencers in their life feel about this?
- Is it really something they want to do or do they feel they have to do this?
- Have they looked at other alternatives like reduced involvement?

Again, most small and very small businesses are going to sell in the broad range of 1.5–3 times the seller's discretionary earnings (SDE) or 3–5 times EBITDA. Basically, what the owner will make in three to four years if the company does not grow. This brings up another broker shorthand: "Owners are sellers when their TIME is worth more than their MONEY."

Most owners are not sellers because their business is how they want to spend their time. Their business is worth more to them than other potential owners. That is why brokers are so concerned about what owners are going to do next. The void of time becomes bigger as closing gets closer if the seller does not have real plans.

Higher Price, Lower Taxes, AND...

Of course, sellers want a higher price and lower taxes. Often there is something more that they want. Often they do not know what it is or maybe how to express it.

Example

One seller had renovated an old country Texaco station into a café. It turned out having a financially strong buyer to "take care of the building" was an important factor.

Helping the seller understand these factors, when possible, is important so the broker and other parties in the transaction can try to obtain that. Again, try to understand the underlying motivations. Often your client will not fully understand this either.

Value versus Price

Valuations are important for planning purposes and verification of reasonableness. Only in rare cases do they prove that the best price was obtained. For instance, a synergistic buyer offered 250% of a reasonable fair market value price. Run, do not walk, to complete that transaction. In the same vein, what if the buyer had offered 125%? More than one broker I talked to reports seeing those become 150% of fair market value, in some cases due to implementation of a proper sales process.

What Do Buyers Want?

One of the most important things for sellers to understand is what buyers want. Many small and very small business owners do not really understand what buyers want. They think 20 years in business or a large database of prior customers will provide value. The short answer to that is … *Buyers are looking for a proven future cash flow so strong it is worth paying for.*

This translates to:

- A "working model" to generate the cash flow. This means systems that work today. People who can operate the systems today who are staying after the sale.
- Simple is better than complex if it meets the test. Annie's Pretzels in high traffic, mall locations (the larger malls that are likely to survive) are wonderful. Simple, organized, profitable.
- A very clear buyer adage is, "If you want to be paid for it, prove it." In other words, buyers pay for what exists. An apple seed has the potential to be an apple tree. But no one pays for the tree when they are getting a seed.
- Along the lines of the last statement, buyers are buying a business for potential. BUT, they pay for what is proven. Without potential, they will just go get a job.
- Some form of competitive advantage and/or Amazon protection. This can be location, distribution chain, supply chain, devoted or repeat customer base, and so on.

In even simpler terms: *people, processes, profits.*

Buyers for small and very small businesses want to step into the owner's shoes and successfully run the business the way the owner has for 6–12 months. Then they will venture off and start changing the business to suit them.

They are the most conservative of entrepreneurs. The most risk-tolerant entrepreneurs tend to be those who do start-ups. Then some franchise buyers for new areas. Then existing business buyers.

Issues in Advising Owners on Creating Value

Often the biggest problems confronting advisors trying to assist clients is helping the client grow personally. The adage, "what got you here may not get you there" is true at certain points in growing a business. An owner's willingness to really look at themselves and take the personal risk to change themselves and their related actions often is the biggest impediment to improvement. Tired owners are just one symptom of this. There are many other varieties. It can sound like, "I know my limits." "We tried that (once)." "My friendly competitor advised me against it." and so on.

A second problem is that you as an outsider may see the problem and solution easily. But, until the owner internalizes it, until they see the problem and, more importantly, until they see the solution as theirs, they are unlikely to act. When doing advisory work, it is really exciting to hear an owner tell you as if it was a brand new idea what you have been suggesting to them for weeks. That is when change begins. When the client has "taken the solution to heart."

Finally, sometimes growth does require a short-term reduction in profits. Some owners are so short-term profit-driven (which is not all bad) that they will not make the investment in people and plant even when they have a long time-line to reap the rewards.

Increasing Business Value

Most business owners think the quickest path to increasing value is to increase sales, namely, to grow. Valuation professionals realize the quickest path is increasing profitability. Make sure your client really understands the difference.

Steps for Short-Term Value Enhancement

Usually there is not enough time to fully absorb the costs of growth when a sale is planned in the next year or two. Rapid customer growth can be expensive in the short term. Often advertising and sales expenses are high to initially obtain a customer who may be around for many years. Same for capital expenses. High capital expenses often take years to fully absorb. Businesses sell based on profitability. Profits are highest when cost of goods sold are low and sales, administrative and overhead costs are low and are fully absorbed. Buyers pay for proven cash flow. Therefore, the advice is:

- Cut expenses, then cut some more[2]
- Hold off on major capital expense other than emergencies, safety, and so on
- Hold sales steady or grow while maintaining reasonable gross or contribution margins (If margins fall too much, do not grow.)[3]
- Document systems and provide limited cross-training
- Recognize the importance of people staying. With a very small business, even a key administrative assistant who is knowledgeable and staying will usually add value. In most instances if everyone leaves, so does the business value
- Maintain energy around staff, namely, lead.

Mid-Term Two- to Four-Year Value Enhancement Steps

Again, improvements allowing a quick return make sense. Major improvements do not. To increase value over two to four years:

- Cut expenses
- Only make "normal" level capital expenses, i.e., replace trucks and equipment but do not fit out a new warehouse or major capital expense requiring three or more years to fully absorb (again, these can be expensive)

- Grow incrementally at a rate that maintains margins
- Look at your products/services, job cost, to understand where you make the largest margins. How can you sell more of those?
- Allocate overhead as best as possible to understand true customer and product costs. Factor this into margin analysis
- Learn the fine art of buying goods and services to increase quality and lower costs. Focus on lowering expenses and costs
- Document and refine systems. "Forever and continuous improvement." Use technology to make videos of systems with your phone or video work being done on the computer, while talking. This simplifies manual creation. Create a video library or operations manual
- If your business involves professional liability make sure you are properly insured
- Train and retain the best people. Some cross-training is helpful.[4] If possible obtain "stay" agreements (usually a bonus plan for key employees if they stay after an event like transfer of the company) and non-solicits of clients and other employees.

Longer-Term Value Creation

Now is the time to develop a strategy and revise capital, human, and sales expenditures. There is time to make those expenditures in the early years and hopefully reduce (at least on a percentage basis) some of these expenditures, thus increasing profits and value as the exit nears. In addition, if a sale is planned to family members or employees, this is the best timeframe to begin those conversations. In those cases, additional focus on both financial ability and developing all the skills a new owner will need is essential.

Follow the two- to four-year strategy above

- PLUS
- Develop a plan and review monthly

- Selectively try new products and services. If something looks good and the likely lifetime value is sufficient, market and sell hard to grow early. In general, growth is expensive and most small businesses are sold on profits. Cut back on expenses the last few years prior to the exit
- Make major capital investments if necessary at least five years before exit. It takes a while to fully absorb the costs and maximize profit
- If long term, consider acquisitions. A patient strategy with constant low-level outreach to prospects can pay off handsomely
- Bring in high-level team members that can grow. Obtain non-solicits and possibly stay agreements with bonus provisions for staying through a transition period
- If the company carries debt, see if it can be refinanced to lower rates and improved terms, including loan covenants.

While not sexy, these strategies will produce profitability which is the primary driver of value with small and very small businesses.

ISSUES WHEN REPRESENTING BUYERS

As mentioned earlier, most buyers of small and very small businesses are not represented by business brokers or business intermediaries. They tend to work on their own. The key for them in the early part of the process is to develop a diligent search methodology. Another important point is for them to look at enough businesses so that they begin to understand pricing, and when they find the right business, they can move forward with confidence. In good markets, good businesses can sell rapidly. Even in tough markets, good businesses sell. A suggested methodology is:

- Search BizBuySell and other business for sale websites. There are a lot of them

- Reach out on all interesting businesses. In the beginning there should be a lot of interesting businesses for most individual buyers who are, "looking for a good business." It is estimated only 35% of the buyers buy the type of business they first started looking for
- Sign the nondisclosure agreements and, when requested, provide simple but clear financial statements. The better and more expensive the business, typically the more thorough the nondisclosure and financial request will be. Certainly, do read the nondisclosure and if particularly egregious, negotiate it, but remember, they are there to protect the seller and they are hard and expensive to enforce. Enforcement is unlikely unless there is a clear breach
- Review the package. These will vary from one-page tear sheets with the last year's summaries and a little key financial information to complete information packages that often include three to five years summarized financials and a reasonable level of detail on the operations of the business
- Reach out to the brokers and owners where you have interest
  - Recognize that most business brokers have a difficult time getting all information on the business too. Often once it is provided, sometimes the broker realizes the listing has little likelihood of selling. Also, if a letter of intent has been negotiated, the listing may still be on the websites but not really on the market
  - Business brokers rarely co-broke, so any broker whose packages and demeanor are reasonable is worth touching base with directly every month or two
  - As a buyer develops a clear vision of some interesting industries or business types, they might want to cold call business owners directly. A certain percentage of sellers will not work with business brokers so this can sometimes be effective. Recognize when using this route that this may take a year or two to go from initial contact to closing. Part of what business brokers do is realign

seller's expectations. Often a good part of that is done before the business goes on the market

- Develop a letter of intent (LOI) for use when the right business is found. Include key business terms but do not get too far into legalese. It is far more important "to get the business off the street," i.e., have the seller working only with you, if possible, than to have all small terms worked out at this stage. This document will mainly be non-binding although some provisions may be binding. Often legal counsel will assist at this stage. Again, focus on business terms
- Develop basic pricing, valuing models for businesses looked at. Talk to sellers and brokers to get questions answered. Understand what drives the business and the numbers as described throughout this book. This is important for understanding the market and for being prepared when the right business comes along
- When a good prospective business comes along, make an offer, then negotiate the best transaction possible. Remember to obtain terms reducing risk wherever possible, such as simple earn-outs
- When the LOI is agreed to, begin due diligence as described below and have counsel prepare a definitive purchase agreement. Make sure the buyer (or seller if representing a seller) understands the business terms and representations and warranties and how indemnifications work if the representations and warranties are breached. Also understand who (company or individuals) stand behind the indemnifications
- Obtain financing
- Go to closing
- Post-closing obligations from both parties.

Each of these steps is far more complex than can be covered here but this is sufficient to allow high-level advisory work to assist buyers.

BUY-SELL AND RELATED AGREEMENTS

One of the biggest issues most inexperienced buyers do not comprehend is the risk posed by their partners. (Note: Partners is used for convenience. It is intended to include shareholders or members.) Even when two employees who have worked together for years are making the purchase, their past relationship is going to change. In all cases, the LLC operating agreement or a buy-sell agreement for corporations should incorporate the relationship between partners, including how to make changes in the relationship over time.

Buy-sell provisions should incorporate what happens if a partner wants or needs to leave. Death, disability, disputes, family changes, and more can happen and should be addressed in an agreement. In the event an owner leaves, how will the company be valued and how will the value be paid out?

Ongoing provisions that need to be addressed include: Who will put in more cash if required? How is that rewarded? (Interest, increased ownership, other?) What is the policy for re-investment? Over time many companies have a partner who really would like to re-invest and keep growing and one who would like to enjoy the fruit now.

This agreement or the agreements should be carefully thought out and negotiated as a fall-back. In many cases the parties can renegotiate as time goes on and specific situations arise but if they cannot agree downstream, the buy-sell agreement is a backstop so the business and owners can move on.

Much like working with potential sellers' emotions and helping them determine what they really want, this is a crux issue for buyer partners. Don't let your clients work it out tomorrow. Make sure they have suitable partner agreements in place.

THE SBA LENDING PROCESS

It is actually hard to separate the Small Business Administration (SBA) 7(a) loan program and current small business values.

The SBA 7(a) loan program is designed to facilitate the financing of the sale of small businesses by financial institutions.

The 1986 1st edition of *Valuing Small Businesses and Professional Practices*[5] has devoted a whole chapter to the lack of financing for small business sales, including how to estimate a value when the seller's price was based on a seller note. This lack of financing meant that most sales were based on the seller taking back financing or taking a very low cash price. The SBA 7(a) program has changed that. The SBA 7(a) program along with the 504(c) used typically for larger asset-based transactions (often with a user real estate component) provides financing for many small business sales.

Currently the SBA programs allow financing of a business purchase with as little as 10% down. For someone with related experience and some assets, the SBA programs shift most of the risk of loan default from the lender to the Federal Government. If the loan defaults, and the bank has followed SBA procedures which are spelled out in the Statement of Policy (SOP), then the Federal Government typically picks up 75% of the loss. (Specific SBA terms and requirements tend to change over time. The overall concepts tend to remain the same.) The Federally insured portion of SBA loans are traded on Wall Street as government-insured loans. This allows banks to originate loans and sell them much like the mortgage markets work. Most 7(a) loans are variable interest loans set at prime plus 2.5 to 3%.

The generous default protection under the SBA program comes at a price. The lender must comply with many SBA rules and must have complete files of detailed underwriting. This often leads to a paper-chase type situation where one document request leads to another question that then leads to another document request. For that reason, most SBA loans for business sales often take 120–150 days to complete.

This chapter will discuss the basics of the 7(a) loan program. The 504(c) program tends to be used for larger asset-based transactions including owner-occupied real estate and is much more complex in execution. The 504(c) program can result in a lower cost, long-term, fixed rate loan but it is very cumbersome in practice. Because most loans are under the 7(a), that program creates the primary pillar of small business value, therefore, that is what will be discussed here.

SBA 7(a) loans can have a principal amount of up to $5,000,000. Unless there are significant fixed assets, most loans are up to $2,500,000 or so. Many are in the $500,000–$1,500,000 range. This is how many small and very small businesses are financed. Of course, there are fees and closing costs but those can be lent to the purchaser along with working capital in many cases.

Banks and non-bank lenders can be approved to make SBA loans.[6] Make sure the lender you work with is designated a PLP (Preferred Lenders Program) lender by the SBA. PLP lenders have the authority to underwrite and close their own loans without further SBA approval. The reality is if there are close calls in the underwriting process, those questions may get referred to the SBA but this process is still much quicker than needing the entire file to go to the SBA for approval. Ask this question very directly as many loan officers have learned to make it sound like they have PLP approval when they do not.

Many businesses with purchase prices below $200,000 tend to sell for cash. Between $200,000 and $400,000, there may be a substantial down payment and a smaller seller note, for example, $250,000 down and $150,000 note. As transactions get larger, it is more likely an SBA loan will be involved up to about $2,500,000, as described above. Financing between $2,000,000 and $5,000,000 can still be difficult as it is too small for middle market lenders and SBA lenders tend to shy away from having so much risk in one loan without significant collateral.

Basic SBA Underwriting

SBA loans for business sales are cash flow loans. They can be granted typically when loan coverage is 1.2 times the available cash flow.[7] 1.2 times means that all costs including principal, interest, and payment of the owner-operators' living expenses are accounted for and covered.

The business must be in an industry that has not had an unusual level of loan losses. For instance, the printing industry which has been under siege due to the internet and the ease of in-house printing (copying to us) is restricted to 50% loan to value loans instead of the normal 90%. Certain industries are restricted for political or economic reasons, such as banking and some areas of finance. Franchises or industries that have had unusual number of losses can be barred or again have a higher equity requirement. Franchises also require a document approval process by the SBA. It is useful to check with a knowledgeable lender to see if the industry or franchise has these types of approval issues. The inability to finance certainly will impact marketability and may impact value.

Another SBA requirement is that the lender must obtain a business valuation for more than the SBA loan amount. If the business has more than $250,000 of goodwill and intangible value or if the parties in the transaction are related (this can be related as in family or in the management structure), then the underwriting requires a third-party business valuation. While the SOP does not specify the standard of value, most appraisers doing work in this area use fair market value. The SOP is clear that the transaction terms need to be specified and the various included and excluded assets and liabilities accounted for.

A factor in the SBA loan process that is hard to fully understand is when an underwriting decision is based on an SBA requirement or a bank underwriter determination. The first tier of consideration with SBA loans is the loan must meet SBA standards or obtain a waiver from the SBA. Then you get to the bank underwriting standards. If the bank has too many defaults, they will run into regulatory issues downstream. So, underwriters often require things above the base SBA standards (i.e., a 20% down payment instead of 10% down payment). Yet they often tell you it is an SBA requirement. Well, what they mean is it is *their* SBA requirement.

The reason this is being brought up is if you bump into an SBA requirement, then all lenders using the program will have to obey the requirement. But often it is a bank requirement, meaning you might solve the problem by shopping around for banks. Experience dictates if you are assisting a buyer or seller, talk to at least three knowledgeable loan officers and banks. Experience suggests talking with a minimum of five if it is a "difficult" loan. Send them all the necessary documentation. Then see what they come back with. If there is interest, obtain letters of intent or term sheets and make sure you understand all the provided terms in order to fully compare. Loan terms extend far beyond interest rate and the payback timeline. Make sure you understand them all. It is extra work and it is often worth it.

Most small businesses obtaining SBA loans do not have reviewed or audited financial statements. Many do not have compiled statements. This means the Federal Tax Returns are often the primary source of financial information. Year to date financial information is usually internal and of varying quality. For many small businesses, balance sheets are prepared on a cash basis without payables or receivables or a balance sheet is even non-existent. This is particularly the case with Schedule C tax filers.

In many cases, the bank underwriter favorably views the business seller taking back 10–15% of the business sale amount, which can be secured by the business assets in a second trust behind the bank. Sometimes the banker will specify that this loan be a "silent second." Silent second refers to the fact that the loan security is second or behind the bank and silent in that no payments can be made for a period of years. This will vary with the bank. Payments might start two or three years out or even once the SBA loan is paid off. Once the payments start, the repayment terms can be from a balloon payment to typically five or seven years of even monthly payments. This request will vary based on the transaction and the underwriter but is frequently part of the bank commitment when a borrower would not otherwise qualify. The view held by the SBA and many bankers is that the remaining owner funds will provide an offset for representations and warranties and keep the seller involved during the transition period.

In addition to the business being purchased, the buyer is also evaluated. Reasonable credit scores, relatable experience to what the business will require, cash to close, and, for larger transactions, collateral will be reviewed.

If the buyer has substantial assets, the SBA SOP requires that they be collateralized as part of the loan. What this means is that the SBA program is much more valuable to marginal purchasers who would be rejected without the SBA guarantees than to strong buyers who end up with their assets collateralized. Strong buyers often end up with the complexities of an SBA loan and a 100% collateralized loan. Not an enviable position for an add-on transaction.

Prior to the SBA most small transactions required the seller to finance as there was no one else. Sellers typically required 50% down on smaller transactions and 20–35% down on larger ones. Sellers who were unwilling to do that generally took very large discounts for a cash sale. Because many of these seller-financed loans defaulted, and all cash sale values were small, the market for business sales was much more limited. In addition, a large portion of the "sale price" may never have been paid, as due to renegotiation of the seller loan, it was hard to know what the "real" price was. This is rarely necessary with cash flowing businesses any more. In the last 25 years the SBA has removed these issues and brought stability to the market.

It appears that part of the reason why transaction sale data has become more useful is because there are more consistent transactions. In the end, most sellers take the SBA's loan amount and the sale price is reasonably close to the loan amount. Few sellers want the risk associated with providing financing. The availability and stability of financing have brought predictability to the small and very small business sale market. This in turn has made business valuation using the market method more accurate. This is a major change from 25 years ago that is not fully recognized by many valuators.

Should the SBA program be restricted or if the terms for obtaining an SBA loan become very restrictive (for instance, requiring 35% down instead of the current 10% down), the value of small and very small business will be greatly impacted. This is yet another assumption underlying most small and very small business valuations that no one even thinks about.

BUSINESS BROKERAGE: HOW TO MAXIMIZE A PRICE

The existence of a financing market for small and very small business sale loans has led to an increase in business brokers and business intermediaries. While there were brokers prior to reliable financing, the market was too scattered and unreliable for many brokers to operate. Stories of improper or poor practices by business brokers abound. Yet, like most industries, most of these infractions are carried out by a very small percentage. This chapter is going to talk about types of business brokers and typical size businesses they might work with. Then the chapter will cover the business brokerage process. Finally, how valuation professionals and business brokers can assist one another will be covered.

In business brokerage, businesses are broadly lumped into a few categories determined mainly by value and related characteristics. These categories are Main Street Businesses, Lower Middle Market Businesses, Middle Market Businesses, and Large Businesses.

Smaller businesses are appropriately called Main Street Businesses. Depending on who is classifying the business, this typically represents a company under $1,000,000 in value although some definitions can cover up to $2,500,000 value range. These usually have 25 or less employees and revenues under $3,000,000. As the name implies, main street businesses tend to be smaller service and retail firms that might appear on Main Street (e.g., restaurants, gas stations, repair shops, retailers, and smaller dealerships). These businesses are typically owner-operated. The larger ones may have somewhat sufficient management teams but owner involvement is usually required. These businesses are sold by business brokers.

The next size up business are those with values between $1,000,000 and $5,000,000. (Yes, there is overlap with Main Street businesses.) These are generally called Lower Middle Market. These can go up to $10,000,000 in value but most fall in the lower range. These businesses are still owner-driven although many will have a home-grown management team that can run day-to-day but usually are weak on strategy and longer-term matters. These are sold by business brokers and business intermediaries. Business intermediaries have the same functions as business brokers, they just sell this size business. The term business intermediary has never become clear in the minds of consumers but is often used by brokers focusing on this size transaction.[8] Many of these transactions will be financed by the SBA.

Most small and very small firm transactions only have sell side representation. Business brokers and intermediaries tend to represent sellers. Buyers are generally unrepresented until they talk to their CPAs, attorney or other business advisor. This is because brokers cannot charge enough fees from small buyers unless a transaction occurs and most "buyers" never buy a business. In addition, most business brokers and intermediaries do not co-broke. The value is in obtaining the listing. While it must be sold, selling a good listing is usually easier to sell than finding more listings. In addition, because small business situations are so fluid, often keeping other brokers current on the subject company changes can be difficult and cumbersome. Finally, confidentiality risks abound when providing data to unknown brokers. These are all valid reasons to restrict co-brokering.

Most Main Street brokers and intermediaries work for small firms. Many only have the owner/broker. There are several franchises in the industry including Transworld, Murphy, and Sunbelt. While the franchises provide some support particularly with new brokers, the reality is your individual broker is the person who is going to bring value or cause headaches in the business sale transaction. Most small businesses and even lower Middle Market businesses are going to be purchased by someone already in the same or an adjacent market area. Therefore, a national network is usually of low additional value. Focus on the individual you are going to work with and their resume. Not the brokerage house or franchise name.

The subsequently sized up businesses are those with values of $5,000,000 (or $10,000,000) up to $50,000,000. These are Middle Market businesses. They are typically sold by investment bankers. Investment bankers usually have SEC licensing and tend to be larger brokerage houses with more support staff. Many may have three to five licensed brokers and then several analysts and consultants. Most of these transactions will be financed through private equity groups and mezzanine or other corporate financing. These transactions quickly become very complex and require very high levels of due diligence.

Upper Middle Market is $50,000,000 in value up to $250,000,000. These larger businesses may be sold by the investment bankers mentioned above although they are often are sold by larger New York-based investment banking firms. These larger transactions will not be discussed here.

There are essentially two processes used by business brokers to sell businesses. The main break point of the processes is between Main Street and Lower Middle Market businesses. Certainly, there are Main Street brokers who use the Lower Middle Market process. But many do not.

Main Street Business Brokerage Process

Main Street business brokers typically charge a 10–12% commission. Many charge an upfront fee of $1,000–$1,500 to offset advertising and other costs of the listing. Most listing agreements also have a minimum fee if the business is sold. This is often in the $10,000–$15,000 range. Due to the complexity of some transactions and the fact that brokers need a "floor" commission to take on selling a business, these are normal. *Check the minimum fee stipulation carefully* as it is an area where unethical brokers may try to hide a much higher fee than the quoted commission. Typically, listings are for a year and any prospect worked with will be protected under a tail provision for another 12–36 months. This means if a sale happens to one of the protected prospects (buyer prospects contacted or worked with by the broker) after the listing period has ended but during the tail period, the commission will be paid.

The process for smaller Main Street businesses is simple. Get the listing. Don't worry about selling price or terms or anything else other than getting a binding listing signed. Collect the details on the business and put it on the market. Typically putting it on the market means listing the business on internet listings sites. BizBuySell is probably the largest and most active site. But, there are other private listing sites and many brokerage houses, franchisors, associations, and other groups have listing sites.

Typically, Main Street brokers will develop a tear sheet which is a one-page summary of the major attributes of the business and the last year's cash flow. After a simple confidentiality agreement is signed, the tear sheet will be provided. The broker then qualifies the buyer, perhaps has a site and owner visit and, if the prospect is interested, will write up the offer. Standardized sales agreements are often used.

It should be stressed that the owner and buyer prospect meeting is essential. With small and very small businesses the buyer and seller really need to work together during the transition. If they do not like each other, it is hard to come to an agreement for the sale and even harder if transition services are necessary.

If the business does not get activity or the activity is not leading to offers, then the broker generally works to get the price lowered by the owner. While this may seem unscrupulous for most small businesses, the owner's belief in an unrealistic value is often the major impediment to a sale. Finally, for a typical Main Street broker 60–75% of the listings will turn out to be unsaleable. With very small businesses it is very difficult to properly estimate a sales price (many of these businesses have less than $75,000 SDE) or determine buyer interest. Often the purchase is more of an almost synergistic type opportunity cost for the buyer than true business value generated by the seller (i.e., "I was going to start a store just like this but yours is ready to go"). Estimating a price for that type of serendipitous event is hard.

While this process sounds harsh, the economics of very small Main Street business brokerage is that brokers must deal with volume efficiently. Most successful Main Street brokers will have 10–25 listings and will often have four or more in some level of serious negotiation at any time. In fact, it is hard to make enough Main Street sales to stay in business without 10 or more listings. It is a numbers game.

Main Street brokers bring the following advantages to the seller they represent

- Knowledge of the local market and they will help position the business
- Confidentiality as the contacts are not going to the business and some level of confidentiality agreement is obtained
- Standardized agreements keeping costs down
- Advice and guidance on all aspects of business sale process
- Show the business to more buyers than the seller could alone (it is estimated 35% of buyers buy the type of business they thought they would)
- Often will help the buyer find a bank or other lender for an SBA loan
- Allow the seller to stay focused on running the business.

Main Street brokers present the following risks:

- Time split many ways
- Strategy revolves around getting price right, based on interest.

It should be emphasized that there are many experienced Main Street brokers who use the process described below for very small businesses and those with values over $500,000. But, economics and what actually can be known in advance about the value and marketability of very small businesses often demand the above process.

The Lower Middle Market Business Brokerage Process

Most brokers representing larger Main Street businesses and up will use a process similar to the one described below. Different firms may focus more or less on certain areas of the process but most must perform all aspects reasonably well to successfully obtain a favorable price for the business being sold. Steps include:

- **Introductory meeting.** The owner and broker meet. Key point is to determine trust and ability to work together. Brokers are constantly trying to understand if the seller will pull the trigger and actually sell the business. Many owners get halfway through the process and change their minds. With very small businesses and tired owners, sometimes the business goes out of business before a sale can be completed. These are huge occupational hazards for business brokers
- **Valuation.** Some firms retain an outside business valuation firm. Most prepare a valuation internally. The valuation can vary from a back of the napkin estimate to an opinion of value. The point is to determine if the owner is a seller at a likely valuation for the business. Some firms tie the valuation price into their contracts for sale. At this point, some lower-level due diligence is likely to be done as part of the valuation
- **Engagement.** Marketing processes and plans are presented. Details of the listing agreement and goals are agreed to. Most brokers require an exclusive agreement for a year with another 12–36-month tail for genuine prospects they have

contacted or worked with.[9] Fees can vary from $2,500 up front to $6,000 per month for 6 months or thereabout. Brokerage commissions can be a Double Lehman (10% on the first million, 8% on the second million, 6% on the third million, 4% on the remainder) or a negotiated amount usually between 10% and 3.5%, depending on the size of the transaction. Minimum fees in the event of a closing can be from $75,000 to $250,000, again depending on the size of the transaction

At this point, the broker does his best to obtain the remainder of documents necessary for due diligence. Knowing problems in advance allows dealing with them strategically. Generally, as business size grows, this process to obtain documentation in advance gets easier as sellers tend to be more organized and have true CFOs with organized files who can provide the information. For most businesses under $5 million in value, detailed documents much beyond the financial statements and tax returns are difficult to obtain until a real buyer is asking for them.

Getting your clients organized in advance for the "paper chase" requirements of selling a business will increase their value as organization does count. The next steps are:

- **Marketing the Business.** Brokers generally prepare a "teaser," being a one-page blind summary and a comprehensive confidential package. Information on the teaser is used publicly to market the business. Typical marketing methods are listing on public listing sites like BizBuySell for smaller businesses. For larger businesses it may make sense to put them on private sites like Axial. Direct mail and email to likely synergetic or industry buyers and cold calling to high-level likely buyers. Ads may be placed in industry magazines
- **Key in the process is verification of the ability of the prospect to perform financially.** The prospect must have a

genuine interest, and a logical connection with the business. Also important is the ability of the buyer and seller to get along, and of course completion of a comprehensive nondisclosure agreement. Confidential sales packages for Lower Middle Market are often thorough enough that the buyer can understand cash flows, business structure, significant contracts, systems, and people. Some brokers provide extremely detailed packages but most do not get too detailed as the broker and seller really cannot be completely sure who they are sending the package to. Common prospects are upper middle-class and moderately wealthy individuals who "just want a good business." As the company being sold gets larger, a more comprehensive deal room will have all documents available for all qualified buyers upon qualification, as there will be smaller pools of buyers who can be researched and verified more thoroughly

- **Part of the qualification process is the buyer and seller meeting.** The focus of the first meeting really is, can these people all work together? Certainly, many details of the business will be covered but the ability of a buyer and seller to work together is essential in small business sales

- **Negotiation.** The point of the brokerage process is to make a market across the likely buyer pool for the business. For most small businesses under $1 million in value, the business will be purchased by an individual. For a typical $2 million value business, this includes potentially being an add-on investment for a private equity group (PEG) or competitor, or selling to an individual who sometimes wants to be more of an investor and sometimes is looking to be an owner-operator. The different groups often view the business differently and experienced brokers will talk and qualify them differently.

The goal is to get three or more LOIs at about the same time to allow negotiating power on behalf of the seller and to verify the market. (Valuations are useful for planning but they are NOT proof of a market.) Quality brokers will evaluate the offers, including underwriting payment likelihood of offered terms. Quality brokers are good negotiators. Fear of loss brought on by multiple bidders is what creates negotiation power. Quality brokers know this and will work to obtain the best price—terms—conditions available based on the sellers' wishes and market realities.

While many negotiations devolve down to multipliers and cash flows, the strongest position a seller can negotiate from is that another buyer may win the sales contest. That is why a business valuation can only be used to determine relative worth, not as proof that it was the best deal possible. Having said this, certainly on some synergistic acquisitions, there are offer prices where it is clear statistically that the best thing the seller can do is close the deal as opposed to making a market

- **Due Diligence.** After the LOI or equivalent level offers are made and negotiations have occurred, a purchaser must be selected. Typically, the non-binding LOI is signed. The non-binding LOI will often have binding provisions around the deposit (deposits are common on Main Street deals and less common on Lower Middle Market) and perhaps a no-shop provision barring the seller from continuing to bring in new buyer prospects. From there, detailed due diligence will begin.

  As negotiations begin on the binding sales agreement, the bank financing or other financing process will begin in earnest. Due diligence tends to take 30 days for all cash small businesses and up to 150 days for larger deals requiring SBA financing. The goal of the seller and business broker is to minimize the time period to closing.

  There are always problems in due diligence. Unfortunately, it is hard to know what exactly they will be before they arise. A frequent problem is the buyer wanting to adjust the price. Sometimes this is based on real newly discovered issues or changes in results during the due diligence period but often it is purely based on the difference in buyer/seller power. The seller has the power during the bidding process. The buyer has more power (restarting the process can be expensive and painful) once selected as the winner. Business brokers assist the seller by adding credibility during these negotiations that if the seller must start again, the seller is ready

- **Closing.** As financing approvals are obtained and the remaining due diligence items are resolved, closing approaches. It is important to make sure all approvals, such as landlord approvals, permits if possible before closing, utility switchovers, franchise approvals, tax releases, and the like are obtained. Inventories and work in process, and any working capital adjustments need to be estimated and agreed to by the parties. Working capital is often more difficult to agree to than price. A closing sheet showing the money flow must be prepared and agreed to. Finally, all schedules and agreements including a seller non-compete must be completed and agreed to. As transactions get larger, this list can be quite daunting but must be completed in order to close

- **Post-Closing.** Generally, the broker does not participate in post-closing. But the buyer and seller need to complete the work under any transition employment or consulting agreements. The seller must abide by the non-compete. Often, in many states, permits and vehicles need to be transferred after closing. Post-closing receivables and payables need to be transferred between parties as agreed and received or paid. Finally, often the seller will have a seller note or escrow tied to successful completion of the representations and warranties and perhaps the result based on an earn-out.

Most brokers are active participants throughout this process. They educate the parties and bridge the rough spots. Keeping clear lines of communication and reducing the effect of personalities and emotions throughout the process form an important part of what brokers provide.

Because of the role brokers play, along with the availability of SBA financing, they have created more uniform markets for the sale of small businesses. Most brokers use Deal Stats, Bizcomp's, and West's Guide by Tom West for market information. Many know the valuation ranges for many businesses in their local market. If valuing a business for sale, it just makes sense to ask a local broker what it might be worth.

Selecting a Business Broker

This is a difficult task. While the company affiliation may have some limited value, in general, the knowledge, experience, and efforts of the individual broker are going to have the biggest impact on results.

Most business owners believe sales experience in their industry is important. For most small businesses outside of restaurants, there may not be enough transactions for real specialists. But, in many cases, if a true industry specialist can be found, they may know the real values, likely buyers, and be able to shorten and simplify the sales process.

If a true specialty broker is not available or if you are uncomfortable with that broker, the above-described brokerage system properly implemented by experts with good professional judgment will result in a high value (at least for that market at that time) for most cash-flow businesses.

Brokers understand how to emphasize and demonstrate those features that support stable upward cash flows whenever they exist. This is what creates business value in the business sale market. It can be viewed as "A belief in future cash flow so strong it is worth paying for"—that is what business buyers pay for.

To select a business broker, you should look at the following:

- How long has the person been a business broker?
- What types of businesses have they sold?

- Are their sold businesses about the same size with similar complexity and issues? (This is far more meaningful than industry in most cases.)
- What difficulties did they overcome selling each business?
- How long have the last three business sales taken?
- Do they have references that can be called?
- What do the references say? (Most people never call the references – you might want to.)
- Ask competitors about them. While most competitors will say nothing or be lightly complimentary, there are always a few brokers (there are two small and one large in my market area) that competitors will give warning about. Run from those warnings
- Will I listen to this person when push comes to shove? Do I trust them? (Many deals fail when sellers stop listening. The sellers have final say but the brokers have experience.)
- How many businesses are they selling now?
- What size are those businesses?
- What type of support staff exists?
- Will I have his or her personal attention or will the transaction be handed off?
- If handed off, who to?
- What percentage of the businesses listed do they generally sell? (Main Street is 30% or so. Lower Middle Market is probably 50% or 80% where the sellers do not change their minds. Again, this may not be much above 35%. This will also vary with the local economy.)

If you are working with potential sellers, introductions to quality business brokers can be very beneficial to your client. For cash-flow businesses, brokers will make a market and create negotiating power. Usually that adds far more to the sale than the broker's fee. (Of course, the fact that the fee is less than the price increase is impossible to prove, like many issues in business valuation.)

Businesses are selling current cash flow. Many a seller becomes so focused on the sales process that their profits fall, reducing value. A good business broker minimizes this distraction. After all, sellers need to run their businesses like they will never sell.

General Negotiation Tips

There are many steps to a well-run or well-won negotiation. Several key points are:

- **Research and background.** Do your research on the parties, including the actual participants. What are their socioeconomic profiles? What do they personally like and dislike? Interests, hobbies, family, philanthropies, and the like can have an influence. What would be success to them and what will they never agree to? Remember emotion and desire drive large parts of negotiations. Use this information in selecting negotiators, room settings, snacks and food, etc. Emotion and the subconscious are underappreciated by all but the most experienced negotiators
- **Determine your lines in the sand.** Think through what is a clear win, what is acceptable, and at what point you walk away. What are the comparative timelines? Do the timelines help or hurt you? Do a SWOT (Strengths, Weakness, Opportunities, and Threats) analysis for each party and/or the matter at hand. Consider alternatives and ways to reduce risk and increase reward. Understand your alternatives if you must walk away and always be ready to do so. Think through requests for chipping, as described below
- **Negotiate the negotiation.** Who sets the agenda? Where do you meet? What are the likely steps? These all set the tone and often allow for agreement to be reached on easy matters. These matters do make a difference, by all means set the agenda and think through one that assists you

- **Build a relationship, ask questions, and listen.** See the section, "How to Ask Questions Effectively" in this chapter
- **When stuck on a point, move on and then circle back.** Bring in different options, tradeoffs, and opportunities. You can even expand this to multiple offers (i.e., package a, or package b). Be open to reasonable mixing and matching from the packages
- **Remember win-win negotiating.** Win-win is when you can find something of low value to you that is high value to the other side and vice versa. Carefully trade those wins away to move negotiations forward
- **When you give something, make sure you get something in return.** Do not concede points without something, even something small in return
- **Chip away.** Ask for one more favor, or I will give you that for X which you have already requested and Y, a new request by me. Depending on the number of points being negotiated, small gains can add up
- **Earn-outs and contingencies—share the risk.** As the price or other valued term increases risk to the other party, be willing to make some of the increase subject to performance guarantees and price adjustments
- **Workability.** Remember reaching agreement is only a starting point. Make sure the agreement can be administered. What are the schedule provisions, responsibilities, meeting and reporting requirements, proof of financing, and other terms and conditions? Make sure these terms are workable.

Strengthening the Negotiation Position of Sellers

Key in any negotiation is the strength of the offering. The stronger the offering, the more aggressive the negotiations can be. Therefore, step one is to have a highly valuable company whenever possible.

Attracting motivated buyers is key. Understanding the level and reason for motivation requires qualification. Even if there is only one prospect, the more that is understood about the other party, the more effective the negotiation. This requires questions. Ask many questions. Ask important questions two or three times. When done properly, you will receive more detailed answers. People deflect questions but if nicely asked in slightly different ways, you can get deeper. The question, "Why?" may be the most powerful word on earth. Ask that often. You will be surprised at what you learn.

Read the "How to Ask Questions Effectively" section of this chapter. Figure 13.1 shows the qualification process which is further explained below.

Qualification is part of the questioning process. The prospect must be properly qualified. This means you must verify that they are ready, willing, and able.

FIGURE 13.1 The Buyer Qualification Process

Ask about:

- Their general background
- How does that relate to looking for a business?
- Do they have direct experience in this type of business?
- Other businesses they have looked at?
- Why did they not buy them?
- Have they made any offers?
- What happened?
- Why are they interested in this business?
- Who is on their team?
- How would they finance?
- What would a win look like?
- What would they change first?

The last question is for a little further in the sale process. Often when people start "seeing" themselves in a situation and thinking through changes, etc., they are becoming involved and motivated. Again, that is emotion showing through. The point is to understand their overall situation, ability, and most importantly, deep motivations.

Two of the biggest questions that need to be answered in any negotiation are:

1. What deep down inside is motivating this person to want to do this? (This is rarely the public answer you are told.)
2. What will this person never do?[10] (If it is a deal breaker for your party, all the rest is a waste of time.)

Once the driving emotion is determined, when things stall, ask a question that ties back into the emotion. For instance, "I know this counter is 5% too high and you are thinking of walking away. But, in the long run, if you did pay that amount, would you still meet your goal of building a business like your dad's?" In all likelihood, you will not get much of a response that day. But, the prospect will think about it and likely come back in a day or two with at least a counter.

Where are the drive and desire coming from? Emotion drives transactions. Desire and need. Driving emotion gets the parties through the tough spots. Any business broker will tell you the problem with the fair market buyer definition is there is no "reasonable buyer." You have to want it bad. You cannot effectively negotiate with someone who does not care.

Finally, multiple prospects and multiple offers create a fear of loss. Buyers cannot help but start counting their money when they put in an offer. Many buyers will tell you they are not willing to engage in a bidding situation. But almost all of them will if really motivated (including the ones who said they would not). Multiple offers allow the opportunity to counter, creating the concern of loss of the deal. This is how to increase value 20% or more. Many negotiations eventually end up in a conversation about multiples and cap. rates but that is a losing battle for the seller. A new offer that might take the deal away from a buyer prospect is much more persuasive.

If representing a buyer in a good market, it is hard to negotiate aggressively for your client and still end up as the winner of the bidding war. Some buyers will do almost anything to win the bidding war and then try to renegotiate in due diligence. At that point, the buyer is the only one left. Restarting the process can be expensive and time-consuming. This strategy can be effective and it can be a huge waste of time depending on the business, the market, and the seller.

Due Diligence in Transactions

A business valuation is the starting and perhaps end point of proper due diligence. The valuation is a starting point using seller-provided data early on. The valuation should be adjusted as due diligence indicates variations from the original facts and assumptions. Due diligence should be performed by sellers BEFORE starting the sale process. The fewer surprises and better preparation, the better the final result. But, most owners of small and very small businesses will not provide the level of detailed documentation necessary early in the process. Helping owners prepare and solve "easy" problems prior to starting the sale process will increase value and reduce timeframes on the market.

Proper due diligence is beyond the remit of this book. It is also rarely performed for small and very small businesses. That said, a starting point for minimum due diligence that should be performed is:

- Employment. Are the employees all legal and reported? Are their taxes being collected and paid to the correct jurisdictions?
- What are the benefits and what will need to be done to transfer them? Health insurance can take a long time to set up. 401Ks, etc. may need to be dealt with
- Are key managers and key employees expected to stay?
- Are there employee contracts, stay agreements, bonus or stock agreements, non-solicits and/or non-competes?
- If a union workforce, are there unfunded pension liabilities?
- Are systems documented?
- Are people cross-trained or is another back-up in place?
- Who is opening up new checking accounts, payroll accounts, forming the new company, etc.?
- What insurance is required? If professional liability is involved, is the seller buying tail insurance? Usually it works best to obtain insurance from the seller's current broker and carrier with small and very small businesses (generally the buyer can get going concern vs. new business rates) but do look around
- Independent contractors. Are they really independent contractors under state and Federal law? (State law rules can be much more aggressive toward employees than Federal law.)
- Is the company properly registered in each state or jurisdiction where it does business per requirements?

- Is the company reporting and paying taxes in those jurisdictions?
- Are there any concentrations of suppliers, referrers, customers? If yes, have they been contacted and does it appear that the relationship will transfer?
- Will the real estate lease be transferred? Can it be modified? Will the seller's personal guarantees be released if on a lease?
- Do any customer agreements, franchise agreements, supply agreements, licensing agreements, co-op agreements or the like require approval to transfer?
- If the buyer is to assume debt, can this really be done?
- How will equipment leases be handled?
- Are there bonds or sureties in place? How will they be handled?
- Are there licenses and permits that need to transfer? Are they pre-closing or post-closing?
- Will software licenses transfer or will new up-front fees be required? (This is becoming less of a problem with software as a service.)
- Is there any other intangible property and is it properly protected?
- Does the company own software outright and are the underlying code and related licenses in order?
- Are suppliers expected to continue to supply the new owner and extend credit?
- How are cut-offs for inventory, work in process, accounts receivable, accounts payable, etc. going to be determined and final amounts and payments agreed to?
- Are normal internal controls in place?
- Are cash controls in place, including proper segregation of duties?
- Review the nature of revenues to ensure they are truly forward-looking revenues as opposed to one-time or ending revenue streams
- What are the credit extension policies to customers?

- Are accounts receivables and accounts payables in good order and current?
- Is working capital agreed between the parties and is it supported by bank statements?
- Tie bank statements and, if applicable, point of sales data into the books into the tax returns. Perform limited sampling of source document
- Are there lawsuits or a history of lawsuits or disputes?
- Any known open reasons a lawsuit might be coming?
- Any other possible contingent liability, over- or undervalued asset?
- What is being missed? Spend some time on this one. Something important is being missed.
- Investigate all expected problems.

It must be noted that most small businesses will have problems when screened carefully. In most cases the buyer is going to have to accept some risk on these matters. Exactly where to draw the line and how to negotiate or accept each separate risk takes experience and a qualified deal team (e.g., lawyer, broker, CPA, tax professional).

One more point, it is reported that most mergers and acquisitions do not result in increases of value to the acquirer. There is a key word that explains why, *culture*. The list above is a page and a half of due diligence items that are comparatively easy to count, estimate, and calculate. So everyone focuses on them. But in most cases what is really being purchased is the combined knowledge and skills of the employees.

Companies and owners can have very different attitudes and values. This can strongly impact the outlook of the employees in both firms. Loss of motivation or of trained efficient people can have strong negative impacts on any acquisition. This is also very hard to access. To evaluate culture look at:

- How have other acquisitions gone?
- What is the reputation of the firm in the industry?

- What financial backing and depth do the buyers have if things go sideways?
- Are office and people policies similar both in what is written and as applied?
- Are office, equipment, and plant fit-out similar or very different?
- Would third parties categorize the companies similarly, for instance, hard charging, relaxed, genteel, and so on?

Culture and the ability of two cultures to merge well are very difficult to evaluate. But, if trained and experienced people are one of the motivations in the merger, it is very important to assess.

As a seller, you would like to reduce due diligence (do not hide things, that rarely ends well). Buyers should perform extensive due diligence. Particularly if the representations and warranties in the agreement of sale are extensive. The seller interviews and questionnaires with clear answers and back-up are very important for proving that a representation was researched diligently vs. being missed. A wrong answer on a questionnaire or interview follow-up letter when a problem later arises strengthens the due diligence case and possible downstream price adjustment.

Included is a sample due diligence checklist (Figure 13.2). Every situation is different. These serve as starting points. But recognize, just sending a 10-page due diligence list in a small transaction is rarely productive. It will likely not be reviewed, much less completed. With small and very small businesses, it is often best to orally review the long list in a meeting, taking clear notes that are provided back to the seller. Then send the written questions of the truly important items. Otherwise sellers, due to the form's length and fear of being wrong, tend not to complete anything.

Business Information Inventory Request

This information is a summary of your business. Please complete this and return it to us as soon as possible. **If the question is not relevant or if you have not information, please denote NA for not relevant and NI for no information.** Where financial information is asked for, a relevant report from your accounting or financial system showing the relevant data may be provided. Please write the heading and number of the question on the report so we can properly link them. This information is used to value and analyze your business. Please make it as accurate and complete as reasonably possible.

General Questions & Market Position

1. We are in the business of _____
2. This has an SIC Code of _____ NIACS of _____
3. Our Dun and Bradstreet number is _____
   If you have a current report, please provide it.
4. Please provide the following documents
   a. Software or other licenses or proof of ownership for all technology used by the company
   b. Patents, trademarks, copyrights, or applications therefore.
   c. Titles to all real property owned.
   d. Leases to all real property used in the business
5. Our greatest strength is:
6. Our biggest weakness is:
7. We see our biggest challenge over the next 3 years as:
8. We see our biggest opportunity over the next 3 years as:
9. The biggest change in our industry in the last 3 years has been:
10. Our 3 strongest competitors are (these may not be the biggest, but are the ones that tend to affect your sales the most):
    a. _
    b. _
    c. _
11. The industry leaders are (these are usually the biggest with perhaps an up- and coming firm):
    a. _
    b. _
    c. _
12. Who are your 5 largest customers on a continuing basis? What products do they buy? What % of total revenues are they? If more than 5% of total revenues each, what is your strategy to retain or recover if they leave?

    a.

    b.

    c.

    d.

    e.

FIGURE 13.2   Due Diligence outline

13. Line card or similar document identifying different manufacturing firms, companies represented, or products produced and sold.
14. Have you performed a market study in the last 3 years? If so, please attach.
15. Please provide copies of sales materials, Web urls, etc.
16. Have you had any business valuations performed in the last 5 years? If so, please attach.
17. Please attach any industry reports or market studies including those from trade association sources that indicate industry statistics and averages. If you rely on any published reports or books, please provide a copy to us.
18. Please provide any industry reports in which the company has participated with regard to industry statistics and averages.
19. Please provide any information on local market conditions for your market territory.
20. Please provide any publications or market information for your customer base that you may have. For instance, if you sell to homebuilders, information on the local housing industry.
21. Please provide pictures and/or plans of facilities and locations.
22. Have you developed any software, trademarks, technology, copyrights or patents? If so, please provide supporting documents and explanation as to use.
23. What proof do you have that your website, software, technologies, are owned by the company outright or are compliant with all licenses and agreements? Please provide all licenses and agreements.
24. Thumbnail History of Firm:
    Please include, year started, by whom, major transitions, recent changes

Financial Information

1. Please provide 3 to 5 years Year End Financial Information including a Cash Flow Statement.
2. Please provide 3 to 5 years Tax Returns and if applicable, Gift Tax Returns.
3. Please provide the most current interim Financial Statements available.
4. Please provide a chart of all payments and benefits to the owners and owner's family members for the last 3 to 5 years.
5. Please provide copies of all notes, factoring lines, lines of credit, leases (real estate and equipment), and other obligations or liabilities.
6. If this is not clearly show on your provided financial information, please provide the following sales information for your primary product lines.

Product Line	Sales Volume	% Sales
1.		
2.		
3.		
4.		
5.		

If more, continue on attached sheet.

FIGURE 13.2   *Continued*

7. Please provide the direct costs for the above product lines.

Product Line	Sales Volume	Direct Cost	Gross Margin
1.			
2.			
3.			
4.			
5.			

8. Please describe what costs may be allocated in the above or in your direct costs in your financial statements and how they are allocated.

9. Did you have any material or major unusual one-time expenses or revenues in the last 5 years? Explain.

10. Do you generate cost accounting, inventory or other detail reports? Please list and explain how they are used?

11. If you had to reduce overhead by 5%, what specific cuts would you make?
 a. Why?
 b. Why have you not made them?

12. If you had to reduce overhead by 10%, what specific cuts would you make?

13. What inventory method do you use?

14. Has this method remained consistent over the last 7 years?

15. Do you feel or know if your inventory is over- or under-valued?

16. How much is it over- or under-valued?

17. Please submit a complete property and equipment list (you may write market information and debt information on a depreciation table)

Asset	Book Value	Est. Market Value	Outstanding Debt
1.			
2.			
3.			
4.			
5.			

18. Are there any assets not listed above? Please remember all licenses, copyrights, real property, etc.

19. Do you use real property or equipment owned by related parties (entities or family members)? Yes No

20. If so, please provide information to identify the property and it's book and market value, the ownership, the relationship, any liens against the property, and any lease or other agreement concerning the use between the company and the property owner.

21. Do you intend to sell that property as part of this transaction or lease it?

22. If you intend to lease it, do you believe your current lease rate is market? If not, what is?

23. Please provide an accounts receivable aging showing current, 30 days, 60 days and 90 days. Please explain if you believe anything over 90 days is collectable and why,

FIGURE 13.2 *Continued*

24. Please list every equipment lease, equipment debt, or other obligation secured by personal property.

Bank or Lessee	Orig. Amt	Rem. Amt	Mo. Pay	Payoff Date
1.				
2.				
3.				
4.				
5.				

25. Please list all unsecured lines of credit.

Bank	Orig. Date	Term	Available	Outstanding
1.				
2.				
3.				
4.				
5.				

26. Please list all mortgages and debts secured by real property.

Bank	Term	Available	Outstanding	Payment Provisions
1.				
2.				
3.				
4.				
5.				

27. Please list any other debts and the related relevant information. These debts could be owner's or officers' debt to the company, factoring, etc.

28. Have you or any officer or owner personally guaranteed the debts? Yes No Please explain if yes.

29. Do the loan documents have restrictions on the sale of any shares or transfer of control of the business? Yes No Please xplain if yes.

30. Please provide an accounts payable aging statement showing current, 30 days, 60 days, 90 days, and over 90 days.

FIGURE 13.2 *Continued*

Human Relations

1. Please provide the following documents:
   a. Please supply a brief resume for each key employee listing his or her experience and job description.
   b. Organization Chart or Management Structure outline.
   c. Employment agreements, non-competes, confidentiality agreements, and other employee contracts.
   d. Schedule of compensation and benefits to all employees.
   e. Copy of employee handbook and manual.
   f. Description of related party transactions within the last three years.
   g. Copies of any lawsuit or letters or notices or complaints from regulatory agencies or other documents indicating possible employee unrest for last three years.
   h. Contact information for all employee benefit providers (retirement plans, health insurance, other) and copies of plans.
2. Do you provide health insurance for your employees? Yes No
3. Do you have any type of Retirement or Profit Sharing Plan? Please attach.
4. Do you provide other benefits? Please list and if phantom stock, or other complex plan. please attach copy.
5. Are you unionized? Yes No
6. Do you have any labor unrest or bargaining issues outstanding? Explain.
7. Have you had any complaints, suits or actions from any regulatory body concerning employment, safety, discrimination, etc. Please explain if yes and specify how it was disposed of.
8. Does the company own key man life insurance on anyone? If so, please include a copy of the face of the policy along with the summary information below.

Person	Face Amount	Whole Life	Term
1.			
2.			
3.			
4.			
5.			
6.			

Insurance, Taxes, and Regulations

1. Insurance - Please provide copies of the following documents:
   a. Copies of all insurance policies including but not limited to property, professional liability, operations, product liabilities.
   b. "Key man" or other life insurance policies.
   c. Director and officer indemnification policies.
   d. Safety rating, if applicable.
   e. Bonding policies and requirements, if applicable.
   f. Documentation on open claims possibly including attorney opinion letters.
   g. Contact information for current agents.

FIGURE 13.2 *Continued*

2. Do you have any open claims? Please explain.
3. Is it expected that those claims will be covered by insurance?
4. Is the insurance market becoming softer or more difficult in your industry?
5. Do you anticipate any major changes in insurance costs and coverages? Please explain.
6. Taxes – Please provide copies of the following documents:
   a. Any notice of assessment, revenue agents' reports from any federal, state, or local authority for any open year.
   b. All Federal and State Tax returns for last three years.
   c. Evidence of payment of all sales tax, unemployment, social security, and other tax payments.
   d. Evidence that 1099s have been properly sent to contractors.
   e. Evidence that all employees have been hired in compliance with Federal laws and have acceptable visas or are citizens or otherwise qualify for employment.
   f. Evidence that all independent contractors qualify for that status under applicable Federal and State laws.
   g. Federal Tax Transcripts for open periods.
7. Are all employees legally employed and are all employment taxes being paid?
8. Have you received any notices or complaints or indications of tax issues with any tax authority?
9. Do your "contractors" qualify as independent contractors?
10. Do you ship goods, make sales, provide services, have locations, have employees located in States or jurisdictions where the company is not authorized to do business and properly registered? Please explain the situation(s).
11. Regulations – Please provide the following documents:
    a. Copies of all licenses and discharge or other permits required to operate.
    b. Summary of OSHA, EPA, EEO, or other government agency inquiries for the past three years.
    c. Reports to government agencies over last three years.
12. Are there any permits, licenses, or investigations occurring?
13. Are permits and licenses expected to continue to be available and issue?
14. Are there grandfathering or zoning or other restrictions on permits and licenses?

Ownership and Control

15. Please provide copies of the following documents:
    a. Articles of Incorporation or other formation documents and all amendments.
    b. Bylaws and amendments.
    c. Minutes of all Board of Director, Shareholder, Partner, or other meetings or consents in lieu of a meeting.
    d. List of states and jurisdictions that the company is qualified to do business in.
    e. Material information or documents provided to equity holders and/or directors in the last two years.
    f. Current certificates of good standing for states that the company is doing business in.
    g. Copies of Corporate Book.
    h. Copy of all stock certificates, transfer book.
    i. Shareholder agreements or restrictions on stock transfer.
    j. Powers of Attorney or other voting agreements or rights.

FIGURE 13.2   *Continued*

16. Please list all shareholders or partners

Shareholder	No. Shares	% Ownership	How Acquired?
1.			
2.			
3.			
4.			
5.			
6.			

17. Does anyone have any right of first refusal to buy shares? Please describe.

18. Does anyone have any type of right to buy stock or have any open stock options at this time? Please describe.

19. Do you have any phantom stock or other benefit plan tied to earnings, business value, or share price?

20. Are your shares collateral for any debt or other liability or right?

21. Do you have a shareholder buy-sell agreement? If yes, please provide a copy.

22. Does the company own life insurance or disability on any officers or owners? If yes, please attach the face page of the policy.

23. Do you have a Board of Directors? If yes, please list each director and if they are a shareholder or if they are related to customers, suppliers, bankers, or an owner.

24. Please list every family member of the owner's family and any senior officer's family working for the business or receiving benefits or compensation along with their title, responsibilities and all compensation and benefits provided to them.

25. Please list all loans to or from the company to owners or directors or employees. Please provide copies of the loan documents.

Original Amount	Current Balance	Rate	Terms

Legal and Contractual

1. Please list each facility that is leased and provide the following information. Please provide a copy of each lease.

Facility	Landlord	Rent	Expires	Options
1.				
2.				
3.				
4.				
5.				

2. Please attach an insurance certificate showing the insurance for each facility.

3. Please attach an insurance certificate for workmen's compensation and general liability insurance.

FIGURE 13.2 *Continued*

4. Please list any professional liability insurance and summarize what risks it covers. Please attach the policy.
5. Who handles your insurance needs? Please provide contact information.
6. Please provide your standard Purchase Order and Sales Agreement.
7. Please provide contracts for any major supplier or customer.
8. Please provide any franchise agreement or agreement providing for the right to use, license, etc. intellectual property, trade names, business system, etc.
9. What is your process to make routine purchases? How big a purchase is a routine purchase? Please define.
10. What is your process to make major inventory, supply, equipment, etc. purchases or acquisitions? Please describe.
11. Do you use an advertising or marketing agency? Do you have a written contract? Who are they and please provide contact information.
12. Do you have ongoing directory or advertising obligations? Please describe.
13. Please list all licenses, the agency issuing, and contact information. Please note if they must be reissued upon change of ownership.

License	Issued By	New required if New Owner	Time to Obtain

14. Do you need or use bonds in your industry? Yes No. If yes, please describe your cost per bond, your bonding capacity, how much of it is outstanding. Please attach a bond schedule. Has this been a limitation on growth?
15. Do you have any other ongoing contractual obligations?
16. Who is your accountant? Do they prepare your taxes also? Please provide contact information for your accountant and, if separate, tax preparer.
17. Do you have any outstanding taxes of any type other than normal period accruals? If yes, please describe.
18. Have you been notified of any audits, administrative actions or otherwise?
19. What state are you incorporated in? What states are you authorized to do business in?
20. Who is your primary attorney? Please provide contact information.
21. Do you have any lawsuits or other legal proceeding not already noted during the last 5 years or currently proceeding? Please list suit, amount in contention, court, filing date, and estimated disposition.
22. Does the company have any contingent liabilities, guarantee agreements, etc.? If so, please describe.
23. Who is the contact person and contact information to handle questions during the analysis at the company?

This Business Due Diligence Outline and all provided attachments and information are complete, true, and correct to the best of my information and belief.
Company:

Signature   Title   Date

FIGURE 13.2 *Continued*

NOTES

1. For an interesting look at body language, read Mike Caro, *Caro's Book of Poker Tells* (Las Vegas: Cardoza Publishing, 2003).
2. Cutting expenses entails a staff review, including downsizing and outsourcing options, rebidding of work from time to time, cost engineering for process and product simplifications and reductions.
3. Update sales price comparisons and make sure pricing is current and competitive, review margins on services and products. Focus growth on high margin areas. In some cases, drop unprofitable work. Refer to the contribution margin analysis early in the book
4. Some cross-training provides a solution for employee concentrations. But the best companies have people do what they do best, i.e., do great athletes cross-train?
5. Shannon P. Pratt, *Valuing Small Businesses and Professional Practices* (New York: Dow Jones-Irwin, 1986).
6. Nonbank lenders and credit unions may also be approved by the SBA and provide SBA loans but I will refer to them all as banks for simplicity.
7. According to SOP 50 10 5(K) Subpart B page 179, Effective April 1, 2019, it is actually 1.15%. But I've never heard of a lender going down that low.
8. The IBBA or International Business Brokers Association has a designation, CBI or Certified Business Intermediary, which is obtained by many business brokers and intermediaries. *See* www.ibba.org. Several other certifications and associations exist.
9. The level of work to qualify for protection under the tail provision may be negotiated. Brokers favor any contact. Sellers favor a requirement of having a nondisclosure signed as proof of working with a prospect. Each side has valid points for their views.
10. PEG buyers often have long lists of "never dos." These often center around no concentrations and minimum revenues or earnings. But most buyers have items that fall in this category based on their experiences. Only buying asset sales (or never buying a business in a stock transaction) is another frequent "never do."

CHAPTER 14

How to Review a Business Valuation

I would rather be approximately right rather than perfectly wrong.

Does this make sense?

Namely, when looking at a business valuation, a sense of curiosity is the starting point of the Art of Business Valuation. A surprising number of times when carefully reviewing valuation reports, the answer to the question is no. This does not make sense.

Sometimes the value determined seems reasonable but the supporting facts and assumptions do not really add up. Other times the value calculated is just wrong. Most of us have read too many reports that seem quite "pretty" and thorough (or at least long) to find upon closer review that they are wanting in their logic, have unsound or incorrectly applied methodology, meaningless subjective weightings, unfounded or unexplained assumptions, and calculations that couldn't be replicated or just don't matter.

Clearly there are multiple levels and reasons to review a business valuation. The steps presented here can be used for internal pre-release checking of the valuation. They can also be used to review other valuators' valuations.

Humans (including analysts) can be swayed and begin to take sides and not even notice they are doing it. Another factor that plays into poor valuation estimates is lack of expertise. Combine a work product that requires many assumptions, multiple methodologies, and a huge variation of types of businesses and size ranges of businesses and it is easy to miss the mark and never even know it.

Mergers & Acquisitions professionals see this all the time with valuations prepared for exit planning purposes. For example, the well-meaning analyst who used large public company guideline comparables for a small engineering firm and then put a control premium on top. Nice theories but the wrong result. (You can't make this stuff up. Even the owner knew that the value did not make sense.)

The aim of this chapter is to allow analysts to overcome these issues in their own work and for all users to be able to spot errors and problems in other professionals' reports.

This section will begin with some larger "jump off the page" type issues and work down to smaller details that may impact value and certainly will impact credibility. I am primarily using a bullet-point format as this is more of a checklist.

WHERE ESTIMATES OF VALUE GO WRONG

Eventually value is calculated with numbers. Because every detail and the fact that every detail and assumption are eventually translated into a number representation, it makes sense that following the numbers is a logical way to review the report and calculations. This does not mean the industry, customer relations, organizational structure, and so on do not impact the value. It means we will look at how they are tied into the numbers with an emphasis on ...

Does this make sense?

Most business valuations are going to be in the ballpark, or satisfactory type of work product and opinion. A few will be exceptionally well done. A few will not represent an accurate business valuation or even be close. Remember, the test is not "will this happen" (though "this cannot happen" is a test) but are the fact pattern, assumptions, and value derived therefrom the most foreseeable from what is *known and knowable* on the valuation date?

Key numbers and areas of emphasis are:

- Selection of the period(s) reviewed
- Cash flow normalization/add-backs used
- Weighting and selection of cash flow measure, including projections
- Selection of methods and then the resulting multiplier, capitalization rate, or discount rate
- Modifying cash flows and valuation method calculations for internal and external soft factors (economy, management, etc.)
- Balance sheet adjustments, such as working capital, inventory, excess assets, including built-in gains tax
- Discounts and premiums.

Each of these areas will be reviewed in detail. There is also the issue of the cumulative effect of assumptions, choices, and even errors that also needs to be monitored.

Jump Off the Page Issues

The following issues need little explanation and, if visible, should be further investigated:

- The wrong standard of value
- The wrong valuation date
    - The above two issues seem technical and they are. But think of the value of a restaurant serving a tourist destination on a far-off island the day before and the day after 9/11. Remember after 9/11 no one flew for three years

- Recognize for some planning and divorce matters, the valuation date might "move" over time.
- The cash flow being applied against the wrong multiplier or discount rate (an SDE cash flow being applied to an EBITDA multiplier; a non-tax adjusted cash flow being applied to a standard buildup)
- Almost miraculously better or worse current year or even last two year data
- Hockey stick projections
- Cash flow weighting that is not supported by facts
- Suspicious add-backs, one-time events, and so on
- Unusual or unlikely discounts, capitalization rates, and market data multipliers
- A final value after all adjustments and balance sheet additions (inventory and/or accounts payable) that is above a 100% financed business at 8% (this is extreme, but it happens). Again, the finance method is a great sanity check
- At the other extreme, a long-term high revenue business in a cash industry with very low gross margins and no value. (While it could be a huge discounter, it could have cash leakage.)
- Cherry picking. Namely, almost every choice was favorable to very favorable for a higher or lower value.

All of these issues, other than the first two issues, could be explainable and even correct. But, if these factors are present, look hard before signing that the value found and report is correct.

Cherry Picking

Cherry picking is when the analyst consistently chooses a favorable assumption or analysis over an unfavorable one to increase or decrease value. This can be an assumption or choice

Cash Flow Weighting	Year 1	Year 2	Year 3	Selected
Base Cash Flow	$175	$250	$225	
Add Backs	$10	$10	$10	
"Correct" with Add-Backs	$185	$260	$235	$227 Average
Additional Add-Backs		$10	$10	
"Little More" with Add-Backs				
Additional Add-Backs	$185	$270	$245	$270 Best Year

	"Correct"	"Little More"	% Difference
Estimated Cash Flow	$227	$270	19.12%
Multiplier	2.4	2.8	16.67%
Value Found	$544.00	$756.00	38.97%

Note:
How small variances are multiplied into large variances.
This is the effect of cherry picking.

FIGURE 14.1   Estimating the Cumulative Effect of Cherry Picking

on any one area but in most cases it is replicated throughout the estimate and report. While performing reviews, keep a tally of the choices made and if they are neutral, unfavorable, or favorable for the direction the preparer may want the value to go, based on the purpose. Also have a column where you check off if the choice was the best choice. Remember, sometimes there really is a very favorable fact pattern for one value or another. Figure 14.1 demonstrates the cumulative effect of cherry picking. Note how small increases in various measures can greatly increase the value found. See Figure 14.2 for a handy form to review a business valuation for cherry picking.

The analysis presented in the chapter will indicate measures of the strength or weakness of the overall valuation. Use the form shown in Figure 14.2 and available on the website to track overall integrity as the review is performed. The remainder of the chapter details issues to look for that can be summarized on the form.

Assumption	Explanation	Favorable	Unfavorable	Neutral	Use?
Basic Accounting					
Periods reviewed reasonable					
Cash or accrual basis					
"Miraculous" up or down results					
Cut-offs adjusted properly (particularly last few periods)					
Revenues and expenses recorded (cash issues)					
Revenues and expenses in correct period					
Math correct					
Add-Backs Normalization					
Add-backs tie into statements used					
Add-backs properly supported					
Owners' compensation / benefits adjusted					
Owned real estate / other adjusted					
One-time revenues / expenses reasonable?					
Consistent margins					
Cogent explanations for change?					
Valuation Matters					
Correct standard of value					
Correct valuation date					

FIGURE 14.2 Cherry Picking Analysis Form

Assumption	Explanation	Favorable	Unfavorable	Neutral	Use?
Premise of value					
Well organized					
Logical case made					
Standards (if any) met?					
Market Method					
Multiplier consistent with profitability, other factors					
Comparable data reasonable for size profitability					
Have comparables been charted by price to cash flow?					
Soft business factors support multiple selected					
Cash flow weighting ties into results and future					
Value found is reasonable					
Balance sheet adjustments performed (see below)					
Income Methods					
Is buildup method accepted and reasonable?					
Basis for specific company premium					
Is growth rate supported?					
Are forecasts supported?					

FIGURE 14.2 *Continued*

Assumption	Explanation	Favorable	Unfavorable	Neutral	Use?
Are forecasts reasonable/ consistent / foreseeable?					
Is the period projected fair?					
Cap of earnings: is the cash flow weighting reasonable?					
Is the method tax affected?					
Do working capital, capital investment, debt support forecast?					
WACC: are the rates representative of this size business?					
WACC: is all interest-bearing debt subtracted?					
Is the value found reasonable?					
Balance sheet adjustments made (if any – see below)					
Business Soft Factors					
Do revenues, gross profits, and profit trends support selections?					
Do people, processes, and profits support selections?					
Risk from concentrations					
Lease, contract, litigation, other deal killers					
Foreseeable caps on growth (capital, key people, etc.)					

FIGURE 14.2 *Continued*

Assumption	Explanation	Favorable	Unfavorable	Neutral	Use?
Owner / management capacity					
Economy / industry issues					
Amazon Effect					
Specific competitor or product issues					
Marketability issues such as certifications, licenses, restricting transfer					
Balance Sheet Matters					
Valuation method consistent with treatment of accounts?					
Inventory taken, merchantable, correct					
Working capital estimated / reasonable					
Accounts receivable collectable					
Excess assets accounted for					
Fixed assets marked to market					
Liabilities paid off or other treatment					
Personal Goodwill, Discounts, Premiums					
Does standard of value allow discounts?					
Are risks double counted?					
Is selected amount reasonable based on comparables?					
Concentrations or other unusual discounts					

FIGURE 14.2 *Continued*

Assumption	Explanation	Favorable	Unfavorable	Neutral	Use?
Definition of personal goodwill					
Reasonableness of factors					
Method Selection, Weighting					
Are method results close?					
Would alternative selection materially change the value?					
Does value relate to price?					
Sanity check, reasonableness test, other					

FIGURE 14.2   *Continued*

Selecting the Periods for Review

This seems pretty straightforward. Select the three or five years before the valuation date. Select the projection period provided by management. In many cases that will be reasonable. However, if data is available, the following review may be very revealing:

- If a year or two was added to either side of the period reviewed, would the resulting cash flows "look" different?
- A quick estimate of the cash flows for those years can be calculated. (EBITDA or SDE using similar add-backs for a very rough cut). Does the resulting revised cash flow support or change your thoughts about the overall cash flow selected? (This will be reviewed in the section, Selection of the Cash Flow.)

- Are the period cut-offs correct?
  - Is the transition from reviewed accounting statements or tax returns to the current year company internal data prepared on the same basis?
  - Does it appear all data is in the right period cut-offs? While this is assumed to be more of a problem with a cash basis, often underlying assumptions for accrual basis can be manipulated (i.e., percentage of completion for contractors and manufacturers, actual capturing of expenses, etc.).
  - Information technology companies often bill and are paid in advance, contractors can have billings in advance of completion (where the liability may not be recorded). These and other factors can require cut-off (and related balance sheet) adjustments.
  - Sniff test work in process schedules when available. Is it consistent over periods? Recognize high-level industry managers can walk a site and quickly access the percentage of completion for most trades. Was that done by impartial people? If multiple WIP schedules can be obtained, do they tend to show losses or reductions in profit first appearing at 80% complete? This often indicates poor management and other problems
  - Beware if current year gross margins or overall results are dramatically changing from historic data. Maybe the current year should not be part of any cash flow weighting
  - Is the cost of goods sold, inventory, work in process, etc. properly established? The retailer that uses 35% COGS because it always seems to work out and has never done a physical inventory has very suspect earnings.
- Do industry and economic data and projections support the periods selected?
  - For instance, doing a cut-off of a projection the year before a recession for an electrical contractor may give

an unfair view. Same with a historic cash flow that selects only one very high cash flow year immediately prior to a recession or for a company that clearly had a one-time boost to earnings.
- Remember, valuation looks to the future with what is known or knowable.
  - Mediators, courts of equity, and other reviewers may view what actually happened in the next few periods as knowable even if different from expert and management projections. If it would influence your thinking, it might influence them
  - Valuators stand up for their valuation conclusion not the client's wishes.

Add-Backs Used

This is an obvious area to examine. Some add-backs are quite basic and straightforward. With small and very small businesses, many add-backs can be difficult to verify and then questionable: does it really meet the definitions and should be added back?

- Start by reviewing all math in the report.[1] Have someone duplicate every addition, subtraction, multiplication, and the like. Surprising things may be found.
- Do the add-backs selected tie into the related expense items on the underlying financial statements? Sounds basic but often they do not.
- Is unreported cash involved?
  - If so, what is the support?
  - If proven for revenues, could there be expenses paid in cash too? (This is very common.)
- Are there support documents such as POS reports or even cash register tapes, credit card statements, delivery tickets, journal entries, reconciliations, sales tax reports, tax accountant work-papers?

- What support is there for discretionary add-backs?
  - Family members' salaries. W-2s show payments but is labor being performed and can it really be determined? Sometimes it is clear such as children who are away at college, though with virtual jobs, even this is less clear.
  - For EBITDA discretionary compensation-type adjustments, does the adjustment include benefits or not? Should it? $25,000 family health insurance plan is a big percentage when it is being given on a $75,000 salary.
  - Is the comparison source for labor value estimates reasonable? (An association representing very large electrical contractors had a typical President's salary at $400,000, which is more than most 15-person electrical firm's SDE – this is not reasonable.)
  - If the building or real estate (or equipment) is owned by a related party, are the payments between parties at market? How was this determined?
  - Is everything properly reflected on the balance sheets?
- One-time revenues/expenses
  - Are they really one-time? Is the claimed item really unusual for the trade or business being reviewed? Does the fact pattern really support "one-time"? What happens if the review period is expanded?
  - Some companies (infrequent with small and very small businesses) "manage" their earnings and have tucked away earnings offset by contingent liabilities. These can be difficult to find (do not assume they show up on reviewed financials as they often do not) but should require at least moving the earnings between periods.
    - An advertising agency offset $500,000 of earnings due to a magazine vendor payment contingency (really?) and recognized the earnings three years later when the business trends were sliding down. The transferred earnings moved EBITDA from $1,000,000 to

$1,500,000. A very material difference in the earnings per period fact pattern.
- Are all add-backs included?
  - Often missed items include the employer portion of payroll taxes.
  - Auto expenses can have many pieces, insurance, repairs, gas, lease.
  - Cost of goods sold can have personal swimming pools, second or new homes and other benefits (often bordering on tax fraud) buried in them. Search contractors' COGS carefully if telltale signs or trust issues (this quickly becomes a forensics matter) when appropriate for the purpose.
  - Question one-time expenses and revenues. Do not assume they will be clearly identified or in other income or expense.
  - Check miscellaneous or other expenses, particularly if very large for hidden add-backs.

Weighting and Selection of Cash Flow Measures, Including Projections

One of the simplest ways to adjust a valuation is to weight the cash flow wrong. This can be very effective and not always obvious to inexperienced eyes. See the section, Weighting the Cash Flow, in Chapter 6, Market Approaches to understand the power of this error. Adjustments include:

- Weighting for the market method or capitalization of earnings method:
  - Do historic result trends support the weighting?[2]
  - Does the weighting tie into economic and industry projections?
  - If the review period was expanded, would you use the same weighting?

- Remember this is future-oriented. There may be major events that will change the future from the historic. (When would these be known or *knowable?*)
- Forecasts (high level review, see the section, Review of Forecasts, in Chapter 8, Income Approaches, for a detailed review):
  - Do the forecasts tie into historic data?
  - Do the gross margins, expenses, profits tie into historic percentages?
  - Was a set ratio (i.e., 3%) used to increase all expenses?
  - Does the forecast form a hockey stick (hard to believe but they often will)?
  - Does forecast preparation date, preparer, purpose, and so on add credibility or reduce credibility?
  - Is there a history of forecasts and, if so, what does that indicate?
  - Do the economy and industry data support the forecast?
  - Do the "reasons" provided for changes make sense and is there supporting evidence?
  - What actually happened since the forecast? (Again, this ties into the known or knowable issue in business valuation. The definition of known or knowable may be liberally construed by courts of equity trying to provide fairness.)

Selection of Methods: The Multiplier, Capitalization Rate, or Discount Rate

Method selection seems basic but results can vary dramatically between different approaches and between the various methods within an approach.

- Method selection and then the multiplier, capitalization rate, or discount rate:
  - **The market method**
  - If the business is in a comparable rich industry, be concerned about why the market method was not used. For all

the cross-examination issues, charting the market method results is quite persuasive and may provide less wiggle room than other methods.[3]

- Do sufficient market comparables exist? While six to ten is often considered a minimum, maybe fewer comparables can still provide guidance.
  - Are the selection criteria reasonable? Remember increasing minimum sales revenues often increases multiples. Was a reasonable sales revenue range selected? Was the earnings stream selected representative and reasonable? For instance, revenues are frequently used for tax preparation firms but rarely for construction contractors.
  - Are the cash flow multipliers based on similar criteria as the subject company or are there many high-revenue low-earning companies in the sample used? (This often produces high cash flow multipliers.)
  - How are "soft factors" tied into the cash flow and multiplier? (See Soft Factors below.)
  - What comparables were eliminated from the set and why?
  - If "specific transactions" were selected and the small set used, do the criteria hold up as impartial vs. all the comparables or vs. other sorting of the comparables?
  - What is the variance from the comparables median or mean multipliers from the selected multiplier?
  - Do the gross margins and other available indicators tie into the selected multiplier indicators?
  - Plot out cash flow and revenue multipliers by profitability. The 75th percentile cash flow multiplier is likely to apply to the 25th percentile performing business. Check, as this alone can be a very big swing.
- The income method: calculating the discount rate:
  - Which buildup method was selected?
  - What is the start date of the data and why was that start date selected?

- If an averaging of methods was used, do the weighting and reasoning make sense?[4]
- Is it consistently applied?
  - First, was the same "chart" or method applied across all buildup tiers and then were the same forward- or backward-looking estimates applied consistently.
- Small company premium: Did the methodology have Section 10 of The Center for Research in Security Prices (CRISP) data further broken down into deciles? Which decile was used and why?
  - Recognize most valuators do not use the smallest deciles under the theory that those are very distressed firms as they report net losses and therefore not comparable. While small company premiums may be arguable for mid-market firms for small and very small firms, very few analysts would suggest there is not small company risk.
- Does the industry premium reflect the conditions of your company? That is, risks to national known restaurant chains may not be the same as an unbranded sub-shop. Should this be in the equation?
- How was the company-specific risk rate formulated? Beyond "experience," what quantitative data was it tied into? If the market method has a reasonable number of comparables, why was that method not used? If it was used as a reasonableness test or otherwise, why not just use the market method entirely? (See Soft Factors below.)
- Income method: calculating a capitalization rate and/or terminal value rate:
  - All factors in the income method determining the discount rate should be reviewed.
  - How was the growth rate selected?
    - This is a very subjective number that can greatly swing value.

- How does it relate to recent actual growth or contraction?
- If it is below 0 or above 6, it is quite suspect in the eyes of the valuation community. Usually 2–3% for mature companies and 3–4% for younger companies.
- For terminal value even though the next year's cash flow is used (with the long-term growth added), remember that the last year of the projection's present value rate is used.
- Are there modifications to the "perpetual" cash flow that should be made (working capital, debt, capital investment) at transition from discrete years cash flow to terminal value cash flow?
- Income methods: all
  - Is the cash flow calculated and used consistent with the capitalization rate or discount rate used?
  - Has the cash flow been tax affected or the discount rate appropriately adjusted for pre-tax cash flow?
  - If WACC (weighted average cost of capital) was used, was the buildup rate increased for additional risk due to leverage and is the ratio of debt reasonable?
  - With WACC, is all interest-bearing debt subtracted from the value found to determine equity values?
  - The specific company adjustment and the growth rate are both highly subjective, hard to tie into data, and can greatly swing value. That does not mean small and very small businesses should not have those adjustments. Yet reasonable may not be right. But it may be hard to overcome that presumption.

Working Capital, Inventory, Excess Assets, Balance Sheet Adjustments

The general rule is that the assets necessary for the business to function, including current assets (usually accounts receivable, inventory, other current assets) and of course fixed assets, need to be conveyed with the business. Otherwise the business could not earn the money or cash flow that is the basis of the value.

This is modified in that the market method for small and very small businesses using the comparables. These often do not include net working capital. Namely, the seller keeps the cash, accounts receivable and other current assets, if any. In addition, in some databases and many industries, good and merchantable inventory is added to the price.

For most small and very small businesses, debts and liabilities will be paid off at the time of a sale. This may vary with the industry custom, valuation method, and standard of value being used.

The Market Method

- The starting point premise, assuming a private transaction database is being used, that is when recording asset sales, is that all current assets are retained by the seller. In addition, all liabilities are retained by the seller.
    - This appears more consistent with smaller companies where SDE is used as a cash flow.
    - As companies get larger and EBITDA is typically used, this is less consistent and reasonableness needs to be tested. The rule of thumb finance method is useful for this check.
- Inventory is reported to be sold above the purchase price in some databases.
    - Carefully check the comparable database for their treatment of inventory.
    - This seems to be more consistent with small companies below $1,000,000 in value.
    - Inventory must be saleable. Often deep inventory retailers or parts suppliers will have huge unsaleable inventory.
        - Take a used parts/junkyard. They had $3,000,000 of "wholesale sales price" inventory that was constantly being added to. Industry custom is that the first sales of parts from a salvage vehicle are applied 100% to cost so there is no real cost record. But, they could not turn it or

discount it to sell at a reasonable pace. Agreed inventory was $400,000 or four months inventory turn.

- Companies with inventory bulges due to seasonality usually have offsetting liabilities and/or reduced capital. Beware of adding the inventory and missing the payable or capital reduction.
- Between $1,000,000 and $2,000,000 of business value inventory is very negotiable.
- Above that, inventory starts tending to be included in the value.
- Check industry custom. Inventory that is the equivalent of "cash," such as gasoline, perishable produce, and other very quick turn inventory, is often added to the value across all transaction sizes.
- Working capital-type adjustments are common for businesses over $1,500,000–$2,000,000 in value. Companies with excessive working capital requirements (or inventory or capital investment for that matter) will have much lower multipliers as they have less cash to distribute to owners. This size guide is probably due both to the size of the bank lines that would need to be borrowed and the sophistication of buyers.
- Excess assets, whether on a net asset basis or as companies get larger on a working capital basis, are added to the value of the business. If there are more liabilities than assets, the liability would be subtracted from the value.

The Income Method

- Typically, the company is assumed to have a "balanced" balance sheet. Namely, reasonably necessary working capital and inventory is included.
- This method is very inaccurate with very small businesses. Particularly with small businesses with inventory and perhaps accounts receivable.
- As a rule of thumb this method becomes more useful for businesses over $1,500,000 in value.

All Methods

- What standard of value is being used to determine hard/fixed asset value?
- Company vacation and sick leave accruals can be substantial. Has that been accounted for?
  - Is inventory merchantable, current, at lower of cost or market, and in reasonable quantities
  - For long-lasting inventory, two years on the shelf is a rule of thumb limit used in many transactions.
- For high inventory or high accounts receivable businesses, the balance sheet adjustments can be huge. A typical $7,000,000 in revenues construction subcontractor can have $1,500,000 of accounts receivable when well managed. Whether this is included or excluded in value is a huge swing.
  - If the SDE of a small subcontractor is $500,000 and the multiple is 2, the value before balance sheet adjustment is $1,000,000. A "typical" transaction might add $900,000 of the receivables to the price and the seller would collect the other $600,000 directly. That collected portion is more likely to be $400,000 after warranty work and negotiations. So the "value" would be $2,300,000 ($1,000,000 + $900,000 + $400,000). In a strong economy that is reasonable. In a weak economy the multiple will be 1 and the value would be $1,800,000. In a very weak economy, the company would be worth the value of the collectable receivables. Once word is out that the company is shutting down, the value of the receivables would probably fall to 70% so the likely value would be $1,050,000.
  - Inventory creates the same issues. Selling the last 50% of inventory in some industries is almost impossible.[5]
- Are all excess assets on the balance sheet known and reported?
- Are assets on the books and records not actually titled to the company?

- Are liabilities being treated properly?
  - They are a usually a subtraction when estimating market value using market methods.
  - Income method:
    - If small amounts or when for sales with small and very small businesses, the debt is usually subtracted.
    - The debt payments may be factored into the cash flow. For small and very small businesses, this often makes more sense for fair value, intrinsic value-type valuations. Sometimes the weighted average cost of capital could be used in these cases.
- Are all liabilities shown on the balance sheet?
  - Check for long-term equipment leases.
  - If union workforce, pension or other liabilities:
    - A small union printer that made $250,000 of SDE had a pension liability of $700,000. The union denied the extent of the liability until a demand letter was presented.[6] It took 60 days to receive the reply revealing the extent of the liability.
  - Unfunded and/or unrecorded warranty liabilities.
  - Unrecorded lawsuits or disputes including employee matters.
  - Are balances of interest bearing debt reported properly?

"Soft Factors"

All methods. How are these factors tied into the cash flow and valuation method?

- Do external "soft" factors support or weaken future prospects of the company. The economy, technological change, industry change all fall in these categories. "A rising tide lifts all boats" is a valid but often hard to adjust for factor.[7]
- Do the company "soft" factors such as management team, history, staff, systems and the like support the multipliers, discount rate, or capitalization rate selected?

- Does the company have concentrations (sales, customers, suppliers, referrers, etc.) that are properly adjusted for?
- How do these two above factors affect the resiliency of future cash flows?
- Does it have a status such as 8(a) or minority owner that might reduce the buyer pool and value?
- Have all material changes such as gain or loss of key accounts and contracts been reported and taken into account?
- Might a franchisor or landlord charge high transfer fees or require expensive upgrades at transfer?
- Check deal killers:
  - State or Federal tax issues, lawsuits, undisclosed legal issues, inability to extend real estate lease or other irreplaceable material contracts, licensing issues, employee issues including key employee availability for transition.
  - These may lower the multiplier, increase the discount rate, or be adjusted against the cash flow. Do make sure they are factored into the business valuation.

Personal Goodwill, Discounts, and Premiums

Personal goodwill, discounts, and premiums are a very subjective area. Clearly a 5–45% discount or more can greatly swing value found. When personal goodwill, discounts, and premiums apply, reasonableness and "Does this make sense?" must be used.

- Check if the standard of value allows for premiums and discounts.
  - Technically, entity-level premiums and discounts may be reasonable even for fair value when comparability or other issues prevail, but this level of parsing may be above a user's comprehension or local court precedent.
  - Does the method used warrant a premium or discount to be comparable to the interest being valued?

- Review for double counting. Namely, if the same risk is being adjusted for multiple times. This can occur in the discount or capitalization rate, in the minority discount, or in the discount for lack of marketability or in all three.
  - For example, the valuator increased the specific company premium for customer concentration and then took a discount for lack of marketability primarily due to customer concentration. Nice when they put it in writing.
  - Is the discount selected on the high, low, or median of the range of discounts?
  - After the premium or discount adjustment, do the overall value, return on investment, and other measures make economic sense? While this may be circular logic, this is the most important factor in reviewing a discount or premium.
- Personal goodwill:
  - What is the definition of personal goodwill being used by your user (state law or Federal tax law)?
  - If there is no non-compete or exit transition agreement or worse yet if the human seller competes, would it damage the company?
  - If the answer is yes, tie into the definition of personal goodwill for your jurisdiction and purpose
    - Many valuators have a "position" on personal goodwill. I too have an opinion. But, if the definition for a purpose is clear in a jurisdiction, we are not legal counsel and should apply the law as provided. Of course, this too can be argued and even I would have exceptions.

Selection of the Method, the Weighting, and Other Factors

This section will look at the selection and weighting of the methods. We will conclude with a few other factors that have an impact on value found and, more importantly, credibility.

- If for estate and/or gift tax, IRS purposes, Revenue Ruling 59-60 specifies selecting the best method.[8]
- Many analysts believe, and standards allow, selecting a range of values for many purposes. Therefore, for many purposes valuators perform a weighting of two or more credible methods.
  - Are there strong reasons to select the weighted methods vs. other methods?
  - If there are large variations between the methods, are the reasons given reasonable?
    - What would the effect have been if one method was selected over the other?
    - Is the other method or is the less weighted method likely to be materially more correct?
  - Is the selected method weighting reasonable?
    - For instance, in a divorce, the "out" spouse's advisor put a heavy reliance on the market method revenues; based on a lifestyle analysis (clearly a forensics not valuation method) that indicated profitability but an inability to account for likely cash and show profitability in the company. Certainly, the forum and rest of the fact pattern will be part of determining if this is really reasonable.
  - Weighting four or seven methods or more indicates a lack of thought and selection. At a minimum, it strikes the appearance of an averaging of rules of thumb. Blind averaging is not supportable.
- Is the application of the discount, premium, or personal goodwill justified and reasonable in the final weighting?
- Other
  - Is the report well organized, does it comply with standards?
    - That assumes the report is prepared by someone with standards. (Note many economists and brokers and other knowledgeable people may not have standards.)

Are there typos and spelling errors? Maybe whole sentences left in from prior uses of the report?

- Check the math (again) throughout
- Is there an overall logic to the story, situation, or case being presented? Is it consistent? Is it fair and reasonable?
- What are the credentials of the analyst? If in a conflict situation, does the analyst appear to have unusual credibility in general or with the reviewer?
  - Take a case where the other valuator was suggested by the judge as a "good guy to use," but both sides were ordered to obtain their own expert.
- Finally, does this make sense?
  - Given the overall fact pattern, would someone pay a price that reasonably relates to the value found, based on the facts and both specified and reasonable assumptions with what was known or knowable on the valuation date?

NOTES

1. Many valuators forget to use the "=ROUND" routine in Excel; when this happens their column of amounts will not properly add to the total disclosed.
2. In a recent review of a report against an oppressed shareholder, the opposing valuator included in the historic data the fifth oldest year with net income of just $10,000. The first through fourth oldest years all had net income in excess of $300,000. The most recent year had the highest net income with expected growth into the future. He weighted all of the historic years equally. The averaged net income that was used to begin the cash flow calculation was "much less" than the most current historic year. Therefore, it appears (subject to other reasoning) the valuator deliberately started with an amount that understated the net income for the cash flow analysis and understated the ultimate enterprise value. He appears to be acting as an "advocate" for his client.
3. *See* Jim Hitchner, "Cross-examination of the Transactions Method of Valuation," *Family Lawyer*, April 29, 2019.

4. If all the methods used to estimate a buildup are based on the same underlying data, is averaging more effective than selecting the "best" data source?

5. Contrast this with furniture "going out of business sales." Specialty liquidators will sell the company inventory and assorted new cheap inventory paying a commission on the new inventory during the sale period. Sometimes this results in a higher liquidation value than otherwise would be estimated.

6. They acknowledged there was "something" due.

7. Commonly attributed to John F. Kennedy who used it in a 1963 speech. His use was more general economic theory than concerns about business cycle effects on valuation.

8. Rule 59-60, Section 7 Average of Factors states that, "Because valuations cannot be made on the basis of a prescribed formula, there is no means whereby the various applicable factors in a particular case can be assigned mathematical weights in deriving the fair market value. For this reason, no useful purpose is served by taking an average of several factors (for example, book value, capitalized earnings and capitalized dividends) and basing the valuation on the result. Such a process excludes active consideration of other pertinent factors and the end result cannot be supported by a realistic application of the significant facts in the case except by mere chance." I do not agree with this statement but it is the rule.

CHAPTER 15

Final Thought

The value conclusion is the result of the appraiser's judgment and not necessarily the result of a mathematical process.[1]

Or as my father would say, "I would rather be approximately right as opposed to perfectly wrong."

Never hesitate to ask, "Does this make sense?"

If the business valuation and resulting opinion do not make sense—keep looking and working with the complete story. Review all the assumptions and facts. *Business valuation is an art*. It is an iterative process that begins and ends with, "Does this make sense?"

Be able to answer yes at every point in the business valuation process and you will have mastered the Art of Business Valuation. The complex is simple and the simple is complex.

NOTE

1. ASA, USPAP STANDARDS Rule 9-5 Comment, 2018–2019 Uniform Standards of Professional Appraisal Practice.

About the Website

*T*he Art of Business Valuation, Accurately Valuing A Small Business includes access to two websites that contain related materials including calculations, checklists, and sample reports demonstrating concepts from the book. These materials should be used as a supplement to the book, not in lieu of the book. Many details are only covered in the book.

www.wiley/go/businessvaluation.com. All original materials are available for download as an archival resource. The password is: Caruso123

www.theartofbusinessvaluation.com/smallbusiness valuation. All original materials are available for download. In addition, the site contains links to related information and updated information pertinent to small business valuation as change and new ideas are a constant. If you would like to submit ideas and links and updates, contact info@theartofbusiness svalution.com. Please only send public information.

The available documents are for educational purposes only. Efforts have been made to ensure reasonableness of the documents provided but no representations or warranties are given as to the work's accuracy or compliance with any credentialing bodies standards or with any jurisdictional, or user (e.g., IRS, SBA, etc.) requirements. It is also understood that there are many opinions, methods, and options on these matters many of which may be correct. We also may have very different views on these matters as business valuation and our knowledge continues to evolve. This is how the profession improves.

Index